HISTORY OF THE
YALE LAW SCHOOL
TO 1915

FREDERICK C. HICKS

INTRODUCTION BY **MORRIS L. COHEN**
Professor of Law, Yale Law School

HISTORY OF THE
YALE LAW SCHOOL
TO 1915

FREDERICK C. HICKS

INTRODUCTION BY **MORRIS L. COHEN**

Professor of Law, Yale Law School

THE
LAWBOOK EXCHANGE
LTD

Clark, New Jersey

ISBN 978-1-58477-175-3 (hardcover)
ISBN 978-1-61619-600-4 (paperback)

Lawbook Exchange edition 2001, 2018

THE LAWBOOK EXCHANGE, LTD.
33 Terminal Avenue
Clark, New Jersey 07066-1321

*Please see our website for a selection of our other publications
and fine facsimile reprints of classic works of legal history:*
www.lawbookexchange.com

Library of Congress Cataloging-in-Publication Data

Hicks, Frederick C. (Frederick Charles), b. 1875.
    History of the Yale Law School to 1915 / by Frederick C. Hicks ; with a
    new introduction by Morris L. Cohen and a new index.
        p. cm.
    Originally published: Yale Law School. New Haven : Yale University
Press, 1935-1938 (Yale Law Library publications ; no 1, 3-4, 7).
    Includes bibliographical references.
    ISBN 1-58477-175-5 (cloth : alk. paper)
        1. Yale Law School--History. 2. Staples, Seth Perkins, 1776-1861. 3.
Hitchcock, Samuel J. (Samuel Johnson), 1786-1845. 4. Daggett, David,
1764-1851. 5. Yale University School of Law. Library Founder's Collection. I.
Title. II. Yale Law Library publications l no. 1, 3-4, 7.

KF292.Y314 Z654 2001
340'.071'17468--dc21   2001016436

Printed in the United States of America on acid-free paper

CONTENTS

INTRODUCTION

Although histories of individual American law schools have attracted some interest in recent years from legal historians and scholars of legal education,[1] this was certainly not true back in the 1930's when Frederick C. Hicks wrote and published his history of the Yale Law School.[2] Aside from puffing institutional histories designed primarily to warm the hearts and open the purses of alumni, the only serious law school histories as of that time were Charles Warren's *History of the Harvard Law School*[3] in three volumes and *The Centennial History of the Harvard Law School, 1817-1917.*[4]

Frederick Hicks was then Librarian and Professor of Law at the Yale Law School having come to Yale in 1928 after serving as Librarian of the Columbia Law School. Hicks had already published a number of books,[5] several of which were historical in nature although designed more for the general reader than the scholarly specialist. His *Materials and Methods of Legal Research,* first published in 1923 and later reissued in

---

1. A search for the subject "law schools-history" in an online periodical index identified 172 articles since 1980. For a critical survey and analysis of earlier law school histories, see Alfred S. Konefsky and John Henry Schlegel, *Mirror, Mirror on the Wall: Histories of American Law Schools,* 95 Harv. L. Rev. 833-851 (1982). Curiously, the authors do not mention the Hicks history of the Yale Law School although it was one of the earliest and most substantial of that genre.
2. The work was originally issued in four paperback volumes in successive years (1935, 1936, 1937, and 1938). It was organized chronologically and was illustrated with photographs and other pictorial matter.
3. *History of the Harvard Law School and of Early Legal Conditions in America* (1908). 3 vols.
4. Harvard Law School Association, c1918.
5. These included: *Aids to the Study and Use of Law Books* (1913); *The New World Order: International Organization, International Law, International Cooperation* (1920);*Men and Books Famous in the Law* (1921); *Materials and Methods of Legal*

second (1933) and third (1942) revised editions, was a pioneering work in that field and probably the most intellectually interesting of those introductory texts. It reflects the influence at the Columbia Law School of legal realism which Hicks, William O. Douglas, and others carried to Yale. Hicks's collection of biographical essays, *Men and Books Famous in the Law*, offers engaging and thoughtful examples of bibliographical detective work.

While at Yale, Hicks also instituted a series of Yale Law Library Publications which were published by the Yale University Press but not widely distributed. After Hicks retired, the series was continued by his successor as Librarian, the distinguished legal historian, Samuel E. Thorne.[6] The first publication in the series, *Yale Law School: The Founders and the Founders' Collection,* was the initial installment of a four-part history of the Yale Law School, all of which were written by Professor Hicks. Not surprisingly, it gave heavy emphasis to the early history of the School's book collection but also described the School's beginnings in the law office instruction associated with the school's founders, David Daggett, Samuel J. Hitchcock, and Seth P. Staples. The second installment, *Yale Law School: From the Founders to Dutton, 1845-1869,* appeared in 1936, as no. 3 in the Publication Series. It was followed by *Yale Law School: 1869-1894*

Research (1923); *Famous American Jury Speeches* (1925); *Arguments and Addresses of Joseph Hodges Choate* (1926); *Human Jettison; A Sea Tale From the Law* (1927); *High Finance in the Sixties* (1929); *Famous Speeches by Eminent American Statesmen* (1929); *Organization and Ethics of the Bench and Bar* (1932); and (as co-author) *Unauthorized Practice of Law: A Handbook for Lawyers and Laymen* (1934).

6. Some of the more noteworthy titles were *The William Blackstone Collection in the Yale Law Library; A Bibliographical Catalogue,* by Catherine Spicer Eller (1938); *Litchfield Law School, 1774-1833: Biographical Catalogue of Students,* edited by Samuel H. Fisher (1946); and *A Catalogue of the Library of Sir Edward Coke,* edited by W.O.Hassall (1950).

Including the County Court House Period (1937, Publication No. 4) and *Yale Law School: 1895-1915 Twenty Years of Hendrie Hall* (1938, Publication No. 7). All four parts are reprinted in full here. Unfortunately, the history was not continued, although Laura Kalman published an important study of a later period in her *Legal Realism at Yale, 1927-1960.*[7]

On the occasion of this reprinting of Hicks's history, it seems only fitting that we give attention to the author who lavished valuable time and attention, during busy days of library administration and teaching, on what must have been a labor of love. Frederick Hicks (1875-1956)[8] was educated in the public schools of Auburn, New York, and later received a Ph.B. from Colgate, an LL.B. from Georgetown, and an M.A. from Brown. In 1922, he also received an honorary doctorate from Colgate. He practiced law briefly and then returned to the library field in which he had worked for six years between college and law school. Before his appointment to the Columbia Law Library in 1915, he served as Librarian of the Naval War College in Newport, Rhode Island, and as Assistant Librarian of the Brooklyn Public Library. During his years as Librarian at the Columbia Law School (1915-1928) and the Yale Law School (1928-1945), Hicks was certainly the most distinguished American law librarian. He wrote and published creditably in law and history, taught at a major law school, and enlarged substantially the library collections of two major law schools. During his librarianship, Columbia's law library grew from "a purely instructional collection of 56,000 volumes" to "become one of the great law libraries of the world, containing almost

---

7. University of North Carolina Press, 1986.
8. For further biographical information, see William R. Roalfe, *Frederick C. Hicks: Scholar-Librarian*, 50 Law Lib. J. 88-98 (1957) and Lawrence H. Schmehl, *Who's Who in Law Libraries; Frederick C. Hicks, Librarian of the Yale Law School Library*, 37 Law Lib. J.16-24 (1944).

150,000 volumes."[9] At Yale, the law library grew under his leadership from 100,000 to 300,000 volumes. His collecting policy at both of those institutions showed significant diversification with new emphases on social science materials and foreign and international law.

In addition to his active professional career, Hicks was an interesting and versatile character. He wrote or edited twenty books (including one novel), fifty- two articles appearing in twenty-three different periodicals, twelve pamphlets, sixteen contributions to encyclopedias or collections of essays, and nineteen book reviews. He was a competent amateur musician, playing the first flute in the Business and Professional Men's Orchestra at Yale. He was also a skilled watercolorist and photographer and his work in those media was frequently shown at exhibitions in New Haven and on Cape Cod where he and wife maintained a summer home. Samuel Thorne said of him: "Quiet of manner, kindly in nature, Mr. Hicks possessed great personal charm."[10]

And what can we say today about Hicks's *History of the Yale Law School*? It is a reasonably objective chronological institutional history, readable and reliable for the period covered. It preserves and makes available to later scholars much basic information about the school that might otherwise have been lost. By modern standards of historical writing, however, its lack of bibliographic references and scholarly apparatus is frustrating and disappointing. The value of otherwise useful but elusive information is frequently diminished by the absence of source citations. For better or worse, Hicks livens the text with anecdotes and sometimes colorful descriptions of the people involved. However, it

---

9. Samuel E. Thorne, *In Memory of Frederick Charles Hicks*, 49 Law Lib. J. 277-278 (1956).
10. *Ibid*, 278.

occasionally reads like a series of "begats" without adequate explanation of changes in policy, curriculum, and pedagogy which undoubtedly followed at least some of the personnel changes. While Hicks tells us much that is useful about the origins of the Yale Law School, he doesn't adequately relate those developments to the proprietary law schools like those in Litchfield and Northampton, which preceded the Harvard and Yale Law Schools. His failure to include at least a name index for the series makes reference to key individuals very difficult. Happily, that omission is corrected by Valerie L. Horowitz of The Lawbook Exchange, Ltd. in this reprinting.

Nevertheless, we owe a great debt to Frederick Hicks for what he did give us, and for his avoiding the institutional vanity and extravagant glorification typical of many law school histories. His study of one of America's great law schools is still one of the best examples of this genre. Further work on the history of the Yale Law School would have been far more difficult without the groundwork that he laid. It is reassuring to know that others at the Yale Law School and elsewhere are now giving long overdue attention to continuing the valuable work which he began.

Morris L. Cohen
New Haven, Connecticut
November, 2000

ALPHABETICAL LIST OF PLATES

LIST OF PLATES

𝔜ale 𝔏aw 𝔏ibrary 𝔓ublications
No. 1 June 1935

Yale Law School:
The Founders and the Founders' Collection

By

Frederick C. Hicks

PUBLISHED FOR THE YALE LAW LIBRARY
BY THE YALE UNIVERSITY PRESS

1935

Yale Law Library Publications

*Issued from time to time for the Yale Law Library with
the coöperation of the Committee on Yale Law Library
Patrons of the Yale Law School Association.*

*Publication No. 1 is issued also as Pamphlet No. XXXIX of the
Committee on Historical Publications, Tercentenary Commission of
the State of Connecticut.*

Catalogue of Saml. J. Hitchcock's

Law Library

No. Vols.		$	cts
3	Anstruther's Reports	3	-
1	American Precedents	5	75
1	Andrews Reports	2	-
1	Anthon's Blackstone $2.00	"	55
1	Angell on Watercourses	2	20
1	Adams on Ejectment	2	75
1	Archbold's Civil Pleading	3	85
2	Archbold's Practice	4	10
1	Anthon's Nisi Prius	1	50
1	Addison's Reports	"	83
1	Abbot on Shipping	3	"
1	Anderson's Reports part first	1	20
1	Adams N. Hamsh Report	1	75
1	Ashmead's Repts	3	21
1	Angel on Limitations	2	92
1	Angel on adverse enjoyment	1	"
1	Angel on Taxing Corporations	"	12
1	Angel on Tide Waters	1	50
1	Angel & Ames on Corporations	3	34
1	American Constitutions	"	87½
2	Aikens Reports 2 Vols	10	"
9	American Jurist	27	"
1	Averaged Marine Insurance	3	75
1	Alabama Digest	4	25
2	Arnold's Maritime Law	1	15
2	American Common Law 2 Vols	12	"
4	do do Vols 3.4.5.6	24	"
2	do do " 7.28	12	"
3	Aikens Reports	4	50
1	Ambler	1	"
1	Aikens Digest on the Laws of Ala.	5	20

FIRST PAGE OF THE CATALOGUE
OF SAMUEL J. HITCHCOCK'S LAW LIBRARY

Yale Law School:
The Founders and the Founders'
Collection

By FREDERICK C. HICKS[1]

I

EXCEPT for manuscript papers, the oldest extant mementos of the early history of the Yale Law School are law books. Professors and students of those days are long since dead; the buildings in which classes are known to have been held have been torn down; but some of the books used by the earliest of its students remain. Curiously enough, these books were not owned by the school until the year 1846, twenty-two years after the names of law students were first listed in the Yale College catalogue, and three years after the degree of Bachelor of Laws was first conferred here. They are books which formerly belonged individually to Seth P. Staples, Samuel J. Hitchcock, and David Daggett, the first, second, and third instructors associated with the private school out of which the Yale Law School

[1] In assembling the material for this sketch, the author has had the invaluable help of Miss Elizabeth Forgeus, Assistant Law Librarian. New matter used is drawn largely from the manuscript papers of Staples, Hitchcock, and Daggett.

I

grew, and they served, in succession, as the law library of both the earlier and the later school.

The segregation of the residue of these books, to form the Yale Law Library Founders' Collection, after more than a century of the school's life, is a belated tribute to these three men, and an event of interest to all Yale men in law, particularly those who are in sympathy with the objects of the Committee on Law Library Patrons of the Yale Law School Association. In the year when Connecticut is celebrating its tercentenary, it is not inappropriate that the school should pay homage to the men and the books that are responsible for its own beginning.

Of the original group of books, only a portion has been salvaged. If henceforth we treat them with reverence, the contrast with their former experiences will be great. They bear the scars of use and misuse, and reflect the lean years through which the law library itself more than once has passed. They have been patched, mended, bound, and rebound until their appearance is pathetic. Now withdrawn from active service, they will nevertheless serve as memorials, not only of their original owners, whose autographs they bear, but also of generations of perspiring students by whom they have been thumbed over, praised, and reviled. Every graduate of the school whose achievements we would emulate has probably given them, by use, an added odor of sanctity.

There is an intimate connection between the careers of the three Founders. All were Yale graduates. Daggett, the oldest, studied law in the New Haven office of Charles Chauncey. Staples studied with Daggett, and Hitchcock with Staples. Daggett, according to the prevailing custom, took into his office a few law apprentices, among whom were Jirah Isham, Elisha Stearnes, and Staples. He did not, however, treat them as a law class. Staples,

2

on his part, soon after the year 1800, met groups of students, much as Tapping Reeve was doing in the Litchfield Law School. Staples was familiar with Reeve's methods, and it is nearly certain that he supplemented his studies with Daggett by a short course in Reeve's school. Hitchcock, in 1820, became Staples' law partner and his associate in the conduct of his school. When Staples dropped out, and the school was loosely associated with Yale College, in 1824, Daggett joined Hitchcock to carry on the law classes. Daggett was then sixty years old, and Hitchcock was thirty-eight.

The limitation of the Founders' Collection to the books owned by these three men should not be understood as failure to give credit to their successors, who on several occasions saved the school from dissolution; nor as unwillingness to recognize the fact that Elizur Goodrich was the first professor of law in Yale College. To this office he was appointed in 1801, in accordance with the plan devised by President Dwight of adding professional studies to the academic courses. Mr. Goodrich, however, had no connection whatever with the Staples school, and his lectures to college students embraced only a general outline of the theory of law, with emphasis on the law of nature and of nations. Goodrich entered Yale College in 1775, and was "uninterruptedly connected with the institution, either as student, resident graduate, tutor, assistant to the Treasurer, Professor, member of the Corporation, or Secretary of that Board, for the space of seventy-one years." He studied law with his uncle, Charles Chauncey, was a member of the Connecticut legislature, a representative in Congress, collector of the Port of New Haven, judge of the Probate Court, and chief judge of the County Court. These public duties and the fact that "the funds of the College would not allow

3

the Corporation to give an adequate salary to their Professor" (it was $200 per year) prevented him from making law teaching a major interest, and he resigned his professorship in 1810. During most of this period, the Staples classes were in all probability being held, but entirely separate from the College. The law professorship made vacant by the resignation of Goodrich was not filled until 1826, when David Daggett was appointed to it.

II

IN the year 1800, Isaac Beers, a New Haven bookseller, imported for Seth P. Staples "a very complete law library, one of the best at that time in New England." This was the first in a series of events which led up to the establishment of the Yale Law School. It is appropriate that books, rather than buildings, or even teachers, should be thought of as the germ of the school, for throughout its early history, as will later be shown, there is constant emphasis on books as the *sine qua non* of a law school. Ten of the volumes in this first shipment to Staples have been identified in the Yale Law Library.

Seth Perkins Staples was born in Canterbury, Connecticut, on August 31, 1776. He was the third child of the Reverend John Staples (Princeton, 1765), pastor of the Congregational Church in Westminster Society. His mother was Susanna, sister of Enoch Perkins, who graduated from Yale College in 1781. The son entered Yale in 1793 and graduated in 1797, in the same class with Lyman Beecher (father of Henry Ward Beecher), United States Supreme Court Justice Henry Baldwin, and United States Senator Horatio Seymour. In 1801, he was the Phi Beta Kappa orator at the College and received the M.A. degree.

Immediately after his graduation, he began the study

4

of law in the New Haven office of David Daggett. Biographical sketches of Staples do not state that he attended the Litchfield Law School, nor does the published list of members of that school, beginning in 1798, contain his name. This negative evidence is not, however, conclusive, since other men, known to have attended the school, are missing also. That he was a student under Tapping Reeve in the fall of 1798 is suggested by a manuscript notebook of 983 pages, some of which are blank, which is now in the Yale Law Library. It is undoubtedly in the writing of Staples, and bears the inscription, "Lectures on Law by T. Reeve, Esq., one of the Judges of the S. Court in Connecticut. Sept. 10th, 1798." It was the method of instruction at Litchfield to read lectures which students carefully took down as nearly verbatim as possible. Seven sets of such lecture notebooks by other students are in the Yale Law Library. It is possible that Staples had access to someone else's notebook, and made a copy of it, but there is no reason to presume this. His notes are not as extensive as those of some other students, indicating perhaps that his stay was shorter; and at the end of the book is a section made up of his own comment on independent readings in criminal law.

If he did study in Reeve's school, he returned to the office of Daggett to complete his preparations for admission to the bar. This event took place in Litchfield, on September 21, 1799.

An incident connected with it is of interest because of the light which it throws on methods of bar examination, on the intense political feeling that existed, and on the close relationship between Staples and his preceptor, Daggett. Staples went by stage from New Haven to Litchfield, arriving on Monday evening, September 16, 1799. On Tuesday, he delivered to the bar his letters of

5

recommendation and his certificate of study signed by Daggett. That evening, Mr. Allen proposed that he be admitted to examination. Thereupon, General Tracy (probably United States Senator Uriah Tracy, who was a major general of militia) objected, because (in the words of Staples) "he had been informed that I was a great Democrat and a violent Disorganizer—that on that account I came to Litchfield to apply for examination, and as proof of this I was strongly opposed to the abolition of the ΦBK Society; & as damning proof Mr. Tutor Day was then in town who would furnish indubitable proof of the whole." Mr. J. C. Smith and several others spoke in opposition to General Tracy, but nevertheless permission to enter the examination was withheld. When these happenings were reported to Staples, who was not present at the meeting, he was "perfectly astonished." "But, it recurring to my mind," he wrote, "that Dr. Dwight had that evening arrived in town, I went immediately to him & stated what had passed in the bar meeting. He laughed very heartily & said he could help me out of that scrape very easily, & wrote me a very full certificate & told me that if Mr. Tracy or any other person wanted any further information either affecting my political or moral character & would call on him in the morning, he would give him or them the fullest satisfaction. Mr. Tutor Day was applied to by Mr. Tracy & others & stated in the fulest manner directly the contrary of every word Mr. Tracy had said." Next day at noon, the bar again took up the matter, but delayed decision because the presence of Mr. Tracy was desired, in order that he might be asked to disclose who was the author of the "vile calumny" against Staples. Mr. Tracy appeared before the bar that evening but refused to give the source of his information, although he said that he was now satisfied.

6

The above account is contained in a letter from Staples to Daggett written on September 20, 1799, with a postscript dated eight o'clock Saturday morning, September 21, in which he said that he was finally admitted to the examination, was questioned very closely by the Committee of Examiners during two evenings, and that at the opening of the Court on that very morning, he was to be sworn. Earlier in the letter, he wrote that "some give hints as if they thought" General Tracy "objected on account of the *good will* he bears my instructor" (Daggett), and in the postscript he wrote that "there is a secret in this business, which if I were not under injunctions of secrecy, I would tell you. The obligation of secrecy will not, however, preclude me from being at liberty to tell you a curious story when I see you, for I promised to observe no injunctions of secrecy that would involve me."

After the successful outcome of his trip to Litchfield, Staples immediately began the practice of law in New Haven, and in November of the same year he married Catharine, daughter of the Reverend Samuel Wales, Yale 1767, who was Livingston Professor of Divinity in the College. They had six children, three sons and three daughters.

While making his way as a lawyer, he found time to represent the town of New Haven in five sessions of the State legislature (1814–16), and he was a colonel of the militia. At a New Haven military muster on May 7, 1810, making a fine figure riding on a horse, he commanded an artillery company of one hundred men with four pieces of artillery.

In law, his success was rapid. It is said that he ranked with the leaders of the profession in New Haven, including such men as David Daggett, Simeon Baldwin,

7

Nathan Smith, William Bristol, and Charles Denison. In 1820, he formed a partnership with Samuel J. Hitchcock by means of which he maintained a connection with New Haven for many years after he moved to New York City in 1824.

A famous New Haven case in which he was counsel was that of the Amistad captives, African negroes kidnapped in 1839 by slave traders, sold by them in Cuba to Spanish subjects, shipped on the schooner *Amistad* which they took by force into their own hands, and captured in Long Island Sound when the schooner anchored there. Anti-slavery philanthropists engaged Staples, Theodore Sedgwick, and Roger Sherman Baldwin to represent the negroes, and they were eventually set free. The argument in the United States Supreme Court (15 Peters 518) was made by Baldwin and John Quincy Adams, in opposition to Attorney General Gilpin.

Staples was an expert in patent law, and was for many years counsel for Charles Goodyear in the series of cases over his patent for vulcanizing rubber. From 1837 to 1855 his name appears constantly in litigated cases along with those of Daniel Webster, Rufus Choate, Francis B. Cutting, Charles O'Conor, and James T. Brady. Staples' granddaughter, Mrs. Harriette S. S. Wheeler, possesses as a reminder of this litigation, a cane of vulcanized rubber with gold tip, given to Staples by Goodyear.

Staples' withdrawal from the law school which he had started in New Haven did not end his interest in teaching, for in 1828 he delivered lectures on commercial law at the Mercantile Library in New York City. In appreciation of this gratuitous service, the directors of the library presented to him a silver pitcher, appropriately engraved. His scholarly habit of mind is further attested by his ownership of a share in the New York Society Library,

8

and by the large law office library assembled by him in New York, which was sold at auction after his death. A copy of Bangs, Merwin and Company's auction catalogue for April 24–25, 1862, now in the Yale Law Library, lists 1,417 volumes of his law books, including not only the usual type of treatises and American law reports, but also many English law reports, long runs of American, English, and Canadian session laws, sets of legal periodicals, works on Roman and international law, and a special group on patents. Included in the sale are the essential furnishings of a frugal law office, pine wood bookcases, a library table, and two black-walnut office chairs.

He died in New York City on February 15, 1861, at the age of eighty-six, and was buried in the Grove Street Cemetery in New Haven.

III

THE story of the Staples law school, as has been said, begins with the importation of a shipment of English law books in 1800. To this first shipment he continued to add both English and American books, so that students deemed it a high privilege to study in his office. They came in sufficient numbers to warrant organization of regular classes. There is a tradition that these were at first held in his own house, before breakfast, and that the students often "assembled before he left his bed-chamber, and awaited 'patiently' his appearance." The earliest of Staples' several residences was at number 75 (now 155) Elm Street, the building known as the Graduates Club. If he did in fact hold classes there, it is an interesting coincidence that Hendrie Hall, where the Yale Law School was housed from 1895 to 1931, should have been located next door. At a later time, his house was on

9

Temple Street, on a site subsequently occupied by the house of Ezekiel G. Stoddard, eventually purchased for the use of the Sheffield Scientific School. And later still, he lived on Church Street, opposite the Green, on the site where the law chambers building now stands.

Without doubt Staples' law office was the center of his law school, serving as a library, classroom, and laboratory of practice. Where this office was prior to 1820, has not been discovered. Beginning with that date, when he formed a partnership with Hitchcock, it was located on Church Street near the corner of Court, where Staples leased from William Leffingwell a building of twenty-two feet frontage. The lease, dated November 11, 1820, was for twenty years, and stipulated that Leffingwell was not to build within ten feet of the line, and that he would deed the property to Staples, his heirs or assigns. This lease was, on October 28, 1831, assigned to Samuel J. Hitchcock, and in 1843, an heir of William Leffingwell deeded the property, but without the agreement not to build within ten feet of the line. The twenty-two feet frontage was between the sites later occupied by the City Hall and the Leffingwell building, the latter of which stood on the northeast corner of Church and Court Streets. The present Powell building occupies the site of these two buildings, running from the corner to the City Hall. In this little building, leased by Staples and later known as the Hitchcock building, the Staples law school and its successor in all probability remained until the year 1850 when the Leffingwell building (Heublein's) was completed.

Here, therefore, we should try to picture Staples and Hitchcock, as carrying on the school, surrounded by books, some of which are now in the Founders' Collection. We are helped to do this by a description of Staples,

10

written by a student who attended classes in this building in 1823–24.[2]

"Those who only saw him in the conflicts of the bar," he said of Mr. Staples, "and heard his bitter sarcasms, could form no true estimate of his character. They saw nothing of his kindlier nature and social qualities, as exhibited in the office and the recitation room. As a teacher he exerted a magnetism over his students unsurpassed by any man I ever knew—a magnetism that drew his pupils into thorough study of first principles. No greater contrast could well exist than that presented by comparison of the formal law lectures of the Litchfield school and the off-hand comments and illustrations of Mr. Staples' class room: Judge Gould read his able and finished lectures with a cold dignity to his students, each seated at his separate desk, intent on copying from his lips the principles laid down and the authorities referred to, embodying a system of law for future reference and use. In the New Haven school, at the time it was made a department of the college, the class recitations superseded in great measure the formal lecture. The student in his study drew the principles from the text book. In the recitation they were sifted, tested and illustrated. It was here that Mr. Staples was perhaps unrivaled as a teacher. His practice at the bar enabled him to illustrate principles and decisions from his own experience and observation, in such a manner as to fix them in the mind in a manner very different from the mere entry of them in a note book. Mr. Staples read few lectures, and they were not of a high order. It was as an off-hand commentator that he impressed *himself* as well as *the law* on the minds of his students."

Who were the students whom Staples taught prior to 1820, and whom Staples and Hitchcock taught from 1820 to 1824? Who were the men who fingered the Staples books now in the Founders' Collection?

In 1824, a tenuous connection between the Staples school and Yale College was made by printing the names

[2] Quoted by Theodore D. Woolsey in his *Historical Discourse* at the Fiftieth Anniversary of the Foundation of the Department of Law, June 24, 1874.

II

of fourteen law students in the College catalogue. Who were the students who went before them?

From a reading of biographies, a few names have been gleaned of men who studied law in the office of Staples. They are

Samuel Johnson Hitchcock, Yale 1809
Ralph Isaacs Ingersoll, Yale 1808
Thomas Burr Osborne, Yale 1817
Thomas Clapp Perkins, Yale 1818

To this meagre list can now be added something more substantial. It is a list of students in the Staples law school from 1819 to 1824. Written by Staples, the list appears in the Cash and Receipt Book of the firm of Staples and Hitchcock for the period April, 1817 to August, 1827. The comments following some of the names are by Staples. Names preceded by an asterisk appear also in the list of law students printed in the College catalogue of 1824.

"LIST OF STUDENTS WHO HAVE ENTERED THE OFFICE"

1819

Edward Chapin (Admitted to Bar Nov. 29, 1821)
Samuel D. Hubbard (Admitted to Bar Nov. 29, 1821)
Hector Humphrey
Rufus Woodward

1820

Apollo D. Bates (June 28. County Court June term took the oath and left)
Horace Foot (Admitted to Bar at Middletown, Sept. 27, 1822)
James S. Huggins (Admitted to Bar Nov. 29, 1821)
Pollard McCormick
Horatio Miller (Admitted to Bar Nov. 29, 1821)

12

1821

John H. Brockway (Admitted to Bar Mar. 22, 1823)
Asa Child of Woodstock (Admitted to Bar June 24, 1823)
Walter Edwards of Hartford (Admitted to Bar, Hartford, Nov. 1822)
Theodore Hinsdale of Winstead

1822

William Barnes of Tolland
Asa Butts of Canterbury (Sickened with a decline and died 2d year)
Joel Hinman of Southbury
Sam C. Jackson of Dorset, Vermont
Oliver A. Shaw (Studied one year and went to Virginia)
*Isaac Henry Townsend
Ira L. Ufford of Huntington (Admitted to Bar Mar. 22, 1823)
G. Fitch Wheeler of Huntington (Admitted to Bar Nov. County Court, 1823)

1823

Charles Atwood
William Barnes of Tolland (Admitted to Bar Nov. County Court, 1823)
*John Boyd of Winchester
*Sherman Crosswell of New Haven
Simeon F. Dixon of Enfield
*Samuel Hayes of New Haven
Charles F. Johnson
John H. Lathrop, tutor
*Henry E. Peck
*Amasa G. Porter (Admitted to Bar June County Court, 1825)
Edward Rockwell
William Rockwell of Sharon
*Aaron N. Skinner of Woodstock, Conn.
Solomon Stoddard, tutor (Relinquished study and paid nothing)
William G. Verplanck of Mount Pleasant, N. Y. (Broke his leg and never attended)
*Daniel Whiting
*Frederick R. Whittelsey of Southington

13

1824

*S. J. Andrews of Wallingford
*Linus Child of Woodstock
William Read of Sparta, Georgia (Returned to Georgia, Sept.
   1825)
George B. Ripley of Norwich
*Wm. P. Skinner of Marietta, Ohio
*Isaac Webb

Although the above is a list of students "who entered the office," there is no doubt that they came not as apprentices but as paying pupils. They came, however, not at stated dates, as though for a fixed term, but whenever they could, to stay as long as they could. They paid for the time that they stayed. Many of them remained two years, a fact shown by Staples' notes, and not usually by the repetition of the name under the date of the second year. They paid in cash when they could; if not, by personal note. That all accounts for the years 1819 to 1824 were eventually cleared is shown in a list headed "Amount due Staples and Hitchcock on Book January 1, 1825." There, students' unpaid bills listed by name and amount are classified among "good" debts, and annotations subsequently made give the respective dates of final payment.

IV

THE moving spirit in the law school for a quarter of a century was Samuel J. Hitchcock. He became an instructor four years before Staples withdrew, and he continued actively in the work until his death in 1845, that is, from his thirty-fourth to his sixtieth year. It was Hitchcock who carried the chief burden of teaching, who built up the law library, who paid rent to Staples for the law building up to 1831, and after that himself owned the

14

lease, and who finally brought about the conferring of law degrees by Yale College. His career both in and out of the school is worthy of attention.

He was born on February 4, 1786, at Bethlehem, Connecticut, the eldest of the twelve children of Benjamin and Mary (Johnson) Hitchcock. It was impossible for the father to give his son educational advantages, and his first work was as a mechanic. The love of reading was, however, born in him. It is related that because the father could not "afford young Hitchcock lights to read by so late as he desired, he . . . accustomed himself to lie down in front of the fire with book in hand, and there gratify his insatiable love of knowledge by studying out the words and sentences from the imperfect light of the dying embers thus afforded. To this is attributed the weakness of his eyes, under which he greatly suffered for years." He attracted the attention of his pastor, the Reverend Azel Backus (Yale 1787), who fitted him to teach school, and eventually gratuitously prepared him to enter the Sophomore class at Yale. He graduated at the head of his class in 1809, appropriately delivering the valedictory oration on the *Wisdom of Aiming at High Attainments*.

For two years after his graduation he taught in the Fairfield Academy and then returned to New Haven to become a tutor in Yale College. At the Commencement exercises of 1812, he became a Master of Arts and delivered an oration on the influence of newspapers. He resigned his tutorship in 1815, the event being marked by a gift of money from a committee of his students. The presentation letter, dated July 20, 1815, concludes with the words, "while we lament your departure, we are consoled with the reflection that you have removed from a circumscribed into a more extensive sphere of action,

15

where your acquirements and goodness of heart will be more useful and conspicuous."

The sphere of action referred to was that of the law. While serving as tutor, he had also read law in the office of Seth P. Staples. On June 4, 1814, at a session of the New Haven County Court, he was admitted to the bar, the court having before it a certificate from Staples, and one from the bar examination committee consisting of Nathan Smith, Bennet Bronson, Cyrus Clark, Curtiss Hinman, Isaac M. Wales, and Ralph I. Ingersoll. At a later date, April 13, 1821, he was admitted to practice before the United States Circuit Court.

Beginning practice in New Haven in 1815, by 1818 he was ready to embark upon the sea of matrimony. One of the preliminaries to this event throws light on his character. The lady of his choice, Laura, the orphaned daughter of Simeon and Parnel Coan, of Guilford, returned his affection, but hesitated to name the day because, being unable to purchase her "furniture," she feared that she might be a burden to him. To overcome this obstacle, Hitchcock proposed to her uncle in a letter dated January 5, 1818, that they conspire together to practice a pious fraud upon her. The plan was that the uncle, Eliakim Fowler, should make a gift of $300 to Laura, telling her that he knew she needed the money for the purpose above mentioned, and that he had always intended to assist her on the approach of that crisis which he had heard was coming upon her. Hitchcock engaged on his part to repay Fowler with interest at any time and in any way that the donor might point out. "If you will do this," wrote Hitchcock, "I am well convinced you will add exceedingly to her comfort and do much, more perhaps than you are aware of, toward making her a happy bride. . . . You will see, dear Sir, that if you can conveniently and

16

SETH P. STAPLES

From Jared B. Flagg's copy, in the Yale Law School, of a portrait by Samuel L. Waldo and William Jewett.

SAMUEL J. HITCHCOCK

From a portrait in the Yale Law School by Jared B. Flagg.

DAVID DAGGETT

From a silhouette made by Samuel Metford, July 5, 1842.

HITCHCOCK BUILDING
(at the extreme lower left), first
home of the Law School.

LEFFINGWELL BUILDING
The second floor of the rear extension
was the Law School's second home.

consistently comply with the above request, it must never be known to your niece that I made it,—or at least that the secret must not be divulged until some future period." The letter closed with a request for a reply within ninety days. The answer must have been favorable, for the marriage took place on May 18, 1818.

As law partner of Staples, beginning in 1820, he divided his time between teaching and practice. An amusing incident connected with the latter is recorded in his "Waste-book," as follows:

Feby. 26, 1821. Norman Munson called and demanded his Bill of fees of S. P. S. for serving writ, H. D. Sewall v. Miles Pickus, indorsed on writ in office as below:—

Travel to make service, 4 mi.	$ 0.20
Travel to return, 13 mi.	0.60
Attachment	0.12
Committing, travel, 13 mi.	2.60
2 Keepers 24 hours	3.00
Necessary expenses for keepers, meat, drinks & Lodgings	3.42
Mittimus	.50
	$10.44

Mr. Staples offered him fees as below:—

Trav. to serve, 4 mi.	$ 0.20
Levy	0.12
Travel to commit, 13 mi.	2.60
Mittimus	0.25
	$3.17

But he demanded the whole and would not take the fees as offered. 4th May gratefully took $3.17 in full.

In later years, Hitchcock's law practice became extensive, and he took a prominent part in the life of the community. He was a judge of the New Haven County Court from 1838 to 1842, chief judge of the City Court, 1842 to 1844, and mayor of the city from 1839 to 1841.

17

For more than a decade (1833–45), he was a deacon of Center Church where he conducted a Bible class for young men. According to Professor Woolsey he was "one of the most decidedly religious men to be found in any department of life."

In developing means of transportation in the State, he played a prominent part for twenty years. From 1825 to 1840, he was concerned professionally with the affairs of the ill-fated Farmington canal. He was a director of the Hartford and New Haven Railroad and its president from 1837 to 1840. These were troubled years. The road, chartered in 1833, was not completed until 1839. The panic of 1837 found the Railroad's treasury completely exhausted, with subscriptions largely unpaid. The cause was not excessive salaries, for Hitchcock received only $1,000 a year. To insure through-service from Hartford to New York City, the road was authorized in 1839 to charter, purchase, and hold steamboats. This development precipitated a rate war in which Commodore Vanderbilt took part. The steamboat fare from New Haven to New York dropped as low as twenty-five cents. In the next year newspaper articles charged official mismanagement of the road. Hitchcock, on July 21, 1840, and again on August 10, replied to the "libelous charges," "industriously circulated among the stockholders," "criminating the officers, and alledging culpable mismanagement." He called upon all stockholders to attend the coming meeting in September, and vote with a knowledge of the "motives and designs" of the accusers. The victory went, however, to the new party, which set about resuscitating the road. They found it useful, nevertheless, to employ Hitchcock professionally, for he was recognized as a specialist in railroad law. Moreover, this was not the end of his official connection with railroads. In

18

1844, he was one of the incorporators of the New York and New Haven Railroad Company, along with Joseph E. Sheffield, William A. Reynolds, Nathan Smith, and others. Launching the new company was difficult business. After the subscription books had been open ten days, there were only three New Haven subscribers, of whom Hitchcock was one. Sheffield and Hitchcock arranged for the first surveys of the route, and prepared a plan for negotiating the stock of the company through the Barings, in England. This latter project failed as a consequence of Hitchcock's death. A part of his last winter was spent in Albany seeking to obtain franchises for the proposed road to enter New York City.

At one time, Hitchcock lived in the house now occupied by the Graduates Club on Elm Street, where Staples had lived before him. At the time of his death, his residence stood next to the Tontine Hotel on Church Street, a house which he had built in 1827–28. He died of a "billious fever," after an illness of three weeks, on August 31, 1845, being then in his sixtieth year. The funeral service in Center Church was attended by the local bar association and the Common Council of the city, and he was buried in the Grove Street Cemetery. By his wife, Laura, he had two sons and three daughters. She died in 1832, and in 1834 he married Narcissa Perry, widow of Joseph Whittemore of Fredericksburg, Virginia, and daughter of Walter and Elizabeth Burr (Sturges) Perry, of Southport, Connecticut. They had one son. In his will, after providing for his surviving widow and children, he directed that the surplus of his estate should be used by the trustees, to the extent of $1,000 per annum, "for the support of indigent pious young men preparing for the ministry in New Haven." Concerning this provision there was litigation as late as the year 1851.

19

IN 1824, when Hitchcock took control of the school, he had formidable rivals. Chancellor Kent was lecturing at Columbia College, the law school at Harvard had already begun to grant degrees, and the Litchfield Law School was in the competent hands of James Gould. In New Haven itself, a competing school was opened by Judge Asa Chapman. After graduation from Yale in 1792, studying at the Litchfield Law School, and being admitted to the bar in 1795, Chapman had settled in Newtown, Connecticut, where for many years, in connection with his practice, he instructed students in law. In the fall of 1824, he moved to New Haven and announced in the *Connecticut Journal* of November 11, that he would receive law students at an annual tuition of $75. The failure of his health and his death in 1825 left the New Haven field free for Hitchcock.

Two fortunate circumstances gave prestige to Hitchcock's school—the listing of his students in the Yale College catalogue beginning in 1824, and Judge Daggett's willingness to join him as a law lecturer. The connection with Yale was further strengthened two years later when a statement descriptive of the law school was added to the list of students in the Yale catalogue, and when Daggett took on the separate duties of professor of law in the College. The first of the annual law-school announcements reads as follows:

The Law School is under the instruction of the Hon. David Daggett, a Judge of the Supreme Court in Connecticut, and Professor of Law, and Samuel J. Hitchcock, Esq., attorney and councellor at law.

The students are required to peruse the most important elementary treatises, and are daily examined on the author

20

they are reading, and receive at the same time explanations and illustrations of the subject they are studying.

A course of lectures is delivered by the Professor of Law, on all the titles and subjects of the Common and Statute Law.

A moot court is holden once a week, or oftener, which employs the students in drawing pleadings and investigating and arguing questions of law.

The students are also called upon, from time to time, to draw declarations, pleadings, contracts, and other instruments, connected with the practice of law, and to do the most important duties of an attorney's clerk.

They are occasionally required to write disquisitions on some topic of law, and collect the authorities to support their opinions.

The students are furnished with the use of the elementary books, and have access, at all times, to the college libraries, and to a law library, comprising very important works both ancient and modern.

The terms for tuition and use of library are $75 per annum. The course of study occupies two years, allowing eight weeks vacation each year. Students are however received for a shorter period.

The Professor of Law will also, for the present, occasionally deliver lectures to the Senior class in College, until arrangements are made for a systematic course to be permanently continued. (Yale College Catalogue, November, 1826.)

In this announcement the name of Judge Daggett is put first, since he was a vastly greater public figure than was Hitchcock. He was not, however, in charge of the school, which was, it will be noted, "under the instruction" of both men. In the catalogue of 1828–29, the word "instruction" was changed to "direction," but still the meaning conveyed is that there was joint responsibility. The same form was used after Isaac H. Townsend joined them in 1842, indicating responsibility divided among three men. There appears to be no doubt that Hitchcock for many years bore the weight both of administration

21

and teaching. The latter was carried on principally by means of textbook reading, lectures, and quizzes. The above announcement states that "students are furnished with the use of the elementary books." This means that Hitchcock provided students with individual copies of such books, without additional cost to them.

Concerning Hitchcock's quality as a teacher, fortunately we have the opinion of two of his pupils, quoted in Woolsey's *Historical Discourse:*

I was a great admirer of Judge Hitchcock (wrote the first). He was a model teacher. He was so clear, you could not fail to understand him fully; so copious in instruction and illustration, that he seemed to exhaust the subject, and you felt that he was master of the principles of law, and of their application and analogies; and yet so compact in style that he never used a word too much. As I had just come from Harvard, I often compared him with Judge Story, and was at a loss to decide which was the most admirable instructor. We recited to him in Cruise's Digest. It was called a book hard to understand, but under his teaching it was all clear and plain; and we wondered how it had got such a name. Recitations to him were for a full half-hour [with] lectures from him on the subjects we were studying.

Another gentleman, who studied law in the school in the years 1838 and 1839, wrote of him thus:

The mainstay of the school was Judge Hitchcock. Many of the students had studied one year at Cambridge, where the school was much larger, and where Judge Story was the great ornament; but they all gave the palm to Hitchcock over Greenleaf, able and learned as the latter was admitted to be. The introductory lecture of Judge Hitchcock always made a great impression. He dwelt upon the distinction between *reading* and *study;* upon the fact that they had not come there to win prizes in the shape of degrees; that a man might read

22

law forever, and not be a lawyer; he must study, and he might study much, but it would be to little purpose unless he accustomed himself to feel that he had the responsibility of some future client [in his hands] whose property or rights would depend upon the accuracy with which the books [he had studied] were comprehended. His running comments, as the recitation progressed, were remarkable, not so much for the matter as for the manner of putting them. There was a tinge of cynicism about him which gave much effect and pungency to his utterances. He had an intense horror of shams. The series of questions with which he tested the students' knowledge were what might be described as searching; they gave an interest to the pages of Cruise and Chitty, which the students, on previously reading them, had never suspected to exist.

The recitations in the first volume of Blackstone's Commentaries had a particular interest for those who did not intend to follow the law as a profession, and many of the theological students were in the habit of coming into the lecture-room at this time.

You are aware there are some chapters relating to subjects which are obsolete or have no possible application to this country. On that account they are not made the subject of recitation in most law schools; but Judge Hitchcock made us [study] them all, as he said that we should find frequent refer ences to them in our future reading, and would better understand some of the influences which had built up the common law. The chapter on the king's royal title, he thought, should be carefully studied by every one who wished to get a clear idea of English history. It was amazing, indeed, to see what stores of illustrations from history, fiction, poetry and the classics were treasured up in the brain of this man, who appeared to the world as nothing but a dry lawyer. (*Historical Discourse* by Theodore D. Woolsey, pp. 19–20.)

A volume of eighty-four pages which has been preserved, containing notes on Hitchcock's lectures taken down by Timothy Merwin, from January 7 to March 5, 1828, shows them to be unlikely to cause students to burst into song. Yet such was the effect on one student

23

who wrote the following in one of the law school's books:

Oh Thou who hear'st the students' prayer
How dark with all its witch-talk
Would seem the Law, if puzzled here,
We could not fly to Hitchcock.

Others had a different reason for gratitude. "To the needy, he was a friend," says an account written at the time of his death. "To the poor young man who listened to his instructions without the ability to compensate him at the time, he was not a hard master; but left them to consult their own time in remunerating him for his services."

In 1830, Hitchcock was made an instructor in the science and practice of law in Yale College. This appointment, it should be understood, gave him merely a title of academic honor, for there is no evidence that he ever taught in the College. The law school, the scene of his constant effort, was still to all intents a separate, private institution. Further recognition came to him in 1842, when the Yale degree of Doctor of Laws was conferred upon him. For some years before his death he was engaged in the preparation of a work on contracts, but despite the desire of Little & Brown to publish it, it never saw the light.

In 1843, the degree of Bachelor of Laws was first conferred by Yale College. The initiative for this step was taken by Hitchcock in the following communication dated August 6, 1842:

To the President and Fellows of Yale College
    The undersigned would respectfully represent
    That from various sources of Information he has learned and believes that the Law Department of the College fails to secure the attendance of many students who enter Law Schools elsewhere, because other institutions confer the degree of

24

Bachelor of Laws upon their students at Law, while Yale College has conferred no degrees in Law except the honorary degree of Doctor of Laws upon distinguished individuals. If equal advantages of Instruction are enjoyed at different Institutions the expected honor of a degree determines the choice of the student. The schools of Law at Yale and Harvard were about equal in numbers until the latter College began to confer degrees, since which time their pupils have rapidly increased, and without any other apparent cause. If it is desirable that a Law Department should be, in any way, connected with the College, it is quite important that such department should not be greatly inferior in numbers and respectability to like Departments in other Colleges. Occasionally also, some restraint upon those who are pursuing professional study, beyond the mere influence of public opinion, or the wish to obtain an instructor's regard, would be salutary. If a favour is sought to be received from the Government of the College, conditions may be prescribed which, while they are not onerous, may secure correct deportment toward all who are officially concerned, and raise the standard of attainments, and of moral conduct, in the candidate for a degree.

With these views I would respectfully present for consideration the accompanying sketch of regulations referring to the above particulars with the wish that the Corporation would act upon the subject at their next meeting.

Samuel J. Hitchcock

On August 16, 1842, referring specifically to Hitchcock's proposal, the Yale Corporation approved the plan, and directed that the specified degree be conferred "on such students in the School, as shall during the year be found to have the qualifications required." The regulations submitted by Hitchcock were given verbal revision during the year, and on August 15, 1843, were adopted by the Corporation as follows:

Voted in regard to the Law Department:
1. *Membership*. Graduates of a College, or those who have been honorably dismissed therefrom are admitted upon proba-

tion upon satisfactory evidence, that they received their degree or dismissal not more than one year previous to their admission. But no person shall be admitted to attend on the lectures or other courses of instruction in the Law School, who has been expelled or disgracefully dismissed from Yale College. Those who have been graduated or honorably dismissed for more than one year and all other applicants must produce testimonials of good moral character. After a residence of three months, and on proof of regular attendance, commendable proficiency, and continued good moral character, the student may be admitted to matriculation.

2. *Degrees.* Matriculated Students who attend all the exercises of the department and fall under no censure as to College deportment after eighteen months membership, if liberally educated, or two years if not, and upon passing a satisfactory examination may be admitted to the degree of Bachelor of Common and Statute Laws. Those who are members of the School and perform their duties in like manner for one year after their admission to the Bar may be admitted to the same degree. Those who are members for a period which does not entitle the student to a degree, and perform their duties in like manner, shall be entitled to a certificate signed by the President and the Professor of Law.

College dues. The Graduation fee shall be four dollars [paid] to the President and the common fee to the Secretary beside diploma, to be furnished by the student.

VI

WHEN Staples moved to New York City in 1824, he took with him most of his law books. What he did not take, books especially suited for school work, Hitchcock bought from him. These books, with others which belonged to Hitchcock, supplemented by books loaned by Daggett, made up the school library in 1824. Thirteen years later, Hitchcock bought these latter books from Daggett at a cost of $325.75. Steadily throughout the years until his death in 1845, Hitchcock added to his

26

collection, always at his own expense. The total cost of the 2,260 volumes which he eventually owned was $7,736.55.

It was Hitchcock's books to which the law school announcement of 1826 referred when it said that "students are furnished with the use of the *elementary books*, and have access, at all times, to the college libraries, and to *a law library*, comprising very important works both ancient and modern." Law books in the Yale College library according to the *Catalogue of Books in the Library of Yale College* (pp. 39–42) published in 1823, numbered about one hundred volumes, most of them books for the general student rather than the lawyer. These could not be depended upon for the regular work of the school. When the announcement refers to "very important works both ancient and modern," it is distinguishing between law treatises, on the one hand, and law reports and statutes, on the other. Of the latter, Hitchcock at first possessed few. Of treatises he continued to purchase many, but not enough to justify the substitution of the word "every" for the word "very." This inadvertent typographical change appeared first in the announcement of 1827, crediting the library with possessing "every important work both ancient and modern."

An announcement which is found in all of the catalogues from 1831–32 to 1837–38, when it was dropped without explanation, is the following:

Arrangements are making and nearly completed, by which the students can at all times examine the Statute Laws of each State in the Union, and all the reported cases which have been published in this country.

"The explanation of this announcement," wrote Professor Henry Wade Rogers (*The Yale Shingle*, 1912,

27

p. 59), "probably lies in the fact that it was expected that the State Bar Library in the Capitol at Hartford would be removed to the State Capitol at New Haven. But this expectation was doomed to sad disappointment. The union of the New Haven and Connecticut colonies had been reluctantly consented to by the former, and as a measure of conciliation, two Capitols were established, one at New Haven, and one at Hartford. This arrangement lasted from 1701 until 1873, when Hartford was made the sole capitol. But the State Law Library was always at Hartford, although in the early thirties there was a scheme on foot to remove it to New Haven."

This particular plan fell through, but nevertheless, the catalogue of 1843–44 not only offered access to "every important work, both ancient and modern," but said that "the law library contains the Revised Statutes, the Reports and the Digests of all the States in the Union." These new accessions were purchased by Hitchcock.

The library, private as it was, was used not only by students, but by members of the bar, under the following simple conditions:

LIBRARY RULES

Members of the Law School cannot be permitted to take the *Reports* and *Digests* from the Library.

Personal application must be made for permission to take away *any other book* excepting the *text books*, which are read and recited in the school.

Gentlemen of the Bar who borrow books, are requested to leave their address in the place from which they take a book.

These rules are necessary, to make the Library equally useful to all.

The textbooks referred to were standard works required to be read by students, for whom copies were

28

provided. They were loaned to the individual students for extended periods, as shown by a receipt, which has been preserved. From this "charge card" we learn that Theodore W. Dwight of the class of 1841, who afterwards became famous as the head of the Columbia College Law School, on January 12, 1841, borrowed from Hitchcock the following books, Blackstone's *Commentaries*, Swift's *Digest*, and Wheaton's *Selwyn*. These he retained until August 15, 1842, when according to the receipt, he returned them. Of such books, when an inventory was taken in 1845, Hitchcock's library contained many copies. For example, he owned of Blackstone's *Commentaries*, thirty sets; of Chitty on *Pleading*, thirty-four sets; of Cruise's *Digest of Real Property*, twenty-five sets; of Starkie on *Evidence*, eighteen sets; of Swift's *Connecticut Digest*, thirty sets; and of Wheaton's Selwyn on *Nisi Prius*, twenty-four sets.

VII

The importance of the part which Hitchcock's library played in the history of the law school cannot well be overemphasized. It was the chief argument by means of which a closer connection with the College was brought about in 1846. After Hitchcock's death, it was frequently said that the school would have to be discontinued unless the library was acquired from his estate for the use of students. The local bar was also vitally interested and took an active part in the events which transpired. Henry White, executor of Hitchcock's will, procured an appraisal of the library, and offered it for $4,227.55, to the instructors then active in the law school, namely William L. Storrs and Isaac H. Townsend. These gentlemen suggested that the offer be made to Yale College. We may surmise that conferences ensued in which the question of

29

funds was prominent, and that the advice of leading members of the bar was asked. They responded by starting a subscription list for the purchase of the library. Storrs and Townsend then presented to the Prudential Committee of Yale College their formal proposal in writing, dated December 23, 1845. Six days later, December 29, Henry White, the executor, gave the Committee the terms on which he would sell the library. So matters stood until the following August, while the amount of the subscriptions was being augmented. Then, on August 11, 1846, came a resolution adopted by the Corporation of Yale College authorizing its Prudential Committee to proceed with the purchase of the library, applying the subscribed amounts to the purchase price, and setting up a plan for amortizing the sum necessary to be advanced to the law school by the College. On the same date the Corporation adopted a resolution, introduced by the Reverend Leonard Bacon, by which the law school was recognized officially as a department in the College "for special instruction in the science of law."

The first three of these documents, telling in detail the story of the purchase of the Hitchcock library, are printed below:

PROPOSAL OF STORRS AND TOWNSEND

The death of Judge Hitchcock, & the consequent necessity of a disposition of his Law Library, present the situation of the Law Institution, which was under his charge, as a matter deserving of the serious consideration of those in any manner interested in the subject, & have suggested to the undersigned (who are now engaged in the instruction of the Law Students,) the propriety of presenting to the Prudential Committee of Yale College their general views as to the course most expedient to be taken.

The Law Library has hitherto been the individual property

30

of the principal Instructor, & there has been no direct connexion between those engaged as instructors of the Law School & the College. Every thing has thus far been conducted in relation to the School with the best understanding with the College, &, it is believed, to the mutual satisfaction of both, as well as for the best interests of Education generally. There is no particular reason to think that this would not be the case in future. Yet it is easy to see that, unless steps are taken to guard against it, embarrassments may possibly arise from the want of a more immediate connexion between the School & the College; and the present is deemed an auspicious time to consider the subject.

As the Study of Law is one of the proper branches of a University education, we deem it very important that facilities for pursuing it should always be at the command of the College, independent of the will or control of any individuals. Those facilities consist mainly of a good Law Library. That is always indispensable. Others in connexion with it may, if not possessed, be supplied by temporary means until permanent ones can be furnished. But without a Library the Law School cannot flourish.

The College, if it owns a Library, can always immediately & properly supply Instructors for any vacancies which providentially or otherwise may occur.

It may also be suggested that a Library would be the foundation for farther endowments, by furnishing a motive for those having the ability, & feeling interested in the welfare of the College generally & the Law department in particular, to add, by donations, to the means of that branch of instruction; while nothing of this kind is to be expected in aid of merely individual enterprize.

It is therefore deemed by us to be of great importance that the College should become the proprietor of a Law Library; & in our opinion none more complete than the present one, as far as it extends, can be procured.

Having obtained a Library, the College, will have the means itself of continuing the Law School in the manner which is considered the most judicious.

The particular manner in which the School should be regulated is left entirely for the decision of the College authorities,

31

who are fully competent to devise the best plan for conducting the Law Department.

But, without intending to be officious, & having, as we trust, mainly in view the best interests of the College, we would take the liberty of adding a further suggestion on this point.

If the College furnish the use of the Library for the Law Institution, it is proper & just that it should have a supervision of the Institution, including the appointment of its Instructors, the terms of their engagement, the direction as to the course of study & the observances of the Students, with the testimonials to be furnished to them, & the terms on which they are to be granted.

Perhaps this Supervision could best be exercised by a Law Faculty, to be appointed by the College Corporation, to consist of the President, the Professor of Law, & such other Professors of the College or Instructors of the Law School, or both, as it shall be deemed best to associate with them for that purpose.

With the Library & such a Board of Supervision, the College would be in a situation to maintain, improve, & carry forward successfully the Law Department.

If these measures should be accomplished, the minor details connected with the subject, such as the necessary additions from time to time to the Library &c. may be safely left for subsequent adjustment.

New Haven,   William L. Storrs
    Dec. 23, 1845.   Isaac H. Townsend
    To the Prudential Committee.

HENRY WHITE TO THE PRUDENTIAL COMMITTEE

Gentlemen,

As executor of the late Judge Hitchcock, it has become my duty to sell his Law Library. As soon as the Inventory of the Library was completed, I thought it my duty to offer it first to the present Instructors of the Law School; and at their suggestion and request I now offer to sell it to Yale College. I am informed that these gentlemen will present a communication to the Prudential Committee which will contain their views of

32

DAVID DAGGETT'S HOUSE ON ELM STREET

the importance of the Library to the College in its relation to the Law School. I would therefore merely express my own increasing conviction of the value of the Law School to the general interests & standing of the College, and of the necessity of the Law Library to the prosperity of the Law School.

The Library of Judge Hitchcock has the reputation of being the best private law library in the country—and of not being surpassed by any public Law Library in actual utility to the student & lawyer.

It has been selected with much labor and discrimination during the whole course of his professional life and is very complete in all works of practical utility to the student & professional man.

The number of volumes including text books is 2,260 and it has been apprised by Dennis Kimberly Esq. & E. C. Herrick Esq. at $5,227 55/100. I will sell it to the College as a whole at a deduction of 1,000 dollars from the above apprisal, payable at any time within ten years in such instalments and at such periods as the College may prefer—with annual interest on the part of the price unpaid. If there are any books of which the College now possesses copies, such may be rejected at the option of the College and their value diminished from the apprisal in the same proportion, deducted from the above price.

Should the Prudential Committee decline this offer, I wish not to be considered bound by it at any future time, although I do not propose to sell the library as a whole for any less sum than the price above named.

I Remain
Very Respectfully
Your obt. sert.
Henry White

New Haven Decr. 29, 1845   *Executor* of S. J. Hitchcock decd.

RESOLUTION OF THE CORPORATION
August 11, 1846

Whereas generous subscriptions have been made, chiefly by gentlemen of the legal profession, to purchase the Law Library of the late Honorable Samuel J. Hitchcock, that the same may be the foundation of a Law School in Yale College,

Resolved that the Prudential Committee be authorised to complete the negotiation with the executors of the last will of the late Judge Hitchcock, and to apply the subscriptions which have been or may yet be made for that purpose, to the purchase of said library, at such a price and on such conditions, as may seem to them reasonable and expedient. Provided that the whole income, whether derived from payments made by the students for the use of books, or from subscriptions for the use of books by the members of the legal profession, shall be devoted if necessary to the payment of the interest of the debt contracted by the purchase, and that such portion of the excess of the income over the interest as may be determined on from year to year by the Prudential Committee, shall be applied in payment of the principal till the debt shall be extinguished.

Resolved that when the Library shall become the property of the Corporation it shall be deposited and kept apart from the general library of the College, in a place convenient for both the instructors and students in the Law Department now to be established, and for those gentlemen of the bench and of the bar who by their subscriptions towards the purchase of the library, have acquired the privilege of using it, and that the library with the additions which may hereafter be made to it by purchase or gift shall be known as the Law Library of Yale College.

Resolved that each of those gentlemen who have paid or shall have subscribed and paid not less than one hundred dollars, severally, towards the purchase of the library, shall have during the continuance of his life the privilege of freely consulting the books in the library and of using, in any court in the City of New Haven, during the trial of any cause in which he is engaged as counsel or attorney, such books in said library as may be needed in such trial; and that the same

34

privilege shall be conceded to annual subscribers of ten dollars each, during the payment of such annual subscription.

Resolved that a committee on the Law Library be appointed, one by the Corporation, one by the Faculty of the Law Department, now to be established, and one by those gentlemen who have subscribed each one hundred dollars or more, for the purchase of the library, which Committee shall devise and recommend to the Corporation such further rules and arrangements as may be requisite to the ends for which the library is purchased and to the convenience of the parties concerned.

Resolved that one-eighth of the fees paid by students in the Law Department annually shall be for the use of the library, and that when the debt contracted by the present purchase shall have been discharged, the entire income from this source, and from the subscription of members of the legal profession, after defraying the necessary expenses of custody, insurance and repairs, shall be appropriated to the enlargement of the library.

The concrete result of these exchanges was, according to the treasurer's report of 1848, that Hitchcock's library was purchased at a cost of $4,188.65, of which sum $2,070 had then been subscribed, the remainder, or $2,118.65, being carried in the report as "balance due the college." In the following years, interest was regularly charged on this balance, by which circumstance and by further borrowings for the purchase of new books, it gradually increased in amount, even though some new subscriptions were made, and even though, at first, one eighth of the receipts from students was credited to the law library account. By 1873, the "balance due to the College," had grown to $4,233.73. The next year it stood at $4,286.38, but then it was recorded in the treasurer's report as a College receipt, being labeled "old debt cancelled." A report to the alumni dated June 1, 1873, gives the probable explanation for this cancellation, when it

35

acknowledges subscriptions for the benefit of the law school totaling about $12,000. Chief among the contributors were William Walter Phelps and Henry C. Kingsley. This sum is not to be confused with the James E. English fund of $10,000 established in 1873, the income only of which was to be, and still is, used for the support of the law library. The Hitchcock library thus finally became an unincumbered possession of the law school. The estate of Hitchcock had been fully paid in 1846, and the principal and interest of loans by the College had now been discharged.

VIII

The public career of David Daggett, the third of the men whose books are included in the Founders' Collection, is so well known that only a brief summary of it is needed to serve as a background for his law-school activities.

Born at Attleboro, Massachusetts, on December 31, 1764, he entered the Junior class of Yale College in 1781, at the age of sixteen. While a student, he supported himself by serving as butler for the College, and by holding a preceptorship in the Hopkins Grammar School. After his graduation in 1783, he studied law in the office of Charles Chauncey in New Haven, and was admitted to the Connecticut bar in 1786. He was a representative in the Connecticut legislature from 1791 to 1797, and again in 1805; from 1797 to 1804, and from 1809 to 1813 he was a member of the Council. From 1811 to 1813, he was state's attorney for New Haven County, and from 1813 to 1819, United States senator. All of these accomplishments were to his credit when he joined Hitchcock in the conduct of the law school in 1824. During the twenty-three years of law lecturing that followed, he also was associate justice of the Connecticut Superior Court

36

(1826–32), mayor of New Haven (1828–30), and chief justice of the Connecticut Supreme Court of Errors (1833–34). He was twice married, first to Wealthy Ann Munson (daughter of Dr. Eneas Munson), by whom he had nineteen children; and second, to Mary Lines, daughter of Captain Major and Susanna (Mansfield) Lines. He died in New Haven, on April 12, 1851, at the age of eighty-seven.

Daggett really lived four separate careers, that of lawyer, judge, statesman, and teacher. The purposes of the present sketch permit dealing in detail with the last only, although nothing could be more fascinating than the story of the bitter political quarrels in which his strong Federalist views embroiled him. Despite this emotional bias, it is said by Lynde Harrison (Atwater's *History of New Haven*, p. 244) that

his success as a lawyer was due to his innate knowledge of human nature, his sound judgment, and his strong common sense. He abounded in wit and humor, and had at command a fund of anecdotes to illustrate his positions and arguments. His manner of speaking was calm and deliberate. His knowledge of the law was thorough and eminently practical. He had no patience with hair-splitting technicalities, which were the delight of many lawyers in the days of the older common law practice. His punctuality was extraordinary, and his integrity was thorough, stern and exact. He was very familiar with the Bible, and frequently used its strong and popular language in his arguments, and even in his charges to the jury when he was a Judge.

Only three men taught in the Staples–Hitchcock–Yale law school from its inception to the year 1842. The periods of their respective service in the school were:

Staples, 1800 (?)–1824
Hitchcock, 1820–1845
Daggett, 1824–1847

37

Between 1842 and 1847, three other men served as teachers, Isaac H. Townsend (1842–47), William L. Storrs (1845–47), and Henry White (1846–47). Daggett, antedating them by many years, and ending his service by retirement when they did in 1847, was the connecting link between the school of the founders and the school which is now Yale Law School.

On November 10, 1824, Samuel J. Hitchcock wrote as follows to Staples, just established in his new quarters at 35 Pine Street, New York City:

> Mr. Daggett began his labours in the School on Monday. He takes hold well. We hope you will send us some students from N. York by and by. There will be one, and perhaps two lectures a week delivered.

Staples and Hitchcock may well have wondered whether Daggett would "take hold" in the way that they knew to be necessary, for he was already sixty years old and to him teaching was a new venture. Apparently it was intended to break him in gradually, and in as comfortable surroundings as possible, for his one or two lectures a week were at first given in his own residence. This house stood on Elm Street, not far from the corner of Temple, where the Trowbridge house later stood, between the present Public Library and the Court House. Later he took on more work and shared substantially in the financial returns of the school. Hitchcock's account books show that payments of $50 and $80 were made to him from time to time, and that in March, 1837, it was agreed that thenceforth he should receive $700 a year. Since he continued to lecture until his eighty-third year, it is not surprising that his lectures became stereotyped, but even then the fascination of his personality carried him through. Evidence of this fact is contained in

38

the recollections of one of his later law students, quoted by Woolsey:

He lectured every morning immediately after Judge Hitchcock's recitation, and the lectures on constitutional law (which were also delivered before the seniors in college) were made very interesting, because his experience in the Senate and intimacy with many of the founders of the Republic, supplied him with many anecdotes which he told with much gusto. He had been a decided federalist, and delighted in giving an occasional slap to Mr. Jefferson, whose character and career were at that time the subject of much discussion in the debating societies of the college and the law school.

His good humor, readiness at repartee and crusty mode of summing up his sentiments in a few words, made him always more interesting in conversation than in the lecture-room. His lectures on the common law, which were read from well-worn manuscripts, were not as interesting. He had been so long out of practice that he had not kept up with the later decisions, and the substance of them was contained in Swift's Digest. (*Historical Discourse*, pp. 17–18.)

IX

It will be recalled that from 1801 to 1810, Elizur Goodrich was professor of law in Yale College. After Daggett had been an instructor in the law school for two years, the professorship of law in the College was revived, and he was, in 1826, appointed to fill it. He signalized that honor by notifying President Day, on October 30, 1826, that he proposed to "attend worship at the College Chapel at least in part. I presume I can be accommodated with a pew," he wrote. "In mentioning it this morning to Mr. Twining, he observed that it belonged to the President to direct. The seat which I have occupied occasionally for the last two years would accommodate me in future. With your permission, I will occupy it hereafter as one of the officers of the College."

39

The new academic professorship in no way affected his connection with the law school. The only relation between the two activities was that, as has been seen, he gave the same lectures on constitutional law to both bodies of students. As a College officer, he received no compensation. The announcement of the law school in the College catalogue for 1826 (see ante), and in later catalogues to 1830–31, states that "the Professor of Law will also for the present, occasionally deliver lectures to the Senior Class in College, until arrangements are made for a systematic course to be permanently continued." In 1831–33, the announcement says that he will lecture to Seniors during the first and second terms, once in each week, and in the 1833–34 catalogue, the information is added that he will also hear recitations in Kent's *Commentaries*. This latter was a welcome task to Daggett, for he said of Kent's *Commentaries*, "this work I cherish with more affection than any other except the Bible and Shakespeare." There was, however, another reason for taking on more regular duties in connection with the College.

This reason is set forth in the following letter dated April 4, 1833:

To the President and Fellows of Yale College.

The Subscriber respectfully represents, that in September 1826, he had the honor to receive the appointment of Professor of law in the College. Since that time, he has delivered lectures to the Senior Class, once in each week, during the principal part of the fall and winter terms in each year. It was then understood that the funds of the College would authorize no salary, and he has, of course, received no emolument. At the Commencement in August last, it was known that a subscription was on foot to raise $100,000 for the College: and it was then suggested that there ought to be some emolument provided for this professorship, as the subscriber has understood,

40

but it was thought not expedient, as the project might fail of success. The subscription was completed on the first of December last: and as that day occurred near the middle of the time of rendering the services, he presumes the Corporation will deem it just that whatever emolument shall be allowed, it ought to be considered payable at that period. The subscriber further represents that there is appropriated by direction of the donors, to this fund the sum of seven thousand five hundred dolls. *absolutely,* and the further sum of Fifteen hundred dolls. if the Corporation should approve of the destination, for the professorship of law.

The undersigned is a subscriber to that fund of $1000, payable in four equal annual payments, commencing on the first of January last. He presumes that the first payment ought to be considered as made on that day by his services the current year. He is not desirous to receive any money from that fund for past or future services, but is willing to perform the duties of the office, & to add recitations to his lectures, as the Corporation or faculty may direct, so long as he shall continue in office & shall be able to officiate in the College, & on those terms he believes it reasonable that no part of his subscription should be demanded of his estate, in case of his inability to perform those duties. The subscriber would further take the liberty of suggesting that the Professorship thus established should be called the *KENT* Professorship of law in Yale College: and that some gentleman be requested to deliver an address on an early day of the next term on its establishment.

David Daggett

The fund of $100,000 referred to is the Centum Millia Fund, still carried in the University treasurer's annual reports with a principal of $82,950, and with the following description:

Established in 1832 from subscriptions received in the first movement for raising a large amount for general endowment. Of the $100,000 subscribed, the above amount ($82,950) was given on condition that the Corporation should hold the amount and use the income only for the general purposes of

41

Yale College. The balance has been distributed among the various departments for which it was subscribed.

As indicated by Daggett, part of this fund was sub-scribed to support the professorship of law, and it is interesting to note that it was Daggett's suggestion, after the money had been raised, that the professorship of law should thenceforth be known as the Kent professorship. Consequently the treasurer's annual reports still list the James Kent Professorship of Law in Yale College, supported by a principal sum of $6,600. According to the arrangement suggested by Daggett, he took on additional duties in the College, thus paying off his subscription of $1,000 to the Centum Millia Fund; but at the same time he agreed to serve without any further compensation while he retained the professorship. His final suggestion was that some gentleman be requested to deliver an address on the establishment of the professorship under its new name. The gentleman selected was Judge Daggett himself, as shown by a letter to him, dated August 3, 1833, from Professor Benjamin Silliman, then secretary of the Centum Millia Fund. The date set for the address was the evening of August 20, 1833, the day before Commencement, and the occasion was the annual meet-ing of the alumni of the College. "As we have no longer to detail our poverty," wrote Silliman, "a short statement from the Pres. of our success and of the general condition of the college will suffice, and we should hope that your address may be the first in a series to go on at that meet-ing year after year, upon appropriate topics." The address, containing an eulogium of Chancellor Kent, was accordingly made by Daggett. Despite its subject and the nature of the occasion, it provoked a bitter editorial attack in the *Columbian Register* of August 24.

42

Judge Daggett made a great impression on his students. Woolsey refers to his striking features, aquiline nose, small clothes and silk stockings, "his courtesy toward all, and that expectation of respect from others which belonged to the gentlemen of the former time." Donald G. Mitchell (Ik Marvel) remembered him on the streets of New Haven, "serene in his top boots." In another place,[3] he affectionately described him more in detail. After referring to other professors of his own college days, he wrote in 1882:

Still more distinctly . . . I have in mind the lithe old gentleman with the springy step and the eager, eagle-like look, which his great Roman nose made vivid, who talked to us of Kent, his *Commentaries*, and of the wide realms of law. He was fast verging on eighty in those days, yet erect and agile, and his voice sonorous. He was bravely outspoken, too, and his political affiliations—for he brought senatorial dignities with him—shone out in little swift gleams of satire that garnished his law talk. He had been judge, senator, and chief justice, and we stood in great awe of him. "Young gentlemen," I think I hear him say—he was always courteous—"Young gentlemen, for more than fifty years I have been engaged in courts and offices of law, and in all that long period I have met with many and many an instance where parents have despoiled themselves for the benefit of their children; but scarce one child, scarce one [a little louder] who has despoiled himself for the benefit of his parents." No figure of the old college days is more present to me than that of this active, brisk, erect old gentleman, in small clothes and in top boots, he being the last, I think, to carry these august paraphernalia of the past along New Haven streets. He picked his way mincingly over the uneven pavements, tapping here and there with his cane, rather to give point to his reflections, I think, than from any infirmness; bowing pleasantly here and there with an old-school lift of the hat; full of courtesies, full of dignity, too; and a perfect master of deportment.

3 Dunn, W. H. *Life of Donald G. Mitchell*, pp. 49–50.

43

When Judge Daggett was eighty years old, he attended the sixty-first anniversary of his graduation from college. This was on June 4, 1844. In a class album for the year 1844, someone made a sketch of Daggett as he then was. An enlarged reproduction of this sketch now hangs in the office of the Yale law librarian. The original sketch was signed by Daggett, and provided by him with a maxim which perhaps should be taken as the guiding rule of his life. It reads: *Via trita est via tuta*, the beaten path is the safe way.

X

THE story of the Founders' Collection—that is, of the extant volumes which formerly belonged to the Hitchcock library—is, as has been seen, inseparable from the history of the law school, as well as from the lives of the Founders, Staples, Hitchcock, and Daggett. Thus the narrative has reached the year 1847. The subsequent history of the school is another story, as is also that of the Yale Law Library developing from the nucleus provided by Hitchcock. The migrations of the books from the year 1847 to the present should, however, briefly be traced.

After the death of Hitchcock in 1845 and the retirement of Daggett in 1847, the books, having been purchased for the school, as has been related, remained in the Hitchcock building, until the completion of the Leffingwell building, on the adjoining lot, on the northeast corner made by the intersection of Church and Court Streets. This building, the first floor of which was occupied by Heublein's Cafe, was completed in 1850. In this structure, beginning in that year, the law school rented quarters on the second floor in the rear, paying a rental of $300 annually. To this place, therefore, the Hitchcock

44

library was moved. There it remained until the year 1873, when the school moved into specially equipped rooms on the third floor of the Superior Court House, now known as the City Hall annex. In April, 1895, it moved again, with the school, to Hendrie Hall, and from there, in May, 1931, to its present resting place in the Sterling Law Buildings.

In these many years, the school passed through great vicissitudes, in all of which Hitchcock's books shared and suffered. That they should have dwindled in number from the original 2,260 volumes is therefore not surprising. It has been noted that the library contained multiple copies of those books which were used as texts and which were loaned to students year after year for their required reading. Such books received hard usage and for the most part were worn out and discarded. Only a few of them have come down to us.

Other classes of books suffered for other reasons. The charging system by means of which members of the bar took away books, leaving their names and addresses on the shelf where the volumes had stood, was subject to great abuses. There was little money to spend on binding, and unsupervised use of books led to injuries that could not be repaired. In 1869, as recorded by Professor Woolsey, "it was found that many sets had become mutilated, that quite a number of books had disappeared, and that others were hardly fit to be used." In later years, many of the Hitchcock volumes were reconditioned, in which process the flyleaves containing marks of original ownership were removed. To identify these positively, so that they may be added to the present Founders' Collection, is difficult. Enough remain and have been identified, nevertheless, to make an interesting collection. Undoubtedly more volumes will eventually be found, as

45

checking is continued, by means of Hitchcock's own catalogue, which fortunately has been preserved.

The Founders' Collection, in April, 1935, including forty-eight volumes which have not physically been transferred to it, subdivides itself, according to the criterion of original ownership, into the following groups:

Seth P. Staples	Volumes
Law Reports	12
Statutes	6
Treatises	21
Trials	1
Digests of cases	1
Manuscript volume	1
	42

Samuel J. Hitchcock	
Law Reports	125
Statutes	25
Treatises	61
Trials	14
Digests of cases	6
Journals of Congress	8
	239

David Daggett	
Law Reports	48
Statutes	1
Treatises	13
Trials	1
Digests of cases	30
International law	12
	105
Total	386 volumes

Included among them are Grotius' *De Jure Belli ac Pacis*, 1650; Bracton's *De Legibus*, 1569; five folio Year Books containing cases for Ed. II, 1–19, Ed. IV, 1–22,

46

H. IV, H. V, Ed. V, Rich. III, H. VII, H. VIII; Rolle's *Abridgment*, 1668; Viner's *Abridgment*, 1791–1806; Beawes' *Lex Mercatoria Rediviva*, 1761; and Domat's *Civil Law*, 1722. Valuable as are these and other volumes in the collection, it is not chiefly for their intrinsic value that we now prize them. Rather it is because of their associations with the Founders and with the long succession of students that have used them. Evidence of wandering thoughts, of budding poetical fancy, of the incipient artist among the students of long ago, appears in them, contrary to approved library regulations, in the form of scribblings, sophomoric verse, and pencil sketches of professors and fellow students. There are dated lists of students present at classes, names of students who read some of the textbooks, anecdotes probably jotted down while listening to lectures, and comments on the professors themselves. All these notations are now preserved as records of voices which spoke in the past, sometimes giving advice to students of the future. Such was the intent of a member of the class of 1867, when he wrote the following in Hoffman's *Chancery Practice:*

Gentle Reader:
Peruse this volume well. It is somewhat old, but nevertheless it is sound law. The immortal class of '67 went through it in one week.
Sic gloria transit mundi.

47

Yale Law Library Publications

No. 3   June 1936

Yale Law School:
From the Founders to Dutton
1845–1869

By

Frederick C. Hicks

PUBLISHED FOR THE YALE LAW LIBRARY

BY THE YALE UNIVERSITY PRESS

1936

[49]

Yale Law School:
From the Founders to Dutton,
1845–1869

FREDERICK C. HICKS[1]

I

WHEN Samuel J. Hitchcock died on August 31, 1845, responsibility for the school fell on Isaac H. Townsend. For a few months, since David Daggett was no longer active, he was the sole instructor, administrator, and financial officer. Even after William L. Storrs joined him later in the year, the initiative in school affairs must at first have come from Townsend, because Storrs was greatly occupied by his judicial duties. These two men successfully appealed to the Yale Corporation to aid in the purchase of Hitchcock's library, thus introducing into the records of the school the name of Henry White, executor of Hitchcock's estate. Part of this estate was the law school itself, including its good will, the law building, and the library. When ill-health incapacitated Townsend,

1. In assembling the material for this sketch, the author has been aided by Miss Elizabeth Forgeus, Assistant Law Librarian, and Miss Ruth E. Bowman, Secretary to the Law Librarian. For the earlier history of the school, see *Yale Law Library Publications*, No. 1, 1935.

I

White found it necessary, as executor, to begin teaching, in order to keep the school running and to complete its contracts with students already enrolled. Other local lawyers were also, in emergencies, pressed into service. On February 12, 1846, Storrs, engaged in court in Hartford, wrote White that he had heard of Townsend's illness, that he, himself, would be detained in Litchfield for two weeks, and that, if possible, he would like to have White, with the aid of two friends, keep the school going.

I would suggest whether you cannot hear the students recite twice a day, except on Wednesdays & Saturdays, & on those days once as at present, and that in addition to these recitations, you call on Genl. K. & Gov. B. to hear them recite as those gentlemen can consistently with their other engagements—and that the lectures be dispensed with until I return.

"Gov. B." was Roger Sherman Baldwin, lately chief executive of Connecticut, and next year to be United States senator. He was the father of Simeon E. Baldwin, who also at a later time came to the aid of the school. "Genl. K." was Dennis Kimberly, a former captain of the New Haven Grays, and major general of the militia of the State. He had been many times an assemblyman, had been mayor of New Haven, and was then State's attorney for New Haven County. It is said of him that "possessing a fine figure, and managing a steed with uncommon grace and skill, he was on public occasions an object of admiration." Baldwin presented an equally impressive figure. Until late in life, he usually wore a full-dress suit of black, but occasionally a blue coat with gilt buttons and buff waistcoat. They were outstanding lawyers, and in their brief rôle as substitute teachers must have given éclat to the school. Such arrangements were, however, only makeshifts. On March 8, 1846, Storrs was still holding court in Litchfield, and writing to

2

White hoping that Townsend had been able to return to duty. After another turn at teaching, he again called on White to aid him. June 25, 1846, he wrote:

I have been on the hunt for you [White] this morning but without success. I am obliged to leave this morning at ½ past 11 or 12 for the Court of Errors at Litchfield & would therefore request you to take charge of the class in the Law School (during my absence) which recites in Jeremy on Equity at 9 o'clock in the morning. If 8 o'clock would accommodate you better I would recommend that you adopt that hour. The lessons I give the class are short—say from 8 to 10 pages. The lesson tomorrow morning (Tuesday) is from page 335 to 346, as marked with pencil. I leave Jeremy on yr. table. Jeremy is very concise & condensed & I have deemed it therefore necessary to make pretty copious verbal explanations & illustrations.

Harassed by such difficulties in carrying on the routine work of the school, Storrs and Townsend, the latter temporarily recovered in health, renewed their suggestion to the Prudential Committee that the school be taken over as a department of the College. On December 23, 1845 (See *Yale Law Library Publications*, No. 1, pp. 30–32), in connection with their proposal that the Hitchcock library be purchased, they had urged that the College have "supervision of the Institution." They now reiterated the suggestion in a letter dated August 4, 1846:

"Taking it for granted," they said in part, "that the Law Library will become the property of the College by the means now in progress for that purpose, or of them in conjunction with the assistance of the College, (without accomplishing which object we suppose that the idea of connecting a Law School with the College would not be entertained) we think that the present is a very favorable time for carrying into effect the object of connecting them, and indeed consider it quite important it should be arranged so as to take effect with the commencement of the Next Term." They then added that the

3

plan had "no particular reference to our being personally connected with the Law School if it shall be placed under the charge of the College."

The efforts of Storrs, Townsend, and White bore fruit in several resolutions adopted by the Corporation on August 19, 1846, including the following, establishing a department of law in Yale College.

Resolved, that there be established in this College a department for special instruction in the science of law, with a reference to the wants both of those who study it as a branch of liberal knowledge, and those who study law as a profession, and that the following regulations be adopted as the constitution of the Law Department.

I. The President and Fellows will appoint from time to time a sufficient number of instructors in the Law Department, whose compensation till other provision shall be made shall be derived exclusively from the proceeds of tuition fees paid by students under their instruction.

II. The President of the College, and the Kent Professor of Law and the Instructors in the Law Department shall constitute the executive faculty of the Law Department, whose duty it shall be to superintend and direct the deportment of the students and to carry into execution whatever laws and orders may be made by the Corporation for the regulation of the Department.

III. The faculty of the Law Department shall arrange the course of studies, and shall assign to the several instructors, their particular duties and subjects of instruction.

IV. None shall be admitted to attend on the lectures or courses of instruction in the Law Department who having been members of any of the academical classes, have not been either graduated or dismissed without censure. In other respects the conditions of admission to the lectures and studies shall be regulated by the Law faculty.

V. Students in the Law Department, who shall be guilty of immoral conduct, of disturbing the order of the City or of the College, or of disrespectful deportment towards any of the

4

officers of the College, shall be admonished, suspended or dismissed at the discretion of the Law faculty.

VI. The degree of Bachelor of Laws may be conferred upon students in the Law Department, who shall be recommended for that purpose by the Instructors to the President and Fellows, as having conformed to the rules of the institution and having passed a satisfactory examination.

Another resolution appointed William L. Storrs, Henry White, and Isaac H. Townsend, professors in the law school. Townsend was to act as treasurer of the school with the duty to collect and distribute its income, and account for the same to the treasurer of the College. For this service, he was to receive such compensation as should be allowed him by the law faculty. The law professors were to receive for their services, out of fees paid by students, not more than $1,200 annually. Storrs and Townsend accepted the appointments, but White, on September 29, 1846, declined, because of the demands of his "professional business." The resignation was accepted by the Corporation on October 20, 1846, and the Prudential Committee was empowered to secure a successor to him.

The several months of illness leading up to the death of Townsend on January 11, 1847, were difficult months for the school. He had been efficient both as a teacher and as an administrator. In the latter capacity, he had as early as 1843 taken charge of advertising the school. Advertisements were run regularly in New Haven papers, the *Courier*, the *Palladium*, the *Herald*, the *Register*, and the *Democrat*; in New York City, in the *Journal of Commerce*, the *Tribune*, the *Daily Express*, and the *Morning Courier and New York Enquirer*; in Washington, D.C., in the *National Intelligencer* and the *Washington Union*; in the *Albany Argus* and the *Albany Evening Journal*; in

5

newspapers of Princeton, N.J., Boston, Detroit, Cincinnati, Richmond, and Philadelphia; in the *Missouri Republican*, St. Louis; and in legal magazines such as the *Law Reporter*, the *Law Magazine*, and the *New York Law Observer*. Townsend advanced the cost of these advertisements out of his own pocket, and both he and Hitchcock, and later the other instructors, individually collected tuition and paid expenses, such as the cost of textbooks furnished to students. This method called for much bookkeeping when the estates of both Hitchcock and Townsend were being settled. From these accounts it appears that Hitchcock was entitled by agreement to two thirds and Townsend to one third of the profits of the school. Taking into account tuition collected and expenses paid, it turned out that the estate of Hitchcock was indebted to the estate of Townsend in the amount of $615.31. As between Storrs, White, and the estate of Townsend, for the two years from October 1, 1845 to October 1, 1847, a different method of distribution was used. A memorandum by White says that during this time,

excluding Sundays and vacations, there were 530 days on which instruction was given, and 1,355 recitations heard, besides moot courts and a few lectures. The general rule was three recitations a day. Of these 1,355 recitations, Judge Storrs heard 614, I. H. Townsend 360, and H. White 381. Their length was ordinarily one hour, frequently longer as conversation was protracted while Judge Storrs was attending court. Mr. Townsend, and after his death, I heard the three recitations a day for two or three weeks in succession.

The income of the school for this period was $3,476.70. The proportion of receipts to which each was entitled was obtained by multiplying the total income by the number of lectures given by each, and dividing the multiple by the total number of lectures. Thus Townsend's estate was

6

entitled to 360/1355 of $3,476.70, or $923.70. Storrs's proportion was $1,575.42 and White's, $977.58. What adjustments were to be made in these amounts for expenses paid and fees collected does not appear. Moreover, it was several years before the accounts were cleared up, and a portion of the tuition fee of each student was remitted for reasons which appear in the following petition presented to Henry White by a committee of students in August, 1847.

Whereas the arrangements of the Law Department of which we are the members have not been such for the past year as to fulfil our just expectations—nor our advantages so great as those extended to pupils who preceded us—to wit: that the course of instruction has been interrupted and unsettled—that we have not had the usual number of recitations and instructors—that the regular courses of lectures have been discontinued—that in short few of the terms of instruction proposed in the catalogue have been complied with—and that the repeated promises of permanent arrangements under which we have been induced to remain remain unfulfilled—therefore
Resolved that we the members of the school have judged a reasonable deduction should be made upon our tuition bills for the year.
Resolved that we consider the proportionate abatement should be one half the usual amount, i.e. forty dollars.
Resolved that in preferring this claim we intend no censure whatever upon our teachers or those who have the management of the institution—for we believe their efforts to improve matters have been energetic, constant & consistent with their promises—but we regret with them, that those efforts have been unsuccessful.
Resolved that we tender our obligations & warmest regards to Mr. White for his courtesy in supplying the place of Mr. Townsend ad interim—& that we feel assured he has been no less faithful than generous in the discharge of this office.
Resolved that we respectfully present these resolutions to the heads of the department for their indulgent consideration, with

7

confidence that they will meet a generous & equitable reception—& that we shall receive an early & favorable reply.

George W. Goddard) Committee
J. C. W. Powell > on the part
A. S. Hawthorn) of the Class

Mr. White did not like the petition, and said so, when he sent it on to Judge Storrs, in Hartford.

"There are some unpleasant features about the document," he wrote, "and I told the committee so—particularly the attempt to fix the price of tuition for the past year. I am not aware of any particular deficiency in the quantity of instruction given during the past year except perhaps in the exercise of drawing pleadings &c and during this last term when there have been only 2 recitations a day."

By November, Storrs and White had come to a conclusion on what should be done. Because, for two months in the summer of 1847, there were only two recitations a day, a deduction of one third in the fee for that term was made.

II

ISAAC HENRY TOWNSEND was a lineal descendant of Sir Roger Townshend of Raynham, Norfolk, England, and was the son of Isaac Townsend and Rhoda (Atwater) Townsend. He was born in New Haven, at 22 High Street, on April 23, 1803. At the age of eleven he and his father, with whom he was returning to New Haven from New York City, were among the passengers on the packet *Susan*, when she was boarded and captured off Bridgeport, on October 10, 1814, by a British brig. The ransom for the father and son was two thousand Spanish milled dollars. The money was sent by messenger from New Haven and paid to the captors who then let the *Susan* sail for New Haven, but only with the threat that after five hours they would attempt to recapture her. By the

8

J. H. Townsend

William L. Storrs

Henry White

use of oars and improvised extra sails the *Susan* won the race to New Haven.[2] Townsend attended the Hopkins Grammar School, entered Yale at the age of fifteen, and graduated second in his class in 1822. He finished his course at the Yale Law School in 1824. His instructors, therefore, were Seth P. Staples and Samuel J. Hitchcock. He entered practice in New Haven under favorable auspices, because his father was one of the prominent businessmen of the town. Public preferments of all kinds were open to him, and he did in fact serve as New Haven common councilman, and as a member of the Connecticut House of Representatives. He was not attracted, however, by contentious contacts with people either in court or in public life, and preferred the scholarly side of his profession. In 1835 he traveled in Europe, observing the operation of legal systems, and returning to devote himself so far as practicable to office practice and arguments in court on points of law. In this field he was eminently successful. "He manifested the acute and solid and strong intellectual qualities, rather than the showy, the ready and the versatile," said the Reverend S. W. S. Dutton, in his address at Townsend's funeral. His arguments in court were "thorough, so much so as often to exhaust the subject." As an illustration of this characteristic, Dutton related the story then current that Townsend's former preceptor, Judge Hitchcock, being associated with him in an important case, rose after Townsend had concluded his argument, and, instead of following him according to previous arrangement, declared the subject exhausted, and declined all further argument as unnecessary and useless.

2. For an account of the Townsend family, see a paper entitled "22 High Street," filed in the New Haven County Historical Society, by Christina H. Baker.

9

Considering Townsend's natural turn of mind, and Hitchcock's high opinion of him, it was not surprising that he should be invited to become an instructor in Hitchcock's law school. This connection began in 1842. The few years following must have been the happiest period of Townsend's life. His father's death had left him well off, and he was engaged in work that he loved. In the following year, August 17, 1843, he founded the Isaac H. Townsend Prize in Yale College, by a gift of $1,000, the income of which is still used to provide an annual prize for excellence in English composition.

That Townsend was a teacher who took his task seriously, even though he carried on at the same time an extensive practice, is shown by some of his papers and law books now in the Yale Law Library. The papers, presented in 1926 by Henry H. Townshend (Yale 1897, Law School 1901), consist of lecture notes on a great variety of subjects: international law, natural law, evidence, domestic relations, bills and notes, and real property, including fines and recoveries, estates, remainders, covenants, and deeds. There is also a series of questions ranging over many fields of law, and one set of nonlegal questions which resemble intelligence tests of the present time.

His lectures were severely practical, but he sometimes prepared a careful introduction for the first of a course. For example, he began his course on natural law as follows:

Among all the ranks and conditions of men, probably not a solitary individual can be found, who will be willing so far to stultify himself to his own heart and before his fellow men, as to claim, that man is self existent, or only the work of chance. As soon as a human being reaches the first stage of consciousness, he hears an internal monitor impressing the sober lesson

10

of a derived origin, and of an external support. And as the days of life advance in their course, the voice within acquires new force and clearness, and speaks in tones of subduing authority of a God Supreme, the Creator and Preserver.

While the relation of man to his God is thus developed by a spiritual guide, during the growth of the human system, and is confirmed through life by the influence of a constantly suggesting reflection; another lesson, of an importance inferior only to the first, is presented by the existence of the circumstances around him, finding and holding him in the relation of fellowship with beings similar to himself. And while with the eye of the mind he sees a God above, with the eye of sight he beholds before and around him a family of brothers, the children of a common Father, impressed with uniformity of character, and destined to a like consummation.

But are these relations of man to his God and to his fellow men, truths of mere abstraction, leading to no action, calling for no duties. Forbid it, heaven. Forbid it, dignity of human nature. Forbid it, aspirations after immortality. No—a Father's love calls for filial reverence and worship; a brother's happiness demands fraternal affection and kindness. To Natural Theology it belongs to teach man's duty to his God; to Natural Law, to exhibit his obligations to his fellows. The holy ministers of the altar will fulfil their solemn functions of showing you the teachings of the Religion of Nature, and the sublimer and holier revelations of the Christian Faith. Be it my task (no humble task) to present to your attention the Law of Nature, as prescribing the duties of man to man, and impelling to their performance.

One of the most interesting of the memorabilia in the Yale Law Library is Townsend's copy of Swift's *Digest*, 1822–23, which he interleaved and fully annotated in his precise and legible handwriting. This copy was presented to the library in 1908 by the widow of Judge William K. Townsend, grandnephew of Isaac H. Townsend, and himself a professor in the law school from 1881 to 1907. Probably these were the volumes which Townsend

11

used in his class on Swift's *Digest*. The book was presented to William K. Townsend in 1874 by N. A. Cowdrey, whose name will appear again in this pamphlet. "Your grand uncle," wrote Cowdrey, "was a very great lawyer—none more so. He stood at the head of his profession. His opinions were sought after by all, both lawyers and laymen and when obtained carried great weight with them. They were respected and deferred to."

One of the students in the law school from October 1, 1846 to October 1, 1847, was Frederick John Kingsbury, who, many years later, was an alumni member of the Yale Corporation (1881–99). From Kingsbury, who listened to Townsend's lectures for about two months, we have the following vivid picture of him (*Yale Shingle*, 1910, pp. 16–18).

He was tall, nearly or quite six feet, with broad shoulders and well filled out, but not much superfluous flesh. He had a pretty large head and must have had a long neck, for he wore a high, sharp-pointed collar, the corners curving up near the corners of his mouth, and a high black silk stock. He never smiled, but at some peculiarly good legal joke he would give a little gurgle which passed for a laugh. He had quite a sense of humor, but it was apparently a strictly legal sense. It was shown by some of the questions drawn up by him for the Moot Court Book, which I hope may still be in existence.[3] His manner in the class was what you might call wooden, very stiff and inflexible. I do not believe that it would have been possible for him to have made a graceful gesture even if he were so much as to venture on a gesture of any kind. He was the soul of honor and had the unreserved confidence of the entire community. His judgment on questions of law, especially everything relating to real estate and to conveyancing was highly esteemed. He was sometimes prolix, but he generally put matters in such a way that they were not likely to be forgotten. . . .

Just in the midst of the school year Mr. Townsend died. His

3. Unfortunately, it has not yet been discovered.

12

death was felt as a loss by the school, the profession and the community. The morning after his death Judge Storrs said a few words concerning his ability and integrity and added: "He was an Israelite, indeed, in whom there was no guile."

III

THE death of Townsend and the declination of White called for prompt action on the part of the college authorities to provide a colleague for Judge Storrs. An active assistant to President Theodore Dwight Woolsey was Wyllys Warner, then treasurer of the College. On January 26, 1847, fifteen days after Townsend's death, he called on Daniel Lord in New York City to discuss the situation. Lord was a graduate of Yale College in the class of 1814, had studied law at the Litchfield Law School, and was in 1847 a leader of the New York bar. He himself was not attracted by law teaching, but was anxious to assist in obtaining the best man for the place. Warner, by letter, reported the conversation to President Woolsey, immediately after its conclusion. "If the School at Yale does not take the lead now," Lord is quoted as having said, "Cambridge and Princeton will have the field and will be likely to retain it." Princeton had in the previous year established a law school fated to last only until 1852. Various possible candidates for the professorship were discussed, among them Judge William Kent, son of Chancellor Kent, Daniel D. Barnard of Albany, New York, lately member of Congress and soon to be United States Minister to Prussia, and Greene C. Bronson of Utica, New York, then chief justice of the New York Supreme Court. They fixed upon the last of these as the best man for the place.

He says Judge Bronson has all the qualifications for the station—learning, reputation, industry, a sound head and a good

13

heart. Judge Bronson associated with Judge Storrs, he says will command all the law students from New York—and will place the school, beyond any manner of doubt, at the head of all law schools in the country.

Mr. Lord offered to write to Judge Bronson if the Prudential Committee wished it. In reporting this fact Warner, with the foresight of a treasurer, suggested that it would be a good thing to accept Lord's offer. "I am satisfied that he will take pleasure in the effort, and will not on that account feel less interest in the School or in the College."

A letter from John F. Seymour of Utica, dated February 1, 1847, shows that President Woolsey, on January 29, sought confirmation of Lord's opinion of Bronson. Seymour, the brother of Governor Horatio Seymour, wrote that Bronson would be a fine choice, but that the bar of the State wished him to continue on the bench. "Whether this depends," he wrote, "upon the qualifications of the Candidate, or other considerations, which can now be brought to bear under our new Constituition, remains to be tried." This reference was to the reorganization of the judicial system of New York under the Constitution of 1846. It is again referred to in a letter of Lord's to Bronson dated February 9, 1847, following approval of the plan by the Prudential Committee.

Not knowing how the recent revolution is likely to affect your taste or pursuits I have ventured to speak of you as one who might possibly be inclined to accept a vacant professorship of law at Yale College in connection with Judge Storrs of the Supreme Court of Connecticut. If such a thing could in any aspect please you, be so good as to drop me a line. It has the recommendation of quiet, agreable associations, refined society, useful and not disagreable labour and very high influence for good. Since the death of Judge Story, it seems to me certain that an Institution at N. Haven for instruction in law

14

would, from its proximity to the City & State of N. York and the more sober atmosphere of industrious learning at N. Haven, be the most considerable in the Union.

Mr. Lord's hopeful view of the future of the law school is further shown in his letter of the same date (February 9, 1847) to President Woolsey.

"I cannot doubt," he wrote, "that with a professor who could add to your Institution the decoration of a reputation extended and deserved, and acquired in the field of active exertion, the Law Department of your college would quickly pass in front of all others out of Europe—if even that exception is to be made. For while in the finish of scholarship the English bar leaves us out of sight, yet the circumstance of instruction in the Law in a scientific way is in England yet to be established and in imitation of us."

Another observation in this letter may account for the fact that the whole plan fell through. "The limitation of salary," said Lord, "would exclude any but worn out or very young men," neither of which Bronson was. He went from the chief justiceship of the Supreme Court of New York, to its newly created Court of Appeals, and after his retirement in 1851 served both as collector of the Port of New York, and as corporation counsel of New York City.

Meanwhile negotiations had been begun with the Hon. Clark Bissell of Norwalk, Connecticut. Formerly a judge in the Connecticut Supreme Court of Errors, he was then actively in practice. On February 22, 1847, a member of the Yale Corporation, the Reverend Aaron Dutton, called upon him in Bridgeport where he was found "surrounded with clients, it being court time." He had already been interviewed by Henry White who, bearing a letter from Judge Storrs, dated November 9, 1846, went to Norwalk to urge him to accept a professorship. Judge Storrs pre-

15

sented his case very strongly, praising New Haven as a place of residence, mentioning its fine opportunities for law practice, saying that attendance at the school was larger than ever before, and ending with the opinion that "the labor which you would perform as an instructor would not, I think, be as great as you endure at present, and I must say that judging from my own experience the business of teaching is much more agreeable than that of practicing law although perhaps not as lucrative." Nevertheless Bissell had not been persuaded. Now the "altered circumstances of the law school presented the question in a new aspect," and he promised to consider it further and give his decision in two weeks. On March 8, he sent to President Woolsey an offer to accept, but on condition that he would not be required to take up his duties immediately. His law business would occupy him until May, and, he added, "should the wishes of my political friends be gratified, I must of course be elsewhere during that month." He was then a Whig candidate for the governorship of Connecticut and in April was elected to that office.

Thus, for a time, the only teacher officially connected with the school was still Judge Storrs and he, unfortunately, was ill. Bissell was urged by President Woolsey to begin his work at the school as soon as possible, but being fully occupied as governor and by private practice, could only write to Henry White who, though he had declined a professorship, was the only one constantly at hand and well acquainted with the affairs of the school. Letters to him on May 1, May 31, June 30, July 20, July 26, 1847, and on October 27, 1848, show that he was the actual administrator of the school, as well as a part-time teacher.

On May 31, 1847, Bissell wrote White that he had heard of Storrs's illness and that there was a rumor both

16

that Storrs was about to resign and that the school would not reopen for its summer term scheduled to begin June 1. "I hope this is not so," he wrote, "as it cannot be otherwise than detrimental to the interests of the institution." Bissell's intention to begin teaching on July 19 was prevented by his own illness. He was confined to his bed with inflammatory rheumatism until August. Then in the middle of the summer term, to complete the series of disasters, came the resignation of Judge Storrs. On August 9, 1847, he wrote President Woolsey.

"Since I last saw you," he wrote, "I have become confirmed in the opinion which I then expressed, that my health will not allow me to discharge the duties of the Judicial Office, and also of the Professorship of Law which I now hold . . . I should have deferred my resignation until the close of the present term, were it not that my judicial duties will occupy me almost constantly until that period, and that it would not therefore be in my power to attend to the duties of the Law School during the remainder of the term."

With regret the Corporation accepted his resignation on August 17, 1847, and without delay, on the same day

Voted, that His Excellency Governor Bissell, and Henry Dutton, Esq., of Bridgeport, be Professors in the Law Department of this College in the place of Isaac H. Townsend, deceased, and Judge Storrs, resigned.

The restriction of law professors' salaries to $1,200 was removed, and Governor Bissell was named treasurer of the department.

So Governor and Mrs. Bissell, after a six hours' journey by private stage, arrived in New Haven on Tuesday, September 28, 1847. The following Saturday, October 2, Mrs. Bissell wrote her children that she and her husband were temporarily installed in rooms in the Tontine Hotel which had been vacated by Judge Storrs. From their

17

windows they had been watching the manoeuvres of the county militia encamped on the green, and they had visited a horticultural and floral fair held in the State House. "Pa seems in good health," she wrote, "and I think feels somewhat encouraged about the Law School. I think he is more troubled about his Thanksgiving Proclamation than anything else at present. He says it is out of his line of business."[4]

IV

FINAL leave should not be taken of Henry White and Judge Storrs without some parting tribute. The progress of the school was by a rule of three. First we had the Founders—Staples, Hitchcock, and Daggett, then Townsend, Storrs, and White, and they were followed by Bissell, Dutton, and Osborne. Later, there was to be the great triumvirate of Baldwin, Robinson, and Platt. *Yale Law Library Publications*, No. 1, deals with the Founders, and Isaac H. Townsend has already been dealt with in the present pamphlet.

Henry White's name is not written large in the political annals of his city and state because he never held public office and seldom appeared in court in the trial or argument of cases which aroused popular interest. In an unobtrusive way he exerted, however, a strong influence both in his professional capacity and in the community generally. He was born in New Haven on March 5, 1803, the son of Dyer White, a successful lawyer and judge of the Court of Common Pleas, and of Hannah Wetmore White. In the class of 1821, at the age of eighteen, he graduated with the highest honors. Two years spent in

4. The originals of Judge Storrs's letter of November 9, 1846, which Henry White bore to Norwalk, and of Mrs. Bissell's charming letter to her children, were made available through the courtesy of Mrs. Oliver Jackson of Norwalk, a granddaughter of Governor Bissell.

18

the Yale Divinity School, and another two years (1823–25) as tutor in Yale College, nurtured his natural taste for scholarship and for social service, both of which interests shaped his subsequent activities. After two years in the law school under Hitchcock and Daggett (1825–26), he was admitted to the bar in 1828 and began practice in New Haven. On January 7, 1830, he married Martha Sherman, daughter of Roger Sherman (B.A. 1787) and granddaughter of Roger Sherman (Hon. M.A. 1768), signer of the Declaration of Independence. They had seven sons, six of whom graduated from Yale College respectively in 1851, 1854, 1859, 1860, 1864, and 1866.

His progress in the law was at first slow.

"The only son of a family in easy circumstances," wrote Simeon E. Baldwin in an obituary notice (47 Conn. Reports, pp. 615–617), "he and they were more anxious that he should make himself a good lawyer, than that he should strive to acquire at once a paying practice. He comforted the writer of this sketch, when he found himself with little or nothing to do soon after his admission to the bar, by telling him [Baldwin] that his own professional income during his first year was precisely six dollars."

The line of his legal development was determined by the fact that, in 1832, he became executor of a large estate, consisting mostly of landed property. In dealing with this estate, he observed the untrustworthiness of the indexes of land records in New Haven, and set about making his own index.

"The result," says Baldwin, "was ten years of patient labor, often carried far into the night, in copying and bringing together in convenient form all the grants, devises, distributions and conveyances of land in the town, from the first settlement to the year 1800. This mass of material derived from the town, colonial and court records, was carefully digested and indexed, and, from that time forward, he was able, without going out

19

of his own office, to trace the title to any land in New Haven down to within a few years, if not days. This soon became, in connection with the settlement of estates, the main business of his life, and the same system of investigation was, in several instances, extended to the records of neighboring towns.

"He was probably the first Connecticut lawyer who deliberately selected a special line of professional practice as most suited to his tastes and circumstances, and pursued it almost exclusively. It was a bold undertaking in so small a place as New Haven then was, but the result showed that he was fully justified in believing that whoever did this one thing well would find it enough. A certificate of title from his office soon came to be required, as a matter of course, in almost all considerable real estate transactions, and though his customary charges were not predicated on the value of the property, and would seem absurdly small to a New York practitioner, he was so often called upon as to be for many years in receipt of a handsome professional income from this source alone."

He never appeared in the trial of contested cases except as a committee, auditor, or arbitrator, but he served, during the period from 1835 to 1875, as executor, administrator, guardian, or trustee more frequently than any other New Haven lawyer.

As has already been related, his executorship of the Hitchcock estate brought about his connection with the law school as proprietor, administrator, and teacher. Not only did he serve the school and the estate from a sense of professional duty, but he contributed from his own pocket the sum of $100 toward the fund for the purchase of the Hitchcock library. In the troubled period in 1846 and 1847 when he came to the rescue of the school as teacher, he performed so acceptably that in August, 1847, the student body presented him with the following resolution:

Whereas circumstances have occurred during the past term which unavoidably deprived us of the services of our regular

20

instructors during a large part of the session; and whereas through the kindness of Henry White Esq. we have been enabled notwithstanding these circumstances to prosecute the studies of the course

Therefore Resolved that the thanks of the members of the school be tendered to Mr. White for his kindness in assuming the task of an instructor & for the uniform kindness & ability which he has displayed in discharging the duties thereby devolving upon him.

He was the first treasurer of the Yale Law Association, organized in July, 1851.

Well established in a congenial type of professional work, he found time to serve in the administration of many local institutions. For example, he was president of the corporation owning Long Wharf, chairman of the Committee of Proprietors of Common and Undivided Lands, trustee of the Old Town Farm and of the Hopkins Grammar School, and auditor of Yale College.

For forty years, he was a deacon of the First Church in New Haven. He was active in local charitable work such as the New Haven Work and Aid Society, was a member of nearly all national charitable societies fostered by the Congregational Church, was president of the Society for Promoting Collegiate and Theological Education at the West, and was in 1854 a member of the American Colonization Society organized to send negroes to a colony in Liberia.

Closely connected with his professional life was his interest in local history and genealogy. For many years he was a vice-president of the Connecticut Historical Society and he was in 1862 an organizer and the first president of the New Haven Colony Historical Society. In its rooms hangs the portrait by Sodersten from which the accompanying cut is reproduced. The two first papers read before the Society were written by him, one on the

21

history of the New Haven Colony, and the other on the history of the Cutler Lot, located on the southeast corner of Church and Chapel Streets, in New Haven.

When he died on October 7, 1880,

"he was the father of the bar in his county, a bar numbering a hundred and eighty-four members," wrote Simeon E. Baldwin. "When he entered it there were but nineteen lawyers in New Haven, four in Waterbury, and eight in other parts of the county. He long outlived all these, and he outlived also the next professional generation which came after them. He habitually worked late, often till past midnight, never was an early riser, and never took bodily exercise for the sake of exercise, but he probably survived his contemporaries because, without doing less labor, he took life more easily than they. He had not the ordinary conflicts of the bar or the excitement of the public platform to disturb the native serenity of his disposition. He was never in a hurry, and seldom had occasion to be. Kindness and courtesy, gentleness and moderation, belonged to his nature, and there was nothing in his professional life to make him ever forget them. It was a life quiet and peaceful, even in its flow, tranquil in its close."

Although William L. Storrs's professorship in the law school was of brief duration, it is not to be supposed that his influence on the school was small. As we have seen, despite the conflicting requirements of his judicial duties and his law professorship, he conducted 614 class exercises in two years' time, a larger number than was credited to either of his colleagues. He not only successfully urged that the school be taken over by the College, and that the Hitchcock library be bought, but he was the largest single contributor to the fund that was raised.

Undoubtedly he was an impressive figure, but with many human attributes and social graces. He was said to have had a Johnsonian power and sententiousness in exposing a sophism and refuting a fallacy, to have been

22

versed in both the English and ancient classics, and to have been happy in his growing popularity as he approached old age. A dry and sometimes sarcastic humor was natural to him, but he used it with kindness and discretion. One of his students in the law school, Frederick John Kingsbury, whose comments on Isaac H. Townsend have already been quoted, draws a revealing picture of him.

"Judge Storrs was a bachelor," wrote Kingsbury (*Yale Shingle*, 1910, pp. 15–16). "He was fond of young men, sympathetic with them in his way and altogether was a most admirable head for the school. He was large, broad and strong, both in mind and body. I think that he and Judge Joel Hinman, who had much the same physique, would have easily, together, tipped the scales at 500 pounds. I think Judge Storrs made pets of all his young men and they were all very fond of him. If they got into any scrapes, as they sometimes did, he was always ready to do everything that was wise and proper to help them out and his advice was so judicious that the young men were ready to take it, and thus to avail themselves of his good offices. I have now particularly in mind one case where a graduate of the college had, in a frolic with some other students, done some damage at the college and generally misbehaved. Judge Storrs knew all the facts. He got another student who was, he thought, on good terms with the misbehaver, to tell him that the facts were known, but if he should go of his own accord to the college officers and confess and apologize the matter would probably be overlooked. The young man saw the point, made the apology and the matter was closed. Otherwise I presume there would have followed a dismissal. This was Judge Storrs in his dealings with the peccadilloes of young men. Though never attempting to be facetious in his class room, he had a keen sense of humor. He chewed tobacco, which he carried in a small oval japanned box. One day, just as he was beginning the recitation, he took this box from his pocket, opened it and, pinching up a good chew between his thumb and forefinger, looked about the class. 'Young

23

gentlemen,' said he, 'there is one habit that I want to warn you against, and that is the use of tobacco; it is a very insidious habit; before you know it, you are wedded to it. If you are trying a case and get out of tobacco you will become restless. The opposing counsel, of whom you might borrow a chew, may not use it; the clerk's box may be empty and you will feel like a cat in a strange garret, wholly lost until you can get another chew. It is a very hard habit to get rid of when once fixed and I seriously advise you not to form it.' Then he placed the chew in his mouth, returned the box to his pocket and went on with the lesson. It was a far more effective sermon against tobacco chewing than it would have been without the accompanying illustration."

Judge Storrs was born in Middletown, Connecticut, on March 25, 1795. He graduated from Yale College in 1814, studied law in the office of his brother at Whitestown, New York, and was admitted to the bar in 1817, beginning practice in Middletown. He served in the Connecticut lower house in 1827, 1828, 1829, and 1834, in the last year as speaker. In 1829 he was elected to the United States House of Representatives, was reëlected in 1838, and resigned in 1840, to become a judge in the Connecticut Supreme Court. From February, 1857, until his death, he was chief justice. Before becoming professor of law at Yale, he had taught law (1841–46) in Wesleyan University, Middletown. He died of a bilious fever, terminating in typhoid, at his home in Hartford, on June 25, 1861. In his memory, on May 25, 1889, his two grandnieces, Miss E. T. Robinson and Miss M. A. Robinson, established the Storrs Foundation to provide for annual lectures dealing with fundamental problems of law and jurisprudence.

V

WITH the coming of Bissell and Dutton in 1847 began a period of comparative tranquillity for the school. The

24

throes of rebirth after the passing of Hitchcock had been survived, and two outstanding lawyers had definitely assumed responsibility. Bissell was destined to remain in service to the year 1855, and Dutton until his death in 1869. The former was governor of the State at the time of his appointment, and the latter was to become governor during his professorship. David Daggett, who had not been teaching in the law school for several years, resigned the Kent professorship of law in Yale College, on August 15, 1848, and on the same day Governor Bissell was elected to be his successor. His annual compensation for lecturing to the Senior Class in college was the income of $6,500, or $390. That the two new instructors commended themselves to the students of the law school is shown by the following resolution adopted at a meeting on August 28, 1849:

Resolved, That, for careful instruction in that profession which is to be at once our means of support and our road to whatever of usefulness and distinction is our destined share in life—for kind and courteous treatment of us as students, and for private acts of friendship and kindness to different individuals of our brotherhood, our hearty thanks are due to the professors of Yale Law School.

Resolved, That those of us now leaving the school, and expecting before long to enter on the practice of our profession, will ever look back to this period of our preparatory training with feelings of pleasure and gratitude; and that we shall regard the time spent here, the examples set before us of legal learning, and the high-toned and correct ideas of a lawyer's duties and responsibilities which we have been taught, as so many living pledges for efforts on our part to do in everything according to the full measure of our abilities and the strict requirements of rectitude.

The great event of this immediate period was the removal of the school from the Hitchcock building, where

25

it had been since 1820, to the Leffingwell building, next door. During Hitchcock's proprietorship of the school, he had carried it on in his own building, and from his death to the year 1850 the school paid rent to his estate for the use of a lecture room. Of this room we may, perhaps, construct an imaginary picture from the details of its furniture. It contained one round table, two other tables, four chairs, ten settees, and a stove. In all probability the law library covered its walls. When the school took possession of its new quarters, on June 1, 1850, it is likely that this same furniture was moved along with the law library. Bissell gave up his law office in the Hitchcock building where it had been since 1848, and moved into the new building. Dutton also took an office there.

The Leffingwell building, standing on the northeast corner of Church and Court Streets, next to the Hitchcock building, was completed in the year 1849. The second-floor rear section was undoubtedly planned to serve as a lecture room for the law school. By 1851, the building was pretty well occupied. On the first floor was Lockwood's Café. Because extant pictures of the building show the sign "Café Heublein," it is usually stated that the law school was located over Heublein's Café. The fact is that Lockwood was not succeeded by Heublein until after the school had again moved to new quarters in 1873. The second floor was occupied by law offices and the law school. The rooms on the third floor were rented for various purposes, some of which will later be noticed. The fourth floor was occupied by the Scroll and Key Society. The rent for the lecture room was $300 a year, paid in two installments, on May 1 and November 1, usually by Henry Dutton.

The lecture room was about thirty feet square, and lighted by five large windows with curved tops. Two of

26

these windows were on Court Street. It was artificially lighted by gas, and its walls, as well as those of the adjoining rooms and halls, were whitewashed. A flight of outside stairs led to the back yard in which were a pump and outhouses.

Available descriptions of the law school quarters picture it as it was about the year 1869, but there is little reason to suppose that they will not serve for the year 1850. In that year, the building was new, and the law-school room, larger than that occupied in the Hitchcock building, must have seemed good by comparison. But certainly it must always have been barren and uninspiring. During the twenty-three years that the school occupied it, the only recorded payments made, in addition to those for rent, books, and salaries, are for whitewashing, repairing broken settees, for coal, carting the ashes, and for cleaning up the yard. Adjoining the lecture room was a small office for the use of the instructors.

The classic description of the situation in the Leffingwell building is by Professor William C. Robinson, given in an address commemorative of the life and character of Dean Wayland, delivered at Hendrie Hall on April 22, 1904.

The assets of the school consisted of a small library of valuable but antiquated books, a dozen dilapidated chairs, an old desk, and a capacious stove whose genial warmth in winter consoled the heels which rested on its girdle. Its lecture hall was a desolate chamber over a saloon where, as a relief in too absorbing studies, the three receptive senses were regaled with glimpses of the guests at the Tontine, with the howls of captive maniacs in the police jail, and with the smell of odorous cooking from the vaults below.

Dean Wayland also has left a description which adds some details.

27

"Up to 1873," he wrote (*Yale Shingle*, 1903, p. 9), "the school occupied two rooms in the rear of this [Leffingwell] building over a restaurant. The larger apartment was at once a library, a recitation, conversation and lounging room. In the intervals between recitations, it is alleged to have been at times the scene of much athletic activity. It was heated by a good-sized stove, around which was an ample box filled with sand designed to receive the frequent expectorations of the faithful few who worshipped at this shrine of Themis.

"The library consisted of imperfect sets of reports of several States and some archaic text-books. On one side of the room was a dais supporting the desk, behind which the instructor (the use of the singular number is intentional) surveyed with a somewhat saddened expression his little band of listeners. A visitor to the scene might well have said to himself: 'These young gentlemen certainly "scorn delights," even if they do not live "laborious days." ' A small adjoining room served as a retreat for the instructor and sheltered the librarian."

Reading these descriptions, one must not assume that Bissell and Dutton in 1850 and thereafter were without resources in energy or were sterile of ideas. They did what they could to carry on the school from day to day, and they were not ignorant of its defects. Busy with practice and the demands of public service, they nevertheless established the school in new quarters, sought to improve the library, organized graduates and students into an association, fostered the formation of student clubs, and kept up the steady grind of classes.

One of Dutton's first acts was to memorialize the Corporation concerning the condition of the law library and ask for help in improving it. Similar requests continued at intervals throughout his professorship. In 1851, the two professors applied to the Corporation for permission to hold public exercises for the law department during Commencement week. The request was granted on July 29, 1851, on condition that there should be no inter-

28

ference with the College exercises. The intention may have been to hold Commencement exercises for the law school, but in view of what was happening on the day when the Corporation voted, we may assume otherwise. On the afternoon of July 29, 1851, the first alumni association of the Yale Law School was organized. At a meeting of graduates and present members of the school a resolution to form an association was adopted, a draft constitution was submitted, and a committee appointed to select a proper name for the Association and recommend honorary members. At an adjourned meeting held the next afternoon, organization was completed by adopting a constitution for the *Yale Law Association* to be "composed of all those persons now or formerly connected with the Law School, and of such honorary members as they may elect." Thus there came to be listed among Yale College organizations the following (*Yale Banner*, October 3, 6, 30, 1851):

YALE LAW ASSOCIATION
Established July, 1851
President
Hon. Clark Bissell
Vice-Presidents
Hon. S. P. Staples, *of New York*
Hon. R. I. Ingersoll, *of New Haven*
Hon. Edward Bates, *of Missouri*
Hon. J. W. Houston, *of Delaware*
Hon. Judge Nesbitt, *of Georgia*
Hon. Lucius C. Duncan, *of New Orleans*
Recording Secretary
Hon. E. K. Foster
Treasurer
Hon. Henry White
Orator at the Commencement of 1852
Hon. John M. Clayton, of Delaware
29

Record has been found of only one other meeting of the Association, that held on the afternoon of July 28, 1852. The *Journal Courier* of the twenty-ninth reported that "the Hon. John M. Clayton, the orator appointed at the last meeting, having neglected to reply to the invitation until it was too late to appoint a substitute, no public exercises were held." The business of the meeting consisted of the reëlection of the officers, and of instructing the standing committee and the corresponding secretary to procure an orator for next year. Apparently they had no success, and there was to be no danger for many years to come of conflict between public exercises during Commencement week held by the College and by the law school.

The eight years of Governor Bissell's professorship ended when the Corporation, on July 24, 1855, accepted his resignation made necessary on account of age and growing infirmities. On the same day Dutton was appointed Kent Professor of Law in the College, and Thomas Burr Osborne was chosen to be a new professor in the law school.

When Bissell died, on September 15, 1857, the Reverend B. Weed, pastor of the First Congregational Church of Norwalk, Connecticut, in a funeral sermon likened him to King David, preaching from the text "For David, after he had served his own generation by the will of God, fell on sleep." (Acts 13.36).

"Our venerable friend," he said, "whose funeral rites have convened us here to-day, has filled, in the last twenty years, an unusual variety of stations and relations. Father of a family, a member of the Church of Christ, a leading member of a social community, chief officer in a banking institution, head of an important law school, a judge in the highest court, and an incumbent of the highest civil office in the State."

This career was made possible by his own efforts. Born

30

in Lebanon, Connecticut, on September 7, 1782, he was the eldest of the four sons of Joseph William and Betsy (Clark) Bissell. The family being in straightened circumstances, Clark prepared himself for college. It is said that when he left Lebanon for New Haven in 1802, he "had only the blessings of his parents and a homespun suit of clothes, dyed with butternut, and made from the fleece by his mother's hands, to take with him." While in Yale College from which he graduated in 1806, he maintained himself by teaching in the city schools. For a year after graduation, he was a tutor in the home of Mr. Singleton on the eastern shore of Maryland, then taught school in what is now Westport, Connecticut, at the same time studying law in the office of Samuel B. Sherwood. In 1808, he entered the law office of Roger M. Sherman of Fairfield, and in 1809, he was admitted to the bar. In June of that year, he began to practice in Norwalk. His marriage to Sally Sherwood, daughter of Samuel B. Sherwood, took place on April 29, 1811. For one year, 1829, he was a representative in the Connecticut legislature, and then, for ten years (1829 to 1839) he was a judge in the Supreme Court of Errors and the Superior Court. He resigned because of the inadequacy of the salary. His law practice thereafter was interrupted again by service in the legislature, in 1841 as representative, and in 1842–43, as senator. From 1842 to 1844, he was a member of the Yale Corporation. The Yale degree of LL.D. was conferred upon him in 1847, soon after he had been elected governor of the State in April, 1847. He was reëlected in the following April. Though nominally leader of the Whig party in Connecticut, the party was in such a state of disorganization that much of his program of legislation failed of passage. On the other hand a bill which he had vetoed was passed over his veto, and in

31

consequence[5] he forfeited his chance of being renominated for governor. The issue was a legislative divorce applied for by Martha Harvey from Alfred R. Harvey, a resident of Georgia. Bissell's temperate, well-reasoned, and judicious message by which he returned the bill to the legislature[6] pointed out that the petitioner had brought no proof that she was a resident of the State, nor that any cause for divorce of which the legislature had jurisdiction had arisen, since she came into the State. His dissent was based also on the further ground that the defendant had not had actual notice of the petition, as required by statute in order to give the General Assembly jurisdiction. Knowing as he doubtless did what the consequences for his political career would be, his message must be viewed as the work of a courageous and disinterested public servant.

When his term of office ended, he thereafter devoted himself to his professorship and to practice, with the exception of one term, 1850, as representative of Norwalk in the legislature.

The picture reproduced herewith shows that he could fix a reciting student or a witness with a penetrating eye. Eyes and mouth in later pictures are softened and more kindly in expression. "In his social intercourse his courteous, unobtrusive manners, his fund of anecdote, his genial humor, made him always a very agreeable companion."[7] He was ready of speech, earnest and impressive in manner, and for forensic discussion was possessed of "a caustic humor—sometimes playful, but when directed against fraud and falsehood often withering."

5. Morse. *A Neglected Period of Connecticut History*, p. 331.
6. *House Journal*, 1848, pp. 119–122.
7. Norton. *Governors of Connecticut*, p. 212.

32

Clark Bissell   *Henry Dutton*

Thos. B. Osborne

DUTTON and Osborne were close political and professional friends. They were of nearly the same age, the former in 1855 being fifty-nine and the latter fifty-seven years old. They had both been elected to public office, and both had practiced at the same bar, that of Fairfield County. Osborne's public career preceded his removal to New Haven to join the faculty of the school, so that during his ten years' tenure, he could devote himself wholly to it, with the exception of time given to practice.

A native of Weston (later called Easton), Connecticut, Thomas Burr Osborne was born on July 8, 1798, graduated from Yale College in 1817, studied law with Seth P. Staples, was admitted to the bar in 1820, and began practice in Fairfield County. On September 6, 1826, he married Elizabeth Huntington Dimon of Fairfield, and in the same year became clerk of the local county and superior courts. He held this office continuously until 1839. In 1836 he served also in the State legislature, and from 1839 to 1842, he was a member of the United States House of Representatives. He was a State senator in 1844, at the same time beginning an extended term as judge of the Fairfield County Court. Later (1850), he was judge of the Probate Court, as well as Connecticut assemblyman. Then came his appointment as law professor (July 24, 1855), his ten years of service, and his resignation on July 22, 1865, on account of ill-health. Four years later, September 2, 1869, he died in his seventy-second year. One of his contemporaries (Charles Ives, 35 Conn. 603) draws an appealing picture of his life in the school and among New Haven lawyers. There,

he was able to follow the law as a student, to learn and teach its philosophy. . . . Thus pursuing the law as a science, his mind

33

was enlarged and disciplined, and it was delightful to see in his old age how pure and calm and philosophic it rose, uncontaminated, above the grosser things of life. As I have met him from day to day, during the last twenty years, and heard him, with his keen reflective, philosophic mind, discourse in regard to local, state and national affairs, the philosophy of life, man and his destiny, he has reminded me, more than any man I have ever known, of Socrates, whose delight it was to converse with young men in the streets and market-places, upon the laws, politics, ethics, religion and other subjects of interest.

For long years of service to the school, Dutton's twenty-two should be bracketed with Hitchcock's twenty-five, and Daggett's twenty-three. Of the three, Dutton probably performed the most difficult task, for he stuck to it, first as junior to Bissell, then with Osborne as colleague, and finally alone, during the school's most trying period, until his death in 1869. Although the school had, since 1846, been a department of Yale College, the Corporation had not taken full financial responsibility for it as an educational institution. Salaries and other expenses were paid out of the income of the school. If the enrollment was small the income was small. That there were financial difficulties is shown by the fact that on July 29, 1856, the Corporation, on the recommendation of the Prudential Committee, voted that "the charging of interest to the Law Library account be discontinued, as the net income from the Law School is not enough to pay any interest." This resolution related to interest due on money advanced to aid in the purchase of the Hitchcock library.

When Osborne resigned in 1865, the Corporation authorized Professor Dutton "to employ such aid in the law school during the coming year as he shall judge best whether he shall prefer to engage lecturers or an assistant in giving instruction—paying such compensation out of the receipts of the department as he shall find to be neces-

34

sary." With this authorization, Dutton employed, as secretary of the school, a graduate of the year 1862, Charles H. Fowler, who served in that capacity from 1867 to 1870. An announcement was published stating that the "Law Department of Yale College has been re-organized, and will commence the ensuing year under a new system. It is designed to furnish advantages for the study of all branches of the law, superior to those of any other similar Institution." The proposed new system consisted in supplementing Dutton's classes by occasional lectures by prominent lawyers and professors. An imposing list of lecturers was given. President Woolsey was to talk on international law, Professor Alexander C. Twining on constitutional law, David Dudley Field on codification, Benjamin Vaughan Abbott on conveyancing, Amos G. Hull on wills, Thomas C. Perkins on conflict of laws, and Loren P. Waldo on domestic relations. No evidence has, however, been found that this ambitious program was carried out.

Friends of the college and of the law school had long been distressed by the school's difficulties. Dutton was aging and could do little more than keep the institution alive. But no one had found the means to help him. One of those who interested himself was Luther Maynard Jones, a Yale College graduate in the class of 1860, who in 1865 had taken his law degree under Theodore W. Dwight at the Columbia College Law School in New York City. Knowing that Dwight had studied law at the Yale Law School (1841–42), and being impressed with his skill as a teacher, Jones wrote President Woolsey on June 5, 1867, suggesting that Dwight might accept a call to return to Yale as head of the law school. Woolsey's reply of June 11, 1867, is an illuminating exposition of the serious problem which confronted the school.

35

An unusual pressure of business at the end of last week, arising out of the burden put on me of commemorating Dr. Hawes who died last week, has prevented me from replying before to your letter of the fifth inst. As to Mr. Dwight I know nothing of his feelings at all, but cannot help thinking that if the school were sure of success he would come here. But to be sure of success it must be endowed. The Library is altogether behind the times. A building containing two or three lecture rooms, a library, a reading room, a hall, etc. is wanted,—a building in short, which could be put up for perhaps 30,000 dollars. Then enough of endowment is wanted to pay, say two professors, about 1500 dollars each and two lecturers 500 each,—enough in short to take off some of the risk which must be incurred if the school is to be pushed on a larger scale. 100,000 dollars properly used would in the end make sure a highly respectable school, and if Mr. D. came the certainty would be more immediate.

A crisis or collapse is coming in the affairs of the school. Judge Dutton told me a few days ago that he did not see how he was to go on if he could not get some pecuniary help. Some years ago the plan was talked of to call in certain young men. Mr. Walter Phelps was conversed with, and there the matter ended. The college authorities have not been at fault in what they have done for the school, or rather in what they have left undone. "The destruction of the poor is their poverty." We could have raised the school by funds and men, but to get the funds we must have the men, and to get the men we needed the funds. There was no leverage.

No one was more conscious of the impending crisis than Judge Dutton. To the Corporation, he presented a "petition or appeal" in regard to the law school, and on July 16, 1867, it was "voted, that Governor English, Lieutenant Governor Hyde and President Woolsey be a committee to confer with Professor Dutton in respect to the matter of his petition, with power to add to the committee from persons outside of the Corporation." Unfortunately the petition itself has not been found. Again,

36

on July 21, 1868, a memorial from him and a letter to President Woolsey "representing the neglected and declining condition of the Law School," was laid before the Corporation, and another committee to confer with Judge Dutton was appointed. It consisted of President Woolsey, Governor English, Dr. Leonard Bacon, and Judge Charles J. McCurdy. This memorial also is missing.

Dutton did not merely send out appeals for help. He was himself busily at work. On March 31, 1868, he procured the adoption by the members of the bar of New Haven of a resolution permitting graduates of the school to apply for admission to the bar without an intervening period of study in a law office. The student body on April 1, 1868, voted him a resolution of thanks for this result. Another of his successful projects was the adoption of a resolution on July 27, 1868, by the Connecticut Assembly providing that copies of the General Statutes and the session laws should be furnished to the Yale Law School to be exchanged by it for the statute books of other states, such books to be kept by the librarian "for the use of Yale Law School, and for the use, at New Haven, of state officers and members of the General Assembly."

His personal efforts and recommendations began to attract attention, but there were many who doubted whether help, if it came, would not be too late. The following excerpt from the *College Courant* of July 17, 1868, quoting an item from the New Haven *Palladium*, is a good commentary on the situation:

The daily *Palladium* announces to the public the following news item, which, we may add, was a piece of news not only to Judge Dutton, but also to all the Faculty of Yale College. We wish in some respects it were true, for certainly it does not look

37

well for Yale to have so many of her graduates seeking other professional schools:

"The many friends of Yale will be gratified to learn that the faculty are perfecting plans which will soon make her Law School worthy of the name of the College. While the College proper has promptly kept pace with the progress of the age, the professional schools connected with it have, until very recently, remained almost stationary. Within the last two years, however, the theological department has been completely reorganized, and it is understood that the same spirit of reform is now to be extended to the Law School. The details have not yet been fully decided upon, but among the changes which are contemplated are the following:—Ex-Governor Dutton, who has long stood at the head of the department, will soon retire, as the duties are more arduous than are pleasant to one of his years. New instructors will be obtained, an entirely new law library secured, and such changes made in regard to buildings and other matters as shall prove necessary. Thus another movement is in progress to make Yale in fact what she already is in name—a university."

VII

DUTTON's death marked the end of an era in the life of the school. Inglorious though the closing years were, the fault was not his, unless it be said that he should have given up the task because it was required to be done under impossible conditions over which he had no control. The resignation of Osborne in 1865 and the disorganizing influence of the Civil War would have given him that excuse. But if he had done so, in all probability, the school would have been abandoned temporarily if not permanently. It should be remembered also that from 1861 to 1866, Dutton was a judge of the Connecticut Supreme Court of Errors, and that in the latter year he became seventy years old. The next three years, until his death on April 26, 1869, were filled, as we have seen, by his attempts to find a solution for the school's future.

38

They were courageous years for one who had already done his life's work.

That life had been an active one, notable for public service, and notable in relation to the law school in that he was the first of its professors who devoted himself extensively to legal authorship. Among works eligible to be put in the Law Faculty Collection, established in the Law Library in 1933, made up of books by members of the Yale Law Faculty, his *Connecticut Digest*, 1833, the editions of Connecticut *Revised Statutes* upon which he worked (1849, 1854, 1866), and his revisions (with N. Cowdrey) of Swift's *Digest* (1849–53 and 1862), precede in point of time, those of any other professor. The literary efforts of his predecessors were confined to legal briefs, judicial opinions, political pamphlets, speeches in legislatures and historical and commemorative addresses. Dutton's output included examples of the above, but also, with industry and learning he prepared or participated in the preparation of eight volumes for the use of the legal profession. All except the first, the *Connecticut Digest*, 1833, were prepared after he became a law professor. This first work, published when he was thirty-seven years old, was constructed after the pattern of Swift's *Digest*, and was intended to serve as a corrective, or continuation of it, in so far as it had become obsolete. This material, along with new matter, Dutton and Cowdrey used when they published in 1849, volume one, and later volume two, of their *Revision of Swift's Digest*. Both works, the *Connecticut Digest*, and the *Revision of Swift*, follow the general order of subjects popularized by Blackstone. In form they stand midway between treatises and modern digests. They laid claim not so much to literary perfection as to accurate statement of decided points of law.

39

Of the three editions of the General Statutes with which Dutton was connected, those of 1849 and of 1866 were genuine revisions, the result of scholarly work applied to the consolidation of existing statutes, the drafting of new statutes for adoption by the legislature and the arrangement of the whole into a consistent system of legislation. That of 1854, though an exacting piece of work, was essentially a compilation based on the *Revision* of 1849. Henry Dutton's name stands first in the list of committee members appointed by the legislature for the preparation of each of these editions.

Henry Dutton was born at Watertown, Connecticut, on February 12, 1796, the son of Thomas and Tenty (Punderson) Dutton. After the family moved to Northfield, Henry divided his time between working on the farm, attending district school, teaching, and individual study, thus preparing himself to enter the Junior Class of Yale College in 1816, at the age of twenty. In College his only pecuniary aid was a legacy of $100 from a maternal uncle. Therefore, when he graduated with honors in 1818, he was in debt. Two years of teaching in Fairfield Academy enabled him to cancel this indebtedness. While there he also studied law in the office of Roger M. Sherman. Then, from 1821 to 1823, he served as tutor in Yale College. As a reminder of this tutorship, Mr. George D. Watrous, Dutton's grandson, has in his library ten volumes bearing the following inscription:

MR. HENRY DUTTON

from the members of the Sophomore Class who were under his care while a Tutor—A tribute of Friendship and Gratitude. Yale College. July 1823.

The choice of books, which included four law reports, five legal treatises, and a digest of laws, presupposes that

40

he was continuing his legal studies, a supposition borne out by the fact that in the same year he was admitted to the bar, and began practice in Newtown, Connecticut. In this year, also, he married Elizabeth E. Joy, daughter of Capt. Melzar Joy of Boston, Massachusetts.

In the early years of his practice, he helped out his income by tutoring young men, some of whom were on "leave of absence" from Yale College. He twice represented Newtown in the legislature. Moving to Bridgeport in 1837, he established a successful practice there, was State's attorney for Fairfield County in 1841, and twice represented Bridgeport in the legislature. Then, 1847, on being appointed professor in Yale Law School, he moved to New Haven. In that year, as has been said, he was also appointed one of the commissioners to revise the state statutes. In 1849, he served as State senator, and later was again an assemblyman. In 1852, he was judge of the New Haven County Court, and two years later was elected governor by the legislature, the people having failed to elect one at the preceding Spring election. He was the last governor elected by the Whigs. Meanwhile he continued his law practice, relinquishing it only when he joined the Connecticut Supreme Court bench in 1861.

The period of the Civil War brought out the mettle of the man. To his country he gave his only son, Lieut. Henry M. Dutton who, at the age of twenty-four, was killed in the battle of Cedar Mountain, Virginia.

"History," wrote John S. C. Abbott (quoted in Atwater's *History of the City of New Haven*, p. 73) "has presented to my view few scenes more sad than the vision of the venerable father of this young man, wandering, a few days after the battle, over this same field in the unavailing endeavor to find the remains of his beloved and only son." But this experience

41

did not embitter him. "Many a student will recall," says the *College Courant*, May 1, 1869, p. 271, "some of his lectures [as Kent Professor in the College] during the war, when he treated upon the live constitutional questions of the day. His eye would often kindle and flash, as he touched upon these subjects and evinced the burning patriotism that dwelt in his heart."

Judge Dutton was above the average height, spare in body, and bold and rugged in countenance. "A slight stoop in posture," says Atwater, "betokened a man of modest spirit, of thoughtful habit, and of earnest purpose. He was affable, gentle and courteous in manner, both in private and official life, and of a kind and generous disposition." When he died both the New Haven County bar and the students of the Yale Law School passed resolutions (*College Courant*, May 1, 1869, p. 271) which expressed respect for his ability, courage, and accomplishments, and affection for him as a colleague and teacher.

VIII

THE events of the period from Dutton's death, April 26, 1869, to the semicentennial celebration of the school, June 24, 1874, will be covered in detail in a subsequent pamphlet. They begin a new era of revival, reorganization, and fresh ideas, rather than conclude the period whose events have just been recounted. Nevertheless, in order to maintain the sequence of outstanding happenings, a brief chronology will here be given.

On July 20, 1869, the Corporation passed four resolutions. The first asked Simeon E. Baldwin, Louis H. Bristol, Johnson T. Platt, and William C. Robinson to take charge of the school. The second authorized President Woolsey to employ an agent to collect funds for the law department; the third authorized the Prudential Com-

42

mittee to pay the rent of the lecture room in the Leffingwell building; and the fourth authorized President Woolsey to appoint an incumbent for the Kent professorship
in the College. In the autumn, the school opened under
the joint control of Baldwin, Platt, and Robinson. On
July 11, 1871, Francis Wayland was appointed a lecturer,
and provision was made for the employment of six others.
Just one year later, July 11, 1872, Wayland, Robinson,
Baldwin, and Platt were promoted from the rank of instructor to that of professor of law. On February 1, 1873,
the last payment of rent for space in the Leffingwell
building was made, and the school moved into the new
courthouse. March 25, 1873, the Corporation adopted a
vote of thanks to the donors of funds amounting to
$20,000 which had been spent to renew the law library
and, on July 31, a gift of $10,000 was received from the
Hon. James E. English, the income of which was to be
expended for the upkeep of the library. In 1874, the balance due the College on its loan to purchase the Hitchcock library was wiped out, and on June 24, the semi-
centennial of the school, reckoning from the date (1824)
when law students' names first appeared in the College
catalogue, was celebrated. The speakers at the exercises
held in Center Church were the Hon. Morrison R. Waite
(Yale 1837), chief justice of the United States Supreme
Court, former President Theodore Dwight Woolsey and
the Hon. Edwards Pierrepont (Yale 1837).

IX

In *Yale Law Library Publications*, No. 1, and in the preceding sections of the present pamphlet, the course of
events in the development of the law school to the year
1869 has been traced as much in detail as available information permits. An impression, perhaps, is given of a

43

continuous uneasy struggle for existence, because difficulties encountered and crises overcome stand out too prominently. To modify this impression, it must be remembered that, for the student, the school went along from day to day, term to term, and year to year, with little interruption of its continuity. Successions of students entered the school, paid their bills, attended recitations, moot courts and debates, sought diversions, passed resolutions, formed clubs and athletic teams, underwent examination tests, received their degrees, and were admitted to the bar.

In view of the fact that Yale law students are today accommodated with rooms in the school's own dormitories which form one section of the Sterling Law Buildings, it is interesting to learn that in the first and second buildings occupied by the law school, sleeping rooms for students were available. The College catalogues, beginning in 1824, list the names of law students, with the location of the rooms which they occupied. In the period ending in 1850 when the school was in the Hitchcock building, the catalogues show that local students lived at home. Those coming from a distance sometimes took rooms with residents or lived in boardinghouses. Names of such public benefactors which frequently appear are Mrs. Laws, Miss Lines, and Mrs. Thompson. Board cost $5 a week. Washing cost sixty cents a dozen. The favored few lived at the Tontine or the Franklin House. But during this whole period, with the exception of four years, there were always students whose addresses were given either as "Law Office," or "Law Building." The former designation was used only in 1824 and 1825. Beginning in 1843, the numbers of the rooms were usually given, e.g., "2 Law Building." In the year 1824, eleven out of fourteen students had rooms in the "Law Office," and in sub-

44

sequent years the number in the "Law Building" varied from one to eight. In the early years the only rival of the "Law Building," in number of students listed, was the establishment of Miss Lines. She took care of from two to eight students annually.

It has been suggested that perhaps students did not in fact live in the law building, but were employed in law offices there and slept elsewhere. As to the Hitchcock building, no proof to the contrary has been found, but after 1850, when the transfer had been made to the Leffingwell building, the evidence is fairly convincing. The College catalogue shows that, as in earlier years, many students had rooms elsewhere in New Haven, some of them living in private homes and boardinghouses, and some at the Tontine, the Eagle Hotel, and the New Haven House. Others found it possible to commute to their homes in Middletown, Wallingford, and New Britain. But there were always, down to the year 1870, students whose addresses were given by room number in the "Law Building." Before 1857 the number of such students varied from four to eight. After that time, the number was sometimes larger. In three separate years the number was eleven, in another, fourteen, and in 1865–66, it was sixteen.

Evidence drawn from the College catalogues is supported by the records kept by the agents of the Leffingwell building, from 1850 to 1858 by Atwater Treat, and thereafter, by Judge Henry E. Pardee. These books are now in the possession of Judge Albert McC. Mathewson (Yale Law School, 1884), by whose courtesy they were examined. From these records it appears that from 1851 to 1853, Miss Lines rented rooms in the building, subletting them to students, and that sometimes a student would on his own account rent several rooms and sublet

45

them. For example, in 1856, Alwin A. Alvord of New York City rented rooms 6, 7, and 11, occupied number 7 himself, and sublet number 11 to James J. Hyde of Baltimore. The agent of the building advertised his rooms in the newspapers, and his record book itemized payments of rent to him by students for rooms whose numbers are the same as those given after their names in the College catalogues. None of these students so listed were already members of the bar, and therefore they had no need of law offices. The cost of these rooms was about $30 a year.

In spite of the gloomy picture usually drawn of the lecture room of the law school, the Leffingwell building must have been something of a social center. The third floor not only contained rooms for students, but also, beginning March 1, 1862, was the headquarters of a club which rented rooms 9, 10, and 11. In 1866, the treasurer of this club was Simeon E. Baldwin. The fourth floor was occupied by the Scroll and Key Society, and the ground floor by Lockwood's Café. What with law and College students, lawyers and clients, clubmen, and patrons of the restaurant, there could have been no lack of activity in the "Law Building" at the corner of Church and Court Streets.

Evidence concerning the extracurricular life of law students is rather scanty. As already noted, they were included in the membership of the short-lived Yale Law Association which was organized in July, 1851. In October, 1856, ten students formed a Law Society, the nature of which has not been discovered. The *Yale Banner* for October 11, 1856, reproduced its symbol, which seems to combine a coffin with a headsman's axe. The symbol of the Theta Upsilon Law Society is reproduced in the number for September 24, 1859. It consisted of two columns supporting a shield on which is a picture of Justice with

46

scales. On the base supporting the columns lie clasped hands, and above the columns floats a ribbon bearing the inscription *Fiat Justicia Caelum Ruat*. There were fourteen members of the Society in 1859. The *Yale Courant* for July 25, 1866, emphasized the cleavage between the Academic department and the law school when it said:

> It is understood a secret society, the Justinian, has been organized in this [Law] department after the manner of the law societies of Oxford,—what manner that is, is not our province to inquire, but we presume and anticipate that it will serve to identify the school more with the other departments of the college, and conduce to the awakening from its semicentennial sleep. The Society contains seventeen members. They will be out with a new pin next term.

The symbol of this society appears in the *Yale Banner* for September 30, 1866. It consists of an oval plaque on which is represented a leaf bearing the word "Justinian." Underneath are the letters L.E.D.D. At that time, there were eight graduate and eleven undergraduate members.

One of the final student events of the period was the organization of the school into a society for the discussion of legal questions, to be named the Dutton Club in honor of Judge Dutton (*College Courant*, January 29, 1868). The organization meeting was held in the lecture room on the evening of January 21, 1868, when Edward DeForest was elected president, Henry H. Wolf vice-president, and John B. Reilly secretary.

If the law school was not closely identified with the other departments of the College, it was neither because it was merely a local school, nor because its students were of a lower order. It is true that there were often more students from New Haven than from any other one town, but usually there were more students from all other Connecticut towns combined than from New Haven, and

47

what is more important, from 1828 to 1869, a period of forty-one years, the number of students from other states exceeded those from Connecticut, except in thirteen of these years. Most of these exceptional years were in the decade including the Civil War. Thirty different states, besides Connecticut and six foreign countries, were represented by students in the school. At the outset, as was to be expected, students came from New England and the Central Atlantic states; but it is interesting to note that they soon came in almost equal numbers from the Southern states, including Alabama, Georgia, Kentucky, Louisiana, Maryland, Mississippi, North Carolina, South Carolina, Tennessee, Virginia, and the District of Columbia. Moreover, more and more came from the Middle West, the Far West, and the Southwest. Ohio was first represented in 1832, Arkansas Territory in 1835, Michigan and Missouri in 1836, Illinois in 1838, Texas in 1841, Indiana in 1845, California in 1858, Wisconsin in 1859, Iowa in 1862, and Colorado Territory in 1863. Out of the total number of students attending the school from 1828, the first year for which the homes of students are indicated in the catalogues, to the year 1869, more than one half of them came from other states than Connecticut.

Although students could enter the school without having been "liberally educated," college graduates occupied a privileged position in the school, and for many years predominated in it. In the years 1824, 1825, and 1826 every entering student had an A.B. degree, and one had also an A.M. In the period from 1827 to 1854, there were in every year except five, more students with A.B. degrees than without them. Twenty also had A.M. degrees and eight had LL.B. degrees when they entered.

Many graduates of Yale College stayed on as "resident graduates" to study in the law department, but certainly

48

an equal number with degrees came from forty-five other institutions, including most of the important colleges of the time. During the years from 1854 to 1869, the number of students having degrees rapidly decreased, and of these the majority were Yale graduates. Nevertheless, during the whole period from 1824 to 1869, when no degree was required for entrance, more than a third of the law students had A.B. degrees.

X

DURING the entire period under review, the course of study in the school is listed in the catalogues as occupying two years. The months of May and September were at first the only vacation periods, but later a recess of two weeks was set down for January. Later still (1851), the vacations were made to correspond with those for the College, so that there was a two weeks' recess in January, a three weeks' vacation beginning about the middle of April, and a summer vacation of seven weeks beginning about August 1. The law-school year began usually on the seventh Monday after the College Commencement, that is, toward the middle of September. The Spring term began usually during the first week of May.

Prior to the year 1843, when degrees began to be conferred, there was little incentive for students to stay the full two years. From 1826 to 1837, the tuition fee was $75 a year. Beginning in 1831, there was an entrance fee of $5, and the tuition for six months was $50. From 1838 to 1842, the annual tuition was $100 with no entrance fee. For periods less than a year the fee was $10 a month. Beginning in 1843, the tuition for two years, payable in advance, was set at $150. For one year the fee was $80; for periods less than one year, $10 a month, and for less than two years, after the first year, $7 a month. The rea-

49

sons for these graded fees appear in the regulations for granting degrees, wherein a distinction is made between college graduates, nongraduates, and members of the bar, specifically as follows:

The Degree of Bachelor of Laws will be conferred by the President and Fellows, on liberally educated students who have been members of the Department eighteen months, and have complied with the regulations of the Institution, and passed a satisfactory examination. Those not liberally educated, will be graduated upon similar conditions, after two years' membership; and members of the Bar, after one year's membership subsequent to their admission to the Bar.

These regulations all refer to the professional course. From 1843 to 1848, there was also a general course. It began on the third Monday in October, and continued six months, with two exercises each week. Additional courses could be started at any time if a class of twenty members could be formed. The fee was $20 for the whole course, or $5 a month for any less time. Students in the professional course were permitted to attend the general course without extra cost. The general course consisted of "lectures and studies on the most important subjects of jurisprudence" for the purpose of communicating "appropriate information to those who wish to attend to jurisprudence as a branch of liberal knowledge." A course on mercantile law, probably dealing with elementary business law, was organized when there was sufficient demand.

The announcement of the professional course as it appeared in the College catalogue for 1826[8] remained practically unchanged for twenty-seven years. It provided for lectures by the instructors, assigned reading in textbooks supplied by the school, recitations on these read-

8. *See Yale Law Library Publications*, No. 1, pp. 20–21.

50

ings, practice work in drawing pleadings and legal instruments, the writing of legal "disquisitions," and moot-court meetings. The backbone of the course was the readings and recitations. As early as 1831, the instructors began to divide the whole number of students into three reading classes. A letter from David Daggett dated December 9, 1831, and written to James Dana of Cambridge, Massachusetts, who attended the school in 1832–33, describes the manner of teaching.[9]

New Haven Dec.ʳ 9, 1831

Dear Sir.

Your letter of 6ᵗʰ current was received this morning. You enquire in relation to our law school "when the next term begins." I reply, we have no regular terms. I lecture every day when not occupied with my official duties which may be considered as taking up about one third of the year. My associate Mr. Hitchcock, during my absence supplies my place in lectures or recitations. We receive students for 6 months or more. The price you will find in the catalogue to which you refer. The Classes are occupied at present thus. First class are commencing 3ᵈ Vol. of Black. Com. & will next begin Cruise Digest. Second class are finishing Cruise Dig. and about to enter on the law of Contracts, & after that Chitty pleadings. The third class is half through Selwins nisi Prius, & will then enter on Phill. Ev. or Starkie. In the course of the ensuing 6 months all the above works will probably be recited as each class recites daily when Mr. Hitchcock is not engaged in Court. I lecture daily as before observed, & my course occupies about 14 or 15 Months. Blackstones Com, are the outlines & I endeavour to fill up certain of his topics such as mortgages, evidence, pleadings, contracts, equity &c. &c.

I, in addition, lecture once a week during the first & second term of the College, to the Students. My lectures in our school

9. I am indebted to Miss Mable C. Weaks of the Manuscript Division of the New York Public Library, where the original is preserved, for calling this letter to my attention.

51

commenced a few days ago—I shall soon be engaged on the 2^d Vol. of Blackstone.

I know not that I can be more particular in answer to your enquiries.

I am respectfully your obed^t.
Servt.
David Daggett

Mr. James Dana
Cambridge

At the foot of the letter is the following in Dana's handwriting, "Since ascertained that we can be received for a shorter period than 6 months."

A memorandum found in the papers of Isaac H. Townsend probably shows how the work was divided about the year 1843.

First year

Recitation No. 1		Recitation No. 2		Recitation No. 3	
Blackstone	5	Swift	2	1 and 2 Kent	2
Cruise	3	Chitty	3	1 Selwyn	2
Archbold	1	Starkie	3	Story on Equity	3
	–		–	Story on Bills	1
	9		8		–
					8

Second year

Same		Same		2 and 3 Kent	2
				2 Selwyn	2
				Story on Equity Pld.	1
				Smith	1
				Admiralty	1
				Civil Law	1
					–
					8

Apparently the plan was to provide three reading courses which together covered enough work to warrant giving a degree. The first and second one-year courses could be taken either in the first or second year, and the third ran

52

through two years. If a student had already done part of the reading elsewhere, he could select whatever course he needed to prepare for his examinations, and the length of the residence requirement depended on whether he was "liberally educated" or not, and whether he was a member of the bar.

In 1845, the announcements began to contain the statement that "the more advanced students are assisted in the study of the laws of the particular states in which they intend to establish themselves," and in this year first appeared the following impressive list of subjects which were "some of the principal studies of the course":

Blackstone's Commentaries	Bills of Exchange
Real Estate	Promissory Notes
Personal Property	Insurance
Contracts	Shipping
Domestic Relations	Corporations
Parties to Actions	Criminal Law
Forms of Actions	Equity
Pleading	
Evidence	Constitution of the United States
Nisi Prius	Law of Nations
	Conflict of Laws

The school prided itself upon its methods of instruction, contrasting them with the supposed greater emphasis at Harvard and at the Albany Law School on lectures. Even as late as 1867, when unfavorable criticism of the school was common, the *Yale Courant* (May 15, p. 260) came to its support in the following editorial paragraph:

The old-fashioned system of instruction by means of recitations, exercises in office practice and the details of conducting suits at law, still prevails in the Yale Law School. We consider this school, in this respect, not excelled. Not only is the theo-

53

retical knowledge acquired by the system of recitations, but also the application and development of the theory of practical questions is afforded in the semi-weekly moot courts, which are presided over by Judge Dutton. It is in these courses that the foundation of the lawyer is laid. One cause of the present limited attendance at this school is that the amount of labor is greater than where the "lecture system" prevails. The exertion of preparing daily recitations and weekly cases for moot courts, involves more effort than to sit in the lecture-room of the professor. Hence the limited attendance. But, after all, personal effort is the only key to success.

Although prizes to stimulate excellence in study and writing were early established in Yale College, similar prizes for law students appear to have been available only during the years 1859 and 1860. The information found concerning them comes from the local newspapers. *The New Haven Morning Journal and Courier* for July 28, 1859, noted that the "Hon. William L. Storrs, Chief Justice, and Hon. Thomas B. Butler and Hon. Origen S. Seymour, Judges of the Supreme Court, have been in town this week to examine Dissertations written by students of the Yale Law School, and award prizes." Eight dissertations were written on the subject, "Implied Warranty in the Sale of Personal Property," the first prize of $30 being awarded to Richard H. Chittenden of Westbrook, Connecticut, and the second prize of $20 being divided between Ezra L. Brainerd of Haddam, and F. Clinton Griswold of Wethersfield, whose essays were considered to be of equal merit. In the following year[10] the judges were the Hon. Charles J. McCurdy and the Hon. John D. Park, judges of the Superior Court, and the former Governor William T. Minor. The subject for the year was "Estoppel in pais," the first prize being awarded to Horatio Nelson Warner of Vicksburg, Missis-

10. *New Haven Daily Morning Journal and Courier*, July 26, 1860.

54

sippi, and the second prize to William Clayton Page of East Haven, Connecticut.

XI

SINCE the printing of *Yale Law Library Publications*, No. 1, further information on the purchase of the Hitchcock library, and the means by which it was brought about, has come to light. It will be recalled that on December 23, 1845, Storrs and Townsend proposed to the Prudential Committee that the library should be purchased and that, on the twenty-ninth, Henry White offered it for sale at a named price.[11] On December 30, 1845, the Prudential Committee appointed President Day, Governor Roger S. Baldwin, and Dr. Leonard Bacon a committee to take the whole matter into consideration, in conjunction with a committee of the College faculty, and report at the next meeting. At a meeting held April 14, 1846, the Prudential Committee authorized and requested President Day "to commission Mr. Tutor Larned and others, if necessary, to obtain money, by subscription or donation," for the purchase of the library.

The tutor referred to was Joseph Gay Eaton Larned, who was born in Thompson, Connecticut, on April 29, 1819, and died in New York City on June 3, 1870. He was a graduate of Yale College in the class of 1839, and from November, 1842 to August, 1847, he was a tutor in the College. The *Quarter Century Record of the Class of 1839*, published in 1865, says that

in 1846, during the vacations, he was instrumental in raising by subscription the money required to purchase for the College the Law Library of Judge Hitchcock, then recently deceased, and thus in establishing as the Law Department of

11. *Yale Law Library Publications*, No. 1, pp. 30–33.

55

Yale College what had previously been merely a private institution, holding but precarious relations to it.

Larned was provided with letters of introduction written by Judge Storrs, and with subscription sheets, at least one of which was headed by the following statement:

We the subscribers hereby agree to pay each the sum of One Hundred Dollars to the President and Fellows of Yale College in New Haven to be applied to the purchase of the Law Library of the late Judge Hitchcock especially for the use of the Law School connected with Yale·College and thereby to increase the facilities afforded by the College for a thorough education in the science of the law—under the following conditions namely,

That the said subscribers shall each have the right during their respective lives to use said Library (together with all additions thereto) in accordance with such regulations as shall from time to time be established by a Committee of three persons, who shall be annually appointed, one by the Corporation of said College—one by the Law Faculty & Instructors of said Law School—and one by the subscribers of one hundred dollars or more for the purchase of said library.

Provided however that such regulations of said Committee shall include the right of each subscriber to consult the books in said Library at all times during the Library hours fixed by said Committee—and to use in any Court in the City of New Haven during the trial of any case in which he is engaged as counsel or attorney, such books in said Library as may be needed in such trial and to draw from said Library at other times such numbers of books as said regulations may prescribe.

Initial subscriptions were readily obtained in New Haven, but when Larned began operations in Hartford, he encountered difficulties. When he wrote Henry White on May 1, 1846, he had been able to get the signatures of only two men, Judge Williams and Mr. Trumbull. Refusals and indecisive answers were the result of a feeling that

56

New Haven lawyers ought to do the whole of this . . . . What they have already done seems to be merely a matter of business—a good investment of a hundred dollars. . . . Over and above their hundred dollars each as a good investment of their money, the New Haven lawyers ought to do as much at least as we out of good will to the College.

To counteract this feeling, Larned suggested that New Haven lawyers who had already subscribed $100 be urged to increase the amount by at least $50 each. No complete record of New Haven subscribers has yet been found, but the names of thirteen persons who had subscribed up to August 27, 1846, appear in a letter of the same date from Larned to White. From this letter and Larned's other letter of May 1, 1846, the following list of known subscribers is made up. Following the name of each subscriber are the dates of his birth and death.

New Haven Subscribers

William Lucius Storrs	(1795–1861)	$500
Isaac Henry Townsend	(1803–1847)	250
Roger Sherman Baldwin	(1793–1863)	100
Alfred Blackman	(1807–1880)	100
William Brooks Bristol	(1806–1876)	100
Eleazer Kingsbury Foster	(1813–1877)	100
Charles Anthony Ingersoll	(1798–1860)	100
Ralph Isaacs Ingersoll	(1789–1872)	100
Dennis Kimberly	(1790–1862)	100
Charles Robinson	(1801–1876)	100
Charles T. Shelton	(–1885)	50
William Joseph Flagg	(1818–1898)	50
Henry White	(1803–1880)	100

Hartford Subscribers

Joseph Trumbull	(1782–1861)	100
Thomas Scott Williams	(1777–1861)	100

$1,950

57

In view of the fact that these men by their subscriptions made it possible to purchase for the law school the Hitchcock library made up of his own books, among which were some which once belonged to Seth P. Staples and David Daggett (the residue of which library is now preserved as the Founders' Collection), it has seemed appropriate to the Committee on Yale Law Library Patrons that these men—together with the Founders, Staples, Hitchcock, and Daggett—be deemed eligible to be named Memorial Patrons of the Yale Law Library.

These subscriptions having been assured, the Corporation, on August 19, 1846,[12] authorized the Prudential Committee to complete the negotiations for the purchase. That Committee, on December 26, 1846, authorized the college treasurer, Wyllys Warner, and Edward C. Herrick, librarian, to purchase the library "excepting certain text books and some others not needed for the law school, at a price not exceeding three thousand five hundred dollars." This sum was considerably less than the price set by Henry White, the executor, who accordingly refused it. Apparently, however, he then offered to accept the sum of $3,750, since the Prudential Committee, on January 18, 1847, authorized Messrs. Warner and Herrick to pay that amount. On the same day the Committee appointed Mr. Herrick a committee on the part of the Corporation for the regulation of the law library. He drew up a plan and sent it to Henry White on January 22, 1847. Part of his suggestions were embodied in the following printed broadside:

RULES OF THE YALE LAW LIBRARY

1. The Library will be open for consultation and for drawing books, from two to three hours on each business day of the week.

12. *Yale Law Library Publications*, No. 1, pp. 34–35.

58

2. No loud conversation can be allowed in the room while any are engaged in consulting books.

3. *Annual subscribers* have the privilege only of consulting the books in the Library Room.

4. *Life subscribers* will be entitled to take books to their offices. Three volumes only can stand charged to any one subscriber at one time.

Reports may be retained *two days* only;—other works *four days* only. A penalty of six cents for each volume will be incurred for each day's undue detention.

Digests and a few other volumes to be especially designated from time to time, can in no case be withdrawn from the room. The signature of each borrower will be required against the name of the book borrowed—or his written order shall be left with the Librarian.

5. Any number of books needed in the trial of any case in court in which any subscriber is employed as counsel, may be had while such case is on trial, by an order sent through the messenger or other officer of the court, and the borrower is to be responsible that the books are returned as soon as the trial is finished.

6. Each borrower shall be liable to supply any loss or repair any injury which may happen to any book while borrowed by him.

7. The Professors in the Law Department may borrow such books as they need for preparing themselves for their duties of instruction.

Members of the Law School are not allowed to remove the books from the Library Room.

8. Judges of the Courts, who do not reside in New Haven, are to be allowed the privileges of life subscribers, during their continuance in office.

9. Subscribers may introduce attornies from other towns to the library for the purpose of consultation.

10. These Rules are subject to alteration by the Joint Committee, appointed by the subscribers, the Law Department, and the Corporation of Yale College.

New Haven, March, 1847.

59

The Corporation's resolution of August 19, 1846,[13] already referred to, provided for life and annual library memberships for members of the bar, at a cost of $100 for the former and $10 a year for the latter. It also stipulated that income from this source and also one eighth of the tuition fees paid by law students should be devoted to paying the interest on the money advanced by the College, and when possible, to reduction of the principal sum owed. On December 28, 1847, the Prudential Committee relieved the law department temporarily of the obligation to reduce the principal debt by providing that "so much of the income of the school as belongs to the College except the payment of the interest on the capital of the law library debt" might be used for the purchase of books. Even so the upkeep of the library was still a problem, for on August 13, 1850, Judge Dutton in a memorial to the Corporation said "that 500 dollars, at least, are needed to supply the Library with such publications as are indispensable," particularly in respect to Law Reports in which the law library, he said, was specially deficient. Moreover, the law professors "had been obliged to expend over 250 dollars for necessary text-books, chargeable, as they suppose, to the percentage due the Corporation." Moved by this information, the Corporation voted that "when the Law Department shall have paid over to the Treasurer of the College that part of the net income of the said Department which is now due, the Treasurer shall be authorized to loan upon interest, to the said Department, an additional sum of 500 dollars, to be secured on the Law Library." Payments were regularly paid by the school to the treasurer down to and including the year 1856, at which time the total payments amounted to $2,180.38. On July 29 of that year, on recommendation

13. *Yale Law Library Publications*, No. 1, pp. 34–35.

60

of the Prudential Committee, as has already been noted, the Corporation voted that "the charging of interest to the Law Library account be discontinued, as the net income from the Law School is not enough to pay any interest."

The income available for the law library from annual memberships could not have been large, since the lawyers of New Haven, for some undetermined reason, less than two years after the Hitchcock library was purchased, took steps to form a library of their own. On November 6, 1848, by voluntary act, forty-two members of the bar founded the New Haven County Bar Library. Included in their number were six of the same men who had subscribed to the Hitchcock library fund, and among them also was Henry Dutton, already a professor in the law school. Each of the forty-two contributed $5 to the fund so that at the outset it amounted to $210. It was provided that on admission to the bar a fee of $5 should be paid to the clerk of the Court by each new attorney to be used for the purchase of books. On July 13, 1849, Charles A. Ingersoll, Alfred Blackman, and John S. Beach were elected to serve as a library committee, and it was resolved that the clerk of the Court, for the time being, be appointed treasurer and librarian. Until 1854, this official was Robert H. Osborne. The first purchase of books was from Little, Brown & Company, and consisted of forty-one volumes, including twenty-five volumes of Connecticut Reports, fifteen textbooks, and one digest. The above information concerning the organization of the New Haven County Bar Library has been taken from the original record book of the Association preserved in the office of the clerk of the Superior Court.[14]

14. See also a report by Harrison Hewitt in the *New Haven County Bar Association Bulletin*, No. 5, September 9, 1929, pp. 1–5.

61

The tentative plans for the regulation of the Yale Law Library drawn up on January 22, 1847, by Mr. Herrick, and sent to Henry White, contained the following paragraph concerning the law librarianship:

Librarian. Mr. Cowdrey to be retained until May, or the time of his leaving. This officer to be one of the students; compensation,—his tuition & $20 pr. annum. As on this plan frequent changes must occur & no provision for vacation; perhaps some elderly man may be found (resident in town) who will act as librarian for $150 a year. In this case pay a student $10 (or more) for locking the door at end of each recitation.

In accordance with the first proposal in the above paragraph, students, with a few exceptions, served as librarians during the whole period covered by the present pamphlet. The incumbents of the office so far as discovered from biographical notices and by reference to the annual catalogues are the following:

1845, October to 1847, June 1	Nathaniel Ackley Cowdrey
1847–1849	Francis Ives
1849–1851	*Unknown*
1852–1853	Enos Nelson Taft
1853–1855	*Unknown*
1855–1856	Jonathan Tillotson Clarke
1856–1857	Alonzo Norton Lewis
1857–1858	William S. Moore
1858–1859	*Unknown*
1859–1860	Richard Handy Chittenden
1860–1861	Washington Frederick Willcox
1861–1862	*Unknown*
1862–1866	Charles Holt Fowler
1867–1868	Fowler, who was Secretary of the Law School, probably acted also as librarian.
1869–1871	William Lyon Bennett

62

𝕻ale Law Library 𝕻ublications

No. 4   April 1937

Yale Law School:
1869–1894
Including
The County Court House Period

By

Frederick C. Hicks

PUBLISHED FOR THE YALE LAW LIBRARY
BY THE YALE UNIVERSITY PRESS

1937

[113]

COUNTY COURT HOUSE   CITY HALL

The third floor was the Law
School's third home

Yale Law School:
1869–1894
Including
The County Court House Period

FREDERICK C. HICKS[1]

I

A LAW SCHOOL never becomes an institution as long as its existence depends upon the life of one man. The Litchfield Law School did not survive the death of Reeve and of his colleague and successor, Gould. The Yale Law School nearly passed away with the death of Hitchcock in 1845, and again at the death of Dutton in 1869. In both cases, emergency measures were required to save the school. From without its own organization, help had to be brought in. During Dutton's last illness, there was no one connected with the school to carry on his classes for the rest of the year. The person drafted into service by him was Simeon E. Baldwin, who was then twenty-nine years of age, and had been at the bar only three years. Without time for preparation, he was called upon, for a few weeks in the spring of 1869, to conduct most of the classes held

1. In assembling the material for this sketch, the author has been aided by Miss Elizabeth Forgeus, Assistant Law Librarian, and Miss Ruth E. Bowman, Secretary to the Law Librarian. Many helpful suggestions have come from former students and from professors formerly or still in the school. The law library would be glad to receive from law alumni, pictures and other memorabilia of the school. For the history of the school from 1800 to 1869, see *Yale Law Library Publications*, Nos. 1 and 3.

I

in the school. "It was with fear and trembling" that he did so, for, said he (*Yale Shingle*, 1898, p. 68), "it was then not long since I had been one of the students there myself, and one or two of the men who recited to me were of almost my own age. However, it is always easier to ask questions than to answer them, and by hard work I believe I contrived to keep a little ahead of my class from day to day."

Later in the same spring, after Dutton's death, the work was taken over by Judge Edward Isaac Sanford of the Connecticut Superior Court. He was fourteen years the senior of Baldwin, had been for two terms Recorder of New Haven, and in 1867 had been elevated to the Superior Court bench. When, on July 21, 1869, he examined the five candidates for graduation, he gave notice that he should resign his position as instructor. (*New Haven Daily Register*, July 21, 1869.) At about the same time, the *College Courant* (July 24, 1869) announced that the school would reopen as usual in September "with competent and distinguished instructors whose names will be announced after commencement." This prospect was due to the intercession of members of the bar, who were stimulated to action by one of the last acts of Dutton. "A short time before his death," wrote Professor William C. Robinson (*Francis Wayland: Commemorative Address*, p. 21), "Governor Dutton, apparently foreseeing conditions in legal education which have since been realized, had sought a closer alliance between the law school and the examining committee of the bar, and had obtained privileges for his students in which no others shared. (See *Yale Law Library Publications*, No. 3, p. 37.) This naturally led the bar committee to take a special interest in the school, and when the rumor of its discontinuance reached their ears some of their number waited

2

upon President Woolsey, deploring the impending catastrophe and offering to carry forward the work of instruction at their own risk, on behalf of the College and the bar. After some negotiations, the offer was accepted."

A committee with which the members of the bar might confer was already in existence, having been appointed on July 21, 1868, by the Corporation, to consider a memorial from Dutton. The Corporation members of the committee were President Woolsey, Governor James E. English, and Reverend Leonard Bacon. They had called to their assistance Judge Charles J. McCurdy of the Connecticut Supreme Court of Errors. The four members of the bar who offered to conduct the school "at their own risk" were Simeon E. Baldwin, Louis H. Bristol, Johnson T. Platt, and William C. Robinson, and these men were by vote of the Corporation, on July 20, 1869, "requested to take charge of the Law School the present, or ensuing year." To reduce the risk that tuition receipts might not be equal to expenses, thus providing no compensation for the teachers, the Corporation on the same date authorized President Woolsey "to employ an agent, to collect funds for the purposes of the Law School, viz., for a library, a building, and endowments for the support of Professors"; and the Prudential Committee was authorized to pay the whole or part of the rent of the rooms used by the law school in the Leffingwell Building. The first payment by the College for the latter purpose was made on August 1, 1870.

All four of these volunteers were young men in active practice, their youth being in marked contrast to the mature or advanced ages of former accessions to the teaching staff. This alone constituted a revolution in ideas concerning the needs of the school. Platt was twenty-five, Baldwin twenty-nine, Bristol thirty, and

3

Robinson thirty-five. Bristol did not accept the invitation to share the responsibility, so that when the school opened on September 15, 1869, it was Robinson, Baldwin, and Platt who took charge. They had no formal academic titles, and no one of them was made Dean by act of the Corporation. By common consent of his colleagues, Robinson, the oldest of the three, served as Secretary of the school for the first year, and thereafter, until 1873, as Dean. On July 19, 1870, and again on July 11, 1871, the Corporation renewed its request that these three men remain in charge for another year, thus filling in the period from Dutton's death to July, 1872. "To any but three sanguine youths, with an ardent love for their profession," wrote Robinson (*Francis Wayland Commemorative Address*, pp. 21–22), "the prospect would have been discouraging. There was no money, not even to pay for necessary advertising. . . . But with three students already on the ground, with the great reputation which the school had gained during its fourscore years, and with the magic name of Yale to conjure by, we could not despair. With what means we could command, the school was advertised. The curriculum was remodelled and enlarged. The number of daily exercises was doubled. Eminent lecturers were employed to give instruction upon special subjects. Students were held up to a rigid fulfillment of their scholastic duties. And when we counted up results in 1872 we found that we had gathered more than fifty scholars, of whom twenty-five had been completely trained and graduated and admitted to the bar. We were astonished at our own success; and we saw then what others since have seen, that if you plant but a dry chip from one of Eli's ancient elms, and water it and nurse it well, it will grow up into a vigorous and fruitful tree."

Thus summarized by Professor Robinson thirty years

4

after the event, and with knowledge of the success of the venture as a background, the accomplishments of the three young teachers may be too lightly accepted. The years 1869 to 1872 were in fact years of intense activity, in which attention was given not only to current administrative details, but to the promotion of interest in the larger future of the school. All this was done while they were engaged with lectures, recitations, and moot courts, which activities were themselves superimposed upon their work as active practitioners. To support the school, it was necessary to attract students. To do this, better library facilities were required. A beginning was made by putting into effect the plan arranged by Dutton in 1868 (See *Yale Law Library Publications*, No. 3, p. 37) for the exchange of Connecticut statutes for session laws and revised statutes of other states. A catalogue of the library was begun, and a few gifts of books and money were received.[2] Three prizes of fifty dollars each were contributed to be awarded for excellence in scholarship, the debate club organized by Dutton was revived, and in 1869, the student body was formally divided in two classes.

But more vital matters than these were in the wind. A careful plan of action conceived by the young triumvirate to establish a policy for the school and provide for its development and support can be reconstructed from the course of events. The first of these was the publication, in April, 1871, of a pamphlet by the Reverend Timothy Dwight, then Professor of New Testament Criticism and Interpretation in the Divinity School. It was entitled "Yale College; Some Thoughts Respecting its Future." Six pages of it, devoted to the law school,

2. For an account of the development of the law library, see *post*, Section VII.

5

are couched in such terms as to suggest frequent contacts of the author with the law teachers. Since President Woolsey's retirement was to take effect in October, Dwight's exhortations were addressed to his successor in the "new era" which was drawing near. Arguing that the "several parts of the University must increase together," he asserted in unequivocal terms that it was the duty of the "central authorities" to put the law school on a firm financial foundation. This could not be done, he said, by passing resolutions setting forth the importance of the object, or by appointing an ordinary financial agent. The "central authorities" must make it their major task, and for the President, "there is here an emergency which requires his personal effort." He and the Corporation should originate the plan and determine to carry it out, but should also consult both lawyers and laymen, and not deliberate among themselves alone. Funds were needed for a building and for a library. The University library was deficient in law books and the law library had been neglected. The teaching staff should no longer be dependent on the fees of students for their compensation, and they should be so well paid that they could give up practice. Professors should give their whole time to the school. "A teacher needs to be wholly a teacher." What the school needs is one or more new professors "of years and eminence and attractive power as teachers," to work with those who are already carrying on with the heroism of youth.

On July 10, 1871, appeared the annual volume entitled *Yale College. Needs of the University. Suggested by the Faculties.* The law section, pages 18–20, was probably written by Simeon E. Baldwin in consultation with his colleagues. It admirably followed up Dwight's opening blast. Since that time some progress had been made. One

6

floor of the new court house, about to be built, would be available for the use of the school. For the present this would serve "although the erection of a separate law building will probably be necessary at some future time." Therefore, increase in the library, and the procurement of an endowment for a body of instructors, were needs immediately more pressing than the formation of a building fund. "It is impossible to sustain a law school which shall acquire and deserve a national reputation, unless the students have access to a library containing at least the principal part of the reports of cases decided in the courts of last resort in England and America, together with the works of the standard writers upon law, and a complete collection of the statutes of the several states. The present library of the Yale Law School, until within two years, had received no additions since about 1852, and includes but two complete sets of Reports—those of the United States Supreme Court, and of the Supreme Court of Connecticut." Turning then to the matter of instruction in law, Baldwin called for funds to sustain four full-time professors who should continue to instruct through the entire year. To these he would add four lecturers, engaged in other occupations, who would serve only as they were called upon. He suggested the following division of labor:

Professor of Real Property and the history of the Common Law, who would also take Equity Jurisprudence.

Professor of Commercial Law, and of Wills and Administration.

Professor of Domestic Relations, and of Public and Private Wrongs.

Professor of Pleading and Evidence, including Admiralty Procedure.

Lecturer on International Law.

7

Lecturer on Constitutional Law.
Lecturer on Civil Law.
Lecturer on Medical Jurisprudence.

For library, for endowment of instructorships and of scholarships and prizes, a total sum of $200,000 was needed. But $80,000 would found two professorships and two lectureships, and would "make the present library complete." Even then a permanent fund of $10,000 would be needed for up-keep of the library.

The pamphlet of which Baldwin's statement was a part, although dated July 10, 1871, must have appeared somewhat later. Its contents, however, were already known to the Corporation, for on July 11, it followed some of the recommendations. It voted that "President Woolsey, Governor Jewell, Rev. Dr. Bacon, and Judge McCurdy be requested to solicit subscriptions in Connecticut in behalf of the Law Department," and it authorized the Prudential Committee to "employ Hon. Francis Wayland and Hon. Henry B. Harrison, and others, as additional lecturers."

The school reopened as usual in September, and on October 11, 1871, the Corporation voted that "President Woolsey, Judge McCurdy, Rev. Dr. Bacon, and Hon. F. Wayland, be authorized to solicit funds for the Law Department and to request any other gentlemen, whom they may desire, to act with them." On that same day President Porter delivered his inaugural address. As marking the beginning of the "new era," Timothy Dwight and the members of the law faculty must have listened intently to this address. Some comfort they found in it because the new President recognized Law as an essential faculty of the University, pointing out the advantage to the University of the continued residence as law students of many of its choicest graduates, and to

8

the law school of association with other departments devoted to ethics, politics, and sociology. "Could a School of Law," he concluded, "avail itself of the wisdom and learning in all these sciences of such teachers . . . as the one who has stood at the head of this university . . . it would have no slight advantage."

This final suggestion came to be realized, for among those eminent lecturers referred to by Robinson whose employment had been authorized by the Corporation, appeared that same year the name of ex-President Woolsey as lecturer on international law. He gave usually about a dozen lectures on general principles of international law, but these were interspersed with special lectures on individual topics, such as the Alabama claims, the Congress of Vienna, and the Virginius affair. These were sometimes attended by President Porter and professors from the other faculties as well as by Governor Ingersoll and other distinguished visitors. Others who lectured were Judge Charles J. McCurdy (Insurance), Dr. Francis Bacon (Medical Jurisprudence), James M. Hoppin (Forensic composition and style), Mark Bailey (Forensic elocution), and James Hadley (Roman law). All of these men except Judge McCurdy were professors or instructors in other departments of the University. The lectures on Roman law by Professor Hadley, who was a professor of the Greek language and literature, were also from time to time delivered to College classes, and once to graduate students at Harvard College. Ex-President Woolsey spoke of them as clear and beautiful, and he thought so well of them that, after Hadley's death in 1872, he edited them for publication. They appeared in 1873, and have been kept continuously in print until the present, the last issue being in the year 1931, by the Yale University Press.

9

The "employment" of these lecturers could not at first be called a financial transaction, for, according to the *Yale Courant* (March 20, 1872), they "lectured gratuitously." "There seems to be a strong disposition on the part not only of the faculty, but of New Haven lawyers to bring up the department if possible." Nevertheless, it was these extra lectures which set the school off from others of the time, and caused President Woolsey to say (*Historical Discourse*, June 24, 1874, p. 12) that "nowhere in the United States are these subsidiary branches of knowledge . . . , these handmaids to a finished legal education, brought more effectively into the service of legal studies and made more useful than in the Yale Law School. . . . By the carrying out of this plan, it is made apparent how much more comprehensive and finished a legal education ought to be, when it is pursued as a department of a university, than when it stands alone."

Mention has been made of the fact that on July 11, 1871, the Corporation authorized the employment of the Honorable Francis Wayland as an additional lecturer, and that on October 11, 1871, he was made a member of a committee to solicit funds for the law school. He threw himself enthusiastically into the task of putting the school on a better financial basis, particularly by raising funds for the law library. He had a special aptitude for this work and was able to put driving force into the plans made public by Dwight, Baldwin, and Porter.[3] With Robinson, Baldwin, and Platt, he was, on July 11, 1872, promoted to a law professorship, and the four teachers were requested by the Corporation "to distribute among themselves, the several branches of instruction, and report the titles of their chairs to this board." The appor-

3. For an account of his success in regard to the law library, see *post*, Section VII.

10

tionment that they made, as follows, was communicated to Mr. Dexter through Professor Baldwin in a letter dated July 15, 1872:

Wayland—Professor of Mercantile Law and Evidence.
Robinson—Professor of Elementary and Criminal Law and the Law of Real Property.
Baldwin—Professor of Constitutional Law, and the Law of Contracts and Wills.
Platt—Professor of Pleading and Equity Jurisprudence.

That the appointments carried no specific compensation, a fact already noted, may be inferred from a sentence in Professor Robinson's letter of acceptance (July 17, 1872): "It is needless to say that I accept the appointment, and shall continue in the future, as in the past, to work for such compensation as the Providence, which watches over law-teachers, may see fit to bestow." For another year, Robinson continued to act as Dean, and then, by general agreement of the faculty, and not by any vote of the Corporation or Prudential Committee, Wayland became Dean, in which capacity, beginning in July, 1873, he continued to serve until his retirement. This was a change which his three colleagues had in mind when they invited him to join them as instructor. He was the first person to accept a Yale law professorship with the intention of devoting himself wholly to it, and he remained unique in this respect for many years thereafter. The administrative organization of the school was completed by the selection of Simeon E. Baldwin as Treasurer.

II

BALDWIN'S statement (*Yale College: Needs of the University*, 1871, pp. 18–20) above summarized, announced that as early as July 10, 1871, arrangements had already been made for the school to occupy a floor of the new

11

court house which was about to be built. This was before Wayland was first connected with the school (July 11, 1871), so that the credit for originating the plan must go to some one else. Wayland, however, must have had much to do in bringing it to fruition. His own account of the consummation of the plan, though lacking in details, probably gives us the essential facts. "By the thoughtful courtesy of the County Commissioners," he wrote (*Yale Shingle*, 1903, p. 11), "with the kindly co-operation of A. D. Osborne, Esq., clerk of the Superior Court, the third story of the new building was arranged for our occupation. . . . As some equivalent for this generous provision, the free use of our library, soon to be greatly enlarged, was granted to the courts and to members of the Bar."

Other accounts seem to indicate that the plan was initiated by the bar and the judges of the courts which were to sit in the building, in order to secure for them the use of the law school library, and that application was made to the Yale authorities to permit this arrangement. For example, a writer in the *New Haven City Year Book*, 1872, p. 378, puts it as follows: "To secure the deposit of the Law School library where it would be most convenient of access to the members of the Bar, and the judges holding court in New Haven, it was suggested, when the erection of a new Court house for New Haven was determined upon, that it would be highly desirable to assign it a place in that building; and, this proposition being favorably received by the College, the architect was directed to plan the third story so as to provide suitable accommodations there for the use of the Law School." While we cannot from correspondence files or reports of conversations, or from the records of the University, say precisely who conceived the plan of housing

12

the law school in the court house, we can from the record of events leading up to the building of the court house, find the names of men who must have been involved.

Up to April, 1861, all courts had sat in the State House which then stood on the Green. After that time they sat in the City Hall. In 1870, the judges were notified that they would have to vacate these premises by May, 1872. The Bar Association met in December, 1870, and appointed a committee headed by Alfred Blackman to confer with the County Commissioners on providing new rooms. At that meeting, it was agreed that a court house ought to be built, and on June 2, 1871, at 11 A.M., a meeting of the Representatives of New Haven County was held in the City Hall, for the purpose of levying a tax upon the inhabitants of the county to build a court house and purchase a lot for it. Arthur D. Osborne, clerk of the Superior Court, called the meeting to order, and George W. Beach of Waterbury was chosen chairman. Charles R. Ingersoll then offered several resolutions which were separately voted upon and passed. By them a tax of two mills on the dollar was levied upon the several towns to be paid by January 1, 1872; the amount to be collected was appropriated for building the court house and purchasing a lot; and James E. English, Morris Tyler, and Luzon B. Morris were appointed a committee to advise with the County Commissioners as to the selection of a site, and to advise with a committee already appointed by the Bar of New Haven County as to the plans and construction of the building. This Bar Committee consisted of Alfred Blackman, Dexter R. Wright, Arthur D. Osborne, John S. Beach, and Luzon B. Morris. The County Commissioners at that time were Archibald E. Rice, Richard Dibble, Charles P. Brockett, Nathan Andrews, and Carlos Smith. The site selected was on

13

Church Street facing the Green, next to the City Hall, being a lot occupied by the former residence of Dr. Jonathan Knight. The sum of $48,000 was paid for it. The one person who had most to do with the planning and furnishing of the building was Arthur D. Osborne. The architect was David R. Brown, and the builders were the firm of Perkins and Chatfield, and Patrick Kennedy. The cost, inclusive of furnishings, but exclusive of the price of the site, was $134,000. The Court of Common Pleas first met in the new building on January 20, 1873, and the Superior Court on January 27.[4]

The building was completed late in the year 1872, and the school was moved into it during the winter vacation. Classes were first held there at the opening of the spring session on Wednesday, February 12, 1873. "There were about thirty present," says the *Yale Courant*, February 15, 1873, "and a number of new members joined. Professors Wayland and Robinson met the class, and President Porter made some remarks congratulating the school on the superior opportunities they now have." These opportunities the *College Courant*, May 3, 1873, took delight in contrasting with those offered in the former building. "Graduates of the Law School will remember," wrote one editor, "the single room in the Leffingwell building which served at once for library, recitations, moot courts, debating societies, and lounging-place. They will not need to be reminded that any apartment more unsuited to what Milton calls 'the still air of delightful studies,' could hardly be imagined. Indeed, one cannot recall its dingy walls, its ill-furnished shelves, and its inadequate accommodations, without wondering that any professional school could maintain even a nominal existence, under such unfavorable conditions."

4. See Superior Court Records. Volume 27, Manuscript, pp. 93–95.

14

The new quarters were indeed palatial in comparison with anything that the school had known. They comprised all of the third floor of the county court house (part of what is now known as the City Hall Annex) except the Supreme Court room, and even this room could be used for moot courts when the Court was not in session. There was a lecture room seating two hundred persons, a library with shelving for 6,000 volumes, offices for the Dean and the librarian, and ample lavatory conveniences. The Dean's office and the library faced Church Street. The building was so constructed that the flooring between the library room and the room below it could be removed if the size of the library required it. It was considered a great advantage that students could so readily attend the trial of cases in the Supreme Court of Errors, the Superior courts, and the Court of Common Pleas in the same building. "At times," wrote Dean Wayland (*Yale Shingle*, 1903, p. 13), "the noise made by the students in their rapid climb [up the long flight referred to as 'those golden stairs'] to reach the recitation room in season for the eagerly awaited exercise provoked an animated protest from the Sheriff, whose duty it was to protect the court from annoyance." The rooms were heated, lighted, and cared for at the expense of the county. Moreover, minor improvements in the building were made from time to time. These were favorably commented upon in the student press, as important items of news. For example, the *Yale Courant*, February 14, 1874, announced that the library room had been improved by the installation of stairs leading to the gallery—"stairs of a peculiar labyrinthine pattern, manufactured by D. P. Calhoun of this city, and they are truly an ornament to our very handsome library." (*See* the picture of the library reproduced herewith.) Also that

15

"an elegant chandelier and reading lamp have been placed over the lecturer's desk in the lecture room"; and that the railing about the well in the main hall had been heightened to prevent accidents by the addition of a handsome silver-plated rail. "Truly, the liberality of the County Commissioners deserves our gratitude."

The event which, in the minds of those interested in the welfare of the school, marked the conclusion of the preliminary stage of its rehabilitation, was the celebration of the semi-centennial of the school's connection with the University—fifty years having elapsed since the names of law students were first included in the college catalogue. It was the one outstanding ceremonial event in the whole history of the school up to that time, and it was the occasion for setting up ideals to which to aspire—ideals then thought to be only possible, not probable, of attainment, but which a half century later were largely to be realized.

The exercises held on June 24, 1874, served also as the first of the school's public Commencement exercises. Many alumni from all parts of the country attended. At four o'clock in the afternoon, a public meeting was held in Center Church, on the Green. On the platform erected around the pulpit were seated Governor English and Governor Ingersoll, the Honorable Morrison R. Waite, Chief Justice of the United States Supreme Court, Attorney General Edwards Pierrepont, President Porter, ex-President Woolsey, Dean Francis Wayland, and Professors Baldwin, Robinson, and Platt. Dean Wayland introduced Mr. Justice Waite who was to preside, prayer was offered by President Porter, and then in succession ex-President Woolsey read a discourse on the history of the school, and Mr. Pierrepont delivered an oration on the "Influence of Lawyers on Free Governments." The

16

LAW SCHOOL LIBRARY IN THE
COUNTY COURT HOUSE

award of school prizes was then made by Chief Justice Waite. William K. Townsend, later to be professor of law in the school, won both the Roman law prize of $30 and the Senior Prize of $50. After a benediction by President Porter, the audience was dismissed, but the alumni were asked to remain seated. Later they marched in a body across the Green to the court house. Here, the new law school rooms were proudly displayed and an "alumni reunion" lasting about two hours, beginning at 6:30 P.M., was held. Three-minute speeches were made by alumni and guests. Mr. Waite thought that "the school should become one of the glories of Yale," and William G. Bates of Westfield prophesied great political futures for graduates of the school, because "lawyers would go to the Legislature, whether they went to the Upper Kingdom or not." Others who spoke were Hon. John Boyd, 1824 L., Hon. Thomas H. Bond, 1827 L., Henry White, 1826 L., Rev. O. E. Daggett, 1830 L., Hon. Cornelius Van Santvoord, 1833 L., Hon. Edwards Pierrepont, 1838 L., Hon. Alphonso Taft, 1837 L., Prof. Cyrus Northrop, 1859 L., then Professor of Rhetoric and English literature in Yale College, and Professor William C. Robinson.

At the conclusion of the reunion, a general reception was held. It was attended by the President and Fellows of the College, the faculties of the other departments, the Governor and Lieutenant-Governor of Connecticut, with the principal State officers and many other invited guests, making an assemblage of about five hundred. According to the newspaper accounts, "ladies were present in great numbers," and "beautiful costumes were the rule."

The ideal picture of a law school, above referred to, was drawn by ex-President Woolsey in his *Historical Discourse*. After tracing the history of the school, he turned

17

in conclusion to consideration of its future. First he answered in the negative the question whether a school located in New Haven could hope to compete in numbers with those located in large cities. Nevertheless, he thought that there was a place for a school of another kind, which would probably not be self-supporting, but which would fill a definite national need. This ideal school he described in the following words:

Let the school, then, be regarded no longer as simply the place for training men to plead causes, to give advice to clients, to defend criminals; but let it be regarded as the place of instruction in all sound learning relating to the foundations of justice, the history of law, the doctrine of government, to all those branches of knowledge which the most finished statesman and legislator ought to know. First of all I would have the training essential to the lawyer by profession as complete and thorough as possible. Let that be still the main thing, and let the examinations together with appropriate theses be a proof that every graduate has fairly earned his degree. But with this let there be ample opportunity for those who wish the aid of teachers in studying the constitution and political history of our country to pursue their studies in a special course by the side of or after the preparation for the bar. Let the law of nations, the doctrine of finance and taxation, the general doctrine of rights and the State, the relation of politics and morals, be within the reach of such as wish to prepare themselves for public life, and of those young men of wealth, of whom there is an increasing number, who wish to cultivate themselves and take their appropriate place of influence in society. Let there be the amplest opportunity for the study of English institutions, even far back into the middle ages, for that of Roman history and Roman law, for that of comparative legislation, and even for less immediately practical subjects, such as feudal and canon law. Let the plan of the library be expanded, so that it shall furnish the best books on all branches and topics connected with law, legislation and government. Can it be doubted that such an institution, of which I have sketched a faint outline, would be of vast serv-

18

ice; that its influence would reach into the halls of Congress, into the departments of government, that it might become a fountain of light through the whole land. (Woolsey. *Historical Discourse*, pp. 23–24.)

III

NOT only Woolsey, but Pierrepont also, in his oration, stressed the point that a law school connected with a University was the best place in which not only to train practicing lawyers, but also legislators, administrators, and executives in government service, and leaders in local communities. This thought was in the air—the idea of preparation for public service and intellectual leadership through a broad legal education. Moreover, that was not a new thought for the school. While emphasis in routine work had always heretofore been laid on training for practice, the men who had conducted the school, in themselves, exemplified public service. Daggett, Storrs, Bissell, Osborne, and Dutton all had had long public careers, while most of the others held municipal offices or were engaged in non-political activities for the social good. Not only that, but a creditable number of the thousand or more students who had been in the school up to 1874, either had already become or were later to become outstanding public figures. Ten of them had been or were later to be governors of states. These were William W. Hoppin (1830 L.), Governor of Rhode Island, 1854–1857; Thomas W. Ligon (1830 L.), Governor of Maryland, 1854–1858; Trusten Polk (1833 L.), Governor of Missouri, 1857; Richard D. Hubbard (1841 L.), Governor of Connecticut, 1877–1879; John G. Smith (1841 L.), Governor of Vermont, 1863–1864; Charles R. Ingersoll (ex-1843 L.), Governor of Connecticut, 1873–1877; Joseph E. Brown (1846 L.), Governor of Georgia, 1857–1865; Henry B. Harrison (ex-1848 L.), Governor of Con-

19

necticut, 1885–1887; Luzon B. Morris (ex-1856 L.), Governor of Connecticut, 1893–1895; and Simeon E. Baldwin (ex-1863 L.), Governor of Connecticut, 1911–1915.

Of future cabinet officers the school had produced three, Alphonso Taft (1837 L.), Secretary of War, 1876, and Attorney General, 1876–1877; Edwards Pierrepont (1838 L.), Attorney General, 1875–1876; and William H. Hunt (1842 L.), Secretary of the Navy, 1881–1882. Maunsell B. Field (1841 L.) was Assistant Secretary of the Treasury, 1863–1865.

Among matriculates who were to be United States senators there were Julius Rockwell (1827 L.) of Massachusetts, 1854; Trusten Polk (1833 L.) of Missouri, 1857–1862; David Davis (1835 L.) of Illinois, 1877–1883; Robert W. Johnson (1837 L.) of Arkansas, 1853–1861, and also in the Senate of the Confederacy, 1862–1865; and Joseph E. Brown (1846 L.) of Georgia, 1880–1891. Thirty-one Yale law students were destined to be representatives in Congress.

To the states and their subdivisions the school had supplied numerous lower court judges. But also there were many others serving in the higher courts. Six of them became chief justices in state supreme courts, William H. Welch (1827 L.), Minnesota Territory, 1853–1858; Benjamin R. Sheldon (1831 L.), Illinois, 1883–1888; Henry Sherman (1831 L.), New Mexico Territory, 1865; Alexander Smith Johnson, New York, 1857–1859; William N. H. Smith (1836 L.), North Carolina, 1878–1889, and George C. Watkins (1836 L.), Arkansas, 1852–1854. In 1874, two of its alumni were associate justices of the United States Supreme Court, William Strong (1832 L.), who served from 1870 to 1880, and David Davis (1835 L.), who served from 1862 to 1877. George Shiras, Jr. (ex-1854 L.) was Associate Justice from

20

1892 to 1903, and Henry B. Brown (ex-1859 L.), from 1890 to 1906.

In foreign affairs, there was also a good showing. Alpheus S. Williams (1833 L.) was Minister Resident at San Salvador, 1866–1869. Francis Schroeder (1834 L.), who later was Superintendent of the Astor Library in New York City, was Minister Resident at Stockholm from 1854 to 1857. Henry W. Ellsworth (1836 L.) was Chargé d'affaires at Stockholm, 1845–1849. Benjamin C. Yancey (1837 L.) was United States Minister to the Argentine Republic, 1858–1859, Edwards Pierrepont (1838 L.) was Minister to Great Britain, 1876–1877, William H. Hunt (1842 L.) was Minister to Russia, 1882–1884, Edward J. Phelps (1841 L.) was Minister to the Court of St. James from 1885 to 1889, and Eugene Schuyler (ex-1862 L.) was Minister to Greece, Roumania, and Servia, 1882.

A well-known journalist, poet, and lecturer was Park Benjamin (1832 L.), who founded the *New World* and edited it for five years. Prominent divines were Horace Bushnell (1829 L.), author of many religious books, and Courtlandt Van Rennselaer (1827 L.), President of the Board of Education of the Presbyterian Church. Five were railroad presidents: John T. Johnston (1840 L.), President of the Central Railroad of New Jersey for nearly thirty years; John G. Smith (1841 L.), President of the Northern Pacific Railroad Company, 1866–1872, and of the Central Vermont Railroad, 1873–1891; Joseph E. Brown (1846 L.), President of the Western and Atlantic Rail Road Company for nearly twenty years beginning in 1870; William D. Bishop (ex-1850 L.), President of the New York, New Haven, and Hartford Railroad, 1866–1879; and George H. Watrous (1855 L.), President of the same road, 1879–1887.

21

In higher education, the school's matriculates occupied an enviable place. John H. Lathrop (1824 L.) was President of the University of Missouri and of the University of Indiana, and Chancellor of the University of Wisconsin. Thomas H. Burrowes (1828 L.) was President of Pennsylvania State College from 1868 to 1871. Robert Emory (1833 L.) was President of Dickinson College, Carlisle, Pennsylvania, 1842–1848. Orsamus H. Marshall (1833 L.) was Chancellor of the University of Buffalo, 1882–1884. Henry Barnard (1834 L.) was Chancellor of the University of Wisconsin, 1858–1860, President of St. John's College, Maryland, 1866–1867, and United States Commissioner of Education, 1867–1870. John Brocklesby (1839 L.) was acting president of Trinity College, Hartford, Connecticut, five times between 1860 and 1874. Theodore W. Dwight (1842 L.) became famous as the head of Columbia University Law School. Cyrus Northrop (1859 L.) went from a professorship in Yale College to become President of the University of Minnesota, 1884–1911. Homer B. Sprague (ex-1853 L.) was President of Mills College, Oakland, California, 1884–1886, and of the University of North Dakota, 1887. Judson S. Landon (ex-1855 L.) was President *ad interim* of Union University, Schenectady, New York, 1884–1888; and Russell H. Conwell (ex-1863 L.) was President of Temple University, Philadelphia, Pennsylvania.

Thirty-three former Yale law students became officers during the Civil War either in the northern or southern armed forces. Of these, four attained the rank of General. These were James S. Wadsworth (1829, 1830 L.), Brigadier General, later breveted Major General in the Union army; Francis S. Barstow (1837 L.), breveted Brigadier General in the Confederate army; William H. T. Walker (1839 L.), Major General in the Confederate army; and

22

Alfred H. Terry (1849 L.), Brigadier and later Major General in the Union army.

Of students in the law school before 1874, forty-one have been deemed of sufficient importance to be included in the *Dictionary of American Biography*.

IV

TAKING stock of the situation after the semi-centennial celebration was ended, the four teachers found cause for encouragement. The presence of alumni whose records already were creditable to the school, the new quarters, the strengthened library, the willingness of well-known men to give special courses without proper compensation; and the picture of a great school delineated by Woolsey and Pierrepont which was before them as an ideal—all these were stimulating to the imagination of the four upon whom the future of the school depended. Only one of them, Wayland, as has been said, was a full-time teacher and administrator, but never before had anyone been able to devote himself exclusively to the school. Despite the fact that professors' salaries were wholly derived from student fees, the other expenses of the school were now less than they formerly were. There was no rent to be paid, there were no repair bills, and light and heat were provided. At this juncture it would have been possible to bend all energies toward enlarging the student body in order to provide proper pay for the faculty. Nothing of the kind was done. On the contrary, the whole trend was toward intellectual improvement and the raising of Academic standards to higher levels.

The first noteworthy step in this direction was brave, bold even, and dramatic. Woolsey had given a view of a law school which he said was "only ideal and possible at present." They would use his words in a different sense.

23

The plan *was* possible. They would make it a reality. They would continue to train lawyers as their chief objective, but they would so add to the work offered by the school that it would indeed be a "fountain of light through the whole land." They would set up a graduate course in law and its allied subjects, the first in the United States leading to the Doctorate in Law.

The proposal was formally presented to the Corporation in a letter, signed by all four members of the faculty, on June 15, 1875. As a reward for one year's additional law study in the school by Bachelors of Law, they recommended that the degree of Master of Arts be conferred, following the practice which they said was already in vogue in the law schools of Harvard and Boston Universities. For two years of graduate study they recommended conferring the degree of Doctor of Civil Law, in preference to that of LL.D., or J.U.D. Their letter was accompanied by two resolutions drawn up in form for the Corporation to adopt, and by a scheme of graduate studies.

This communication was read to the Corporation on June 29, 1875, and on motion of the Honorable Henry B. Harrison, a committee of conference with the law faculty was authorized, and ex-President Woolsey, President Porter, and Mr. Harrison were appointed to consider the plan and report upon it. In the conferences that ensued, it was agreed that a degree more appropriate to be conferred at the end of the first year of graduate study would be that of Master of Laws (M.L.) instead of Master of Arts (M.A.). The Corporation committee favored the degree of J.U.D. to be conferred at the end of the second year, instead of that of D.C.L., but the law faculty held to its original recommendation and so stated in a letter dated May 17, 1876, in which it urged that favorable action upon the whole plan be taken at the Corporation

24

meeting to be held on that day. At that meeting formal approval was given, and the law school bulletin for 1875–1876 (actually covering the calendar year 1876) announced that "a post-graduate course has been recently organized, which will go into full effect at the commencement of the Fall Term in the present year (1876)."

The announcement for the next year (1876–1877) described the new course in detail, listed ten students who were candidates for the M.L. degree, and let it be known that "greater advantages are now offered at Yale College for following the study of public law, Roman law, comparative jurisprudence, style in oratory and composition, constitutional history, and political science, than have ever been afforded before at an American law school, or than can be given at any school where the term is less extended, or where—from its want of connection with a University—the staff of instructors must be less numerous."

Candidates for the M.L. degree were required to be Bachelors of Law, and to study at the school at least one year. Bachelors of Law who also were Bachelors of Arts or of Philosophy were to be permitted, after taking the M.L. degree, to continue study for another year leading to the degree of Doctor of Civil Law. Since no college degree was required in those days for admission to the Yale Law School, it was necessary to make some special regulations for good students who had no Academic degree, to take graduate work. By the above rule, they could become candidates for an M.L. but not for a D.C.L. degree. It was therefore provided further that Yale law students who in the final examination for the LL.B. degree ranked in the first quarter of their class in scholarship could, after taking the M.L. degree, be admitted to candidacy for the D.C.L. All candidates for this degree

25

were required to have a good knowledge of Latin, and also of either the French or German language. All graduate work by candidates for degrees was to be done in New Haven, and included a final examination and the presentation of a satisfactory thesis. For all graduate students, one class ·exercise each day was provided, the rest of the students' time to be devoted to reading and the preparation of their theses.

The first year of the graduate course was frankly stated to be supplementary to the undergraduate course, affording further instruction in the branches of study there pursued. It was the forerunner of the three-year course which, however, did not go into effect until September, 1896. The second year was intended to embrace genuine graduate work, regardless of its applicability to the needs of the practicing lawyer.

Since the law school was thoroughly proud of the new courses offered and of the men who were brought in to supplement the regular faculty, it is worth while to list below the whole array of courses and professors.

FOR CANDIDATES FOR THE DEGREE OF M.L.

Prof. WAYLAND
 Administration of estates
 English constitutional
  history
 Evidence in equity

Prof. BALDWIN
 Practice in the U.S. courts
 Railroad law
 American constitutional
  history

Prof. ALBERT S. WHEELER
 Roman law

Prof. ROBINSON
 Admiralty law
 Medical jurisprudence
 Forensic oratory and rhetoric

Prof. PLATT
 General jurisprudence
 Corporations
 Practice in states having a
  civil code

Prof. ARTHUR M. WHEELER
 English history

Prof. WILLIAM G. SUMNER
 International law

26

President PORTER
  Ethics
Prof. WAYLAND
  Parliamentary law
  Political science
  Hermeneutics
Prof. BALDWIN
  Comparative jurisprudence
  Modern European legis-
    lation
  Political history
  Roman law
Prof. WILLIAM H. BREWER
  Relations of Physical
    geography to
    political history

Prof. ROBINSON
  Conflict of laws
  Early history of real property
  Forensic oratory
  Canon law

Prof. PLATT
  General jurisprudence
  Principles of legislation

Prof. ALBERT S. WHEELER
  Roman law

Prof. WILLIAM G. SUMNER
  Sociology

Prof. FRANCIS A. WALKER
  Political economy

Of the ten candidates for the M.L. degree in the first year, two completed their work and were awarded the degree on June 28, 1877. These men, who were the first to receive graduate degrees in the Yale Law School, were Alexander Rieman Hack, LL.B., University of Maryland, 1875, Yale Law School, 1876, and John Howard Whiting, LL.B., Yale Law School, 1876. Whiting continued his work for another year, and on June 27, 1878, became the first recipient of the Yale degree of Doctor of Civil Law.

At the Commencement on June 27, 1878, the M.L. degree was conferred on five men. Three of them later were awarded the D.C.L. degree, George Gluyas Mercer of Philadelphia, in 1879, and Kazuo Hatoyama of Tokyo, and William Kneeland Townsend, in 1880. In that year the first change in the regulations took place. A letter

27

dated June 26, 1880, from Dean Wayland to the Corporation, pointed out that the existing rule tended to prevent graduates of the school who had no Academic degrees from applying for the D.C.L. degree, because most of those ranking in the first quarter of their class had Collegiate degrees. It was proposed, therefore, to admit to candidacy for the degree, those who at their final examination for the LL.B. degree, were marked as high as three on a maximum scale of four. The Corporation approved this change on June 29, 1880. The new rule, not quite so definitely stated in one respect as the vote would have permitted, and going beyond it in another, was printed in the law school announcement for 1880–1881 as follows:

Those who receive this degree [M.L.] can proceed in their studies for another year with a view to applying for the degree of Doctor of Civil Law (D.C.L.), provided they have been graduated as Bachelors of Arts or Philosophy, or, *on graduating at this Law School, attained a prescribed standard of scholarship* on their examinations *both for the degree of LL.B. and M.L.*

No further change was made in the rules pertaining to graduate degrees until the year 1892, when on June 27, at the request of the law faculty, the rule prescribing an LL.B. as a prerequisite for admittance to the first-year course leading to an M.L. was relaxed so as to admit also "any attorney at law, on the presentation of a certificate of a Judge of the highest court of his State that he has been in active practice during the previous five years, and has a creditable standing at the bar."[5]

V

THE general scheme of instruction in vogue from the year 1826 to 1869 has already been described in an earlier

5. The history of graduate work at the Yale Law School will be continued in a later pamphlet.

28

pamphlet.[6] Two years of study were provided for, and the work was allotted to three reading courses which to some extent duplicated each other, so that students entering at different times could begin the subjects that they needed. One of the first things done under the new regime in 1869 was to divide the school formally into two classes, called the Junior and Senior class respectively. The two courses were, however, not mutually exclusive, because all students were expected to attend the lectures and recitations in both courses, though they recited only in the courses for which they were registered as Juniors or Seniors. This doubling up of courses enabled students having a college degree to graduate in three terms; but others were required to remain for the full two years' period. It should be noted that at this time "no examination, and no particular course of previous study" was required for admission. The next year, 1870–1871, students were no longer required to attend all courses given, but they were urged to do so. "Members of either Class may attend the exercises of both, and, so far as they are able, are recommended to do so." The traditional scheme of instruction in the school was adhered to. It consisted chiefly of recitations on required reading supplemented by lectures and moot court work. Wednesdays and Saturdays were devoted exclusively to the two latter activities. On the other week-days there was a recitation for each class, "accompanied with oral explanations or prefaced by a lecture." In the announcement for 1874–1875, for the first time, a definite schedule of exercises was given. For purposes of record these should be listed, omitting the names of professors because there was a considerable shifting of courses from one to the other.

6. *Yale Law Library Publications*, No. 3, pp. 49–55.

29

JUNIOR YEAR

JUNIOR YEAR

FALL TERM:

Recitations: Elementary law; Torts; International law.

Lectures: History of American law; General jurisprudence and the Common law; Forensic elocution; Methods of study and mental discipline (given by President Porter).

SPRING TERM:

Recitations: Contracts; Mercantile law; Evidence; Pleading.

Lectures: Life insurance; Forensic composition; Wills; English constitutional law; Medical jurisprudence.

SENIOR YEAR

FALL TERM:

Recitations: Equity; Contracts; Mercantile law.

Lectures: International law; Comparative jurisprudence; Roman law.

SPRING TERM:

Recitations: Contracts; Mercantile law; Real property.

Lectures: American constitutional law; Ecclesiastical law; Political economy; Patent law; Criminal law.

In the next year there was a tightening of requirements both for entering the school, and for graduation from it. College graduates could still be admitted without examination, but others were required to be eighteen years of age, and to pass an entrance examination in English grammar, English history, United States history, and on the text of the Constitution of the United States. All applicants for admission to advanced standing were required to have studied law for at least one year under a competent instructor, and to pass such an examination as was held at the end of the Junior year. Once in the school, Juniors were required to write essays at stated intervals, the first subject assigned in October, 1875, being "Remainder and Reversion." An acceptable thesis was required of Seniors before graduation. The faculty also in October, 1875, strengthened its hold on the stu-

30

dents by introducing what was called "the marking system," which meant compulsory attendance at classes. The *Yale Courant* (October 9, 1875) thought this to be a backward step, in view of the fact that it tended to postpone the abolition of the same system in the College. The law faculty, it was inferred, had "decided that voluntary study is a failure. It is rather surprising in an institution composed of college graduates or at least of men much older than the average undergraduate that the sense of individual responsibility is not strong enough to keep the student at work. . . . In view of the action in the Law School, the time when the experiment of appealing to the [Yale College] students' independence and exciting their enthusiasm for intellectual pursuits for their own sake, is indefinitely postponed."

In explanation of the published curriculum, the law school announcements, beginning in 1874–1875, laid emphasis on the necessity for the study of law as a science, as well as for the training of practicing lawyers. Thus they justified the inclusion in the regular course of Roman law, medical jurisprudence, ecclesiastical law, international law, and comparative jurisprudence. Such an attitude prepared the way for, and perhaps necessitated, in order to provide time for study, the establishment of the graduate courses which have already been described as having been begun in the fall of the year 1876.

Incentives to exceptional work were provided in 1882, when by vote of the Corporation (October 26), provision was made for the granting of honor degrees to students of unusual merit. Such degrees were first conferred in June, 1883, when the LL.B., *magna cum laude*, was awarded to Nathaniel T. Guernsey, Daniel W. Lawler, and Sain Welty; and the LL.B., *cum laude*, to Howard J. Curtis, Louis B. Hasbrouck, and George W. Wheeler.

31

Prizes for best work in the regular courses, as shown by final examinations, and also for essays on prescribed subjects, were also awarded. In 1884, a variation in the method of final examination was instituted when one day for each class, in addition to the written tests, was devoted to an oral examination, conducted by members of the bar, not connected with the school. In that year the oral examiners were Julius B. Curtis, David Torrance, and William E. Simonds.

Discussions of general methods of legal education first began to appear in the public announcements of the school in 1885. At first they had to do with the question, which had lately been discussed in meetings of the American Bar Association, whether a law school or a law office was the better place in which to study law. Resolving the question in favor of the schools, the conclusion was for some years given under the heading, "The True Method of Acquiring a Legal Education," followed by a statement of the facilities offered at Yale, and the assertion that "the Law Department of Yale College is the only Law School in America or England which has a four years' course of daily exercises leading up to the degree of doctor of laws."

A more vital question was, however, pressing for an answer. The case method of instruction had been introduced in the Harvard Law School in 1871, and had since been making converts in other schools. Should this method be adopted at Yale? The question was carefully considered and the answer was given in the School's Announcement for 1887–1888, under the heading "Method of Instruction," describing a plan which for many years was referred to as the Yale System. Only gradually and after the turn of the century, was it abandoned for the case method of instruction. Since it was the educational

32

covenant to which all of the faculty of that day devoutly subscribed, and since it succinctly sets forth one side of an argument which rocked the law school world, this statement must be reprinted here:

The method of instruction, especially in the undergraduate course, is mainly that of recitations. It is the conviction of the Faculty of this Department, as well as the tradition of the University, that definite and permanent impressions concerning the principles and rules of any abstract science are best acquired by the study of standard text-books in private, followed by the examinations and explanations of the recitation room. Hence, although certain subjects are separately taught by lectures, either because the want of proper manuals, or the constant and rapid advance of learning, or economy of time, requires the adoption of that method, care is taken that the same topics shall be covered by recitation work in connection with the wider branches of the law to which they belong. The recitation hours, however, are not devoted entirely to the questioning of the student. While this is done with sufficient thoroughness to hold him up to his work of preparation, ample opportunity is afforded for a free colloquial discussion of the subject of the lesson and for the presentation and solution of the difficulties which he may have encountered in his private study. In this manner each student is brought into personal communication with the instructor in reference to his daily work, and as far as practicable receives the benefits which would be obtained if he were placed under the individual tutorship of his professor.

Subsidiary parts of the above system were required participation in weekly moot courts, debating, and review work carried on in quiz clubs. These latter clubs, beginning in September, 1892, were put under the direction of Instructors in Quiz Clubs, the first of whom was John A. Hoober, M.L. 1892. Before that time, quiz work had been supervised by assistant librarians, and by others serving without title. Among them was Edward G. Buckland.

33

The fact that, in the above statement, no mention whatever is made of the use of cases may be explained as due to a desire to emphasize the merits of the Yale System. Cases were in fact referred to and discussed in class, and students were urged to read them in the law reports. In certain courses, such as contracts and criminal law, special emphasis was laid on the need for reading cases decided since the date of publication of the textbooks used. A little later (1892–1893) there was added to the description of the method of instruction the statement that "reported cases of special importance as illustrating the development of law into leading branches are also referred to, and many of these are separately printed and distributed for more ready consultation." There were groups of cases, so printed, on wills, constitutional law, corporations, contracts, and Roman law. Each case was separately printed with its own paging, and the respective groups of cases for particular courses were laced together in binders. Baldwin's *Cases on Railroad Law*, 1896, was published by the West Publishing Company as a bound case book, but there were no footnotes or explanatory statements, and the preface explained that the book was prepared for use in connection with a textbook, *Pierce on Railroads*.

Although the faculty remained true to its conviction that a student's introduction to a subject should be by means of textbooks, recitations, and lectures, using cases only to illustrate texts, the same subjects, in the second year and in the first graduate year (later the third undergraduate year) were sometimes gone over again using a case book as the basis of study. From this practice came a modification in the description of the Yale System, so that in 1895 (*Yale Alumni Weekly*, 4:1, May 1) it was said to combine "the case system and the textbook

34

system in a way which appeals to reason and common sense. It teaches and believes in the logic of the law, and it illustrates the theories taught and believed in by cases which contain the recent utterances of the best judges and that emanate from the highest courts in America and England." But there was yet no idea of complete surrender. Emotional loyalty to their system still throbs in the assertion that the school "does not believe in putting a single flake of gold in a pan of dust and then in placer mining the pan to recover what is there concealed. Men know gold; so do minds know the truth. And it is not necessary to conceal either one to make the finder more sure of his discovery." One of the means by which the school sought, not to conceal, but to expose to the light, supposed nuggets of wisdom, was to issue, in leaflet form, syllabi of lectures and outlines of subjects. These, with textbooks, separately printed illustrative cases, and readings in the law reports, were the means by which recitations and lectures were buttressed. The System was on the defensive, and as will be seen in a subsequent pamphlet, it finally went down to certain but dignified defeat.

It has already been noted (*Yale Law Library Publications*, No. 3, p. 50) that beginning in 1843, non-professional courses were offered for those who wished to study law "as a branch of liberal knowledge," and for those who wished to engage in business. Such courses, in one form or another, continued to be offered during the whole period covered by the present pamphlet. There is no evidence leading us to suppose that this was done to provide a means of taking all comers in order that their fees might be added to the income of the school. On the contrary, it seems to have been dictated by a liberal educational policy which sought to provide the means of

35

legal study to meet all kinds of needs, even when the student did not seek a degree or intend to become a lawyer, and even when his pre-legal education would not enable him to enter the regular courses. In the early years of the school little emphasis was placed upon the desirability of earning a degree, and there are therefore many students annually listed as non-graduates. Such listing carried with it no stigma.

In 1887 a new type of special course was inaugurated for which a degree was granted. On April 14, 1887, Dean Wayland and Professor Robinson appeared before the Corporation to request that it establish the degree of Bachelor of Civil Law in the Law School, to be conferred on students who have pursued a prescribed course of two years, covering instruction in elementary "and American law, international law, public and private, general jurisprudence, political science, the Institutes of Justinian, and the Pandects." A committee composed of President Dwight, Mr. Kingsbury, and Mr. Farnam, to which was delegated power to pass upon the request, reported on May 25, 1887, that it had consented that the degree be established. The School's announcement for 1887–1888 described the course as one designed "for those not intending to enter any active business or professional career, but who wish to acquire an enlarged acquaintance with our political and legal systems, and the rules by which they are governed." No examination was required for entrance, but the passage of regular examinations and the preparation of a thesis were specified as prerequisites for the degree. It was announced also that work in this course by persons having a satisfactory Academic degree might be counted toward the degree of Doctor of Philosophy in the University. Although the course was regularly offered from 1887 to 1916, when on June 16, it

36

was discontinued on the recommendation of the Governing Board of the Law School, the degree of B.C.L. was not conferred until 1905, when it was received by John Robert Waller. It was conferred on only eight other persons.

VI

FREQUENT references have been made to the fact that the amount of compensation received by professors, instructors, and lecturers depended wholly upon the amount of students' fees paid. The account books of Simeon E. Baldwin, Treasurer of the Law School, show that the balance in his hands, after all other expenses had been paid, was disbursed to the regular staff in the form of "dividends." These were reckoned sometimes on a percentage basis, and sometimes on the basis of exercises conducted at so much an exercise. All plans for the financial security of the school laid emphasis on the need for endowed professorships, but no success in obtaining funds for that purpose was achieved until the year 1880. In September of that year, the will of the Honorable Lafayette S. Foster of Norwich, Connecticut, who had been a law lecturer since 1875, bequeathed "to the Corporation of Yale College, to found a Professorship of English Common Law in the Law Department of that institution," the sum of $60,000 subject to a life interest. In addition to the customary duties attached to a professorship, the will provided that "said professor, as often as once in four years, shall deliver a public lecture at some convenient time and place, notice of which shall be previously given, upon any branch of the Common, Civil, Municipal, or Ecclesiastical Law, the Law of Nature, of Nations, of political economy, or general politics; the professor to select his own subject."

37

This bequest did not become available to the school until August 26, 1903, and therefore the effective endowment of the professorship was preceded in point of time by another which was established in 1887. This was the Edward J. Phelps Professorship, endowed by an anonymous gift of $25,000 made through Mr. Phelps, who was then United States Minister to Great Britain. It was specified in the agreement, approved by the Corporation on April 14, 1887, that the fund should be held in perpetuity by the University and that the income should be paid to the law faculty for the maintenance of a professorship of contracts and commercial law. The Corporation minutes of May 12, 1891, show that the original gift was from Junius S. Morgan of London, and that on the above date, his son, J. Pierpont Morgan of New York City, increased the fund to $50,000. The Foster and Morgan gifts were encouraging events, but nevertheless, during most of the period under review, the financial security of the faculty was not much improved. In view of what these men accomplished under such circumstances, it is appropriate to outline their careers more fully than has yet been done in the foregoing pages.

Important as were the men who appeared in the annual law school announcements as special lecturers both in the undergraduate and graduate courses, the backbone of the school was supplied by the men on the regular faculty. Wayland, Robinson, Baldwin, and Platt constituted this faculty until 1876, when they were joined by Theodore S. Woolsey as Instructor in Public Law. With this title, Woolsey continued the work in international law which formerly was carried on by his father, Theodore Dwight Woolsey. On April 1, 1878, the Corporation on recommendation of the law faculty, established a professorship in international law in the law school, and elected

38

Woolsey to it, making the condition, however, that his salary should be provided out of fees accruing to the school. Woolsey was then in Europe and when Mr. Dexter's letter announcing the appointment reached him in Venice, he wrote, on April 22, 1878, the following graceful note of acceptance:

I need not say that I was surprised at my election to this chair. I was thoroughly contented with the tutorship in international law which I held, and hoped to work quietly in it, until I felt more confident of myself, and better able to undertake larger responsibilities. However, as I understand from your letter that my duties at the Law School remain the same but that the style of my position simply is changed, I do not see that I can do otherwise than accept my election.

The next appointee to the regular faculty was William Kneeland Townsend, who on June 29, 1881, became Professor of Pleading. In the same year Edward J. Phelps was appointed Kent Professor of Law in Yale College and began lecturing in the law school. In 1889, George D. Watrous began his long term of service as instructor, assistant professor, and professor, extending to the year 1919; and in 1892, both George E. Beers and Edward G. Buckland joined the faculty. Further account must be given of all of the above, including Simeon E. Baldwin, Francis Wayland, and others, in a subsequent pamphlet dealing with a period into which their law school connections extended. This is, however, the proper place in which to comment at some length on the work of two of the original three, Platt and Robinson, both of whom ended their work at Yale during the period under review.

Johnson Tuttle Platt, the youngest of the three who took over the school in 1869, was the first to be taken by death, and the only one who did not live to see the school

39

installed in Hendrie Hall. He was born in Newtown, Connecticut, on January 12, 1844. His preliminary education was acquired in private schools particularly the Staples Academy, at Easton, Connecticut. Preparation for college was, however, prevented by a serious accident which undermined his health and left him slightly lame for the rest of his life. After a short business experience in New York City, he entered Harvard Law School in 1863, and received his LL.B. in 1865. On January 11 of that year, he was admitted to the Boston bar, and thereafter studied for six months in the law offices of the Honorable James D. Colt, in Pittsfield, Massachusetts. In the autumn of 1865, he moved to New Haven, where he began practice, specializing in equity cases. For a time he had offices with John S. Beach in the Exchange Building. Later he formed a partnership with Morris F. Tyler, the offices of which, at the time of his death, were in the *Palladium* building. He served as United States Commissioner and as Master in Chancery from 1870 until his death, and beginning in 1877, was Register in Bankruptcy. He was repeatedly a member of the New Haven Common Council, and in 1874 was corporation counsel of New Haven. In politics he was a Republican until the year 1884, when he became an ardent supporter of the candidacy of Grover Cleveland for the Presidency of the United States. He was an active and alert practitioner, and tried many important cases in both the Federal and State courts.

Being of a studious turn of mind, he was interested in the plight in which the Yale Law School found itself, and, as has been said, he joined with three others in offering his services, and thus, in July, 1869, became an instructor in the school. July 11, 1872, he was promoted to a professorship, with the subjects, pleading, evidence, and

40

Simeon E. Baldwin

William C. Robinson.

Francis Wayland

equity jurisprudence assigned to him. Other subjects that he later taught were civil procedure, general jurisprudence, history of the common law, torts, municipal corporations, business corporations, code procedure, statute law, criminal law, and charities and trusts. In 1873, Yale University conferred upon him the honorary degree of Master of Arts. Engrossed in his law practice and in teaching, he wrote no books, but occasionally published an article. Two of these were on the general subject of jurisprudence, one was on the "Assertion of Rights," and another was on "English Factory Legislation." In the summer of 1889, he overworked on legal business involving a trip to Chicago, and in December, while still in a weakened condition, he suffered an attack of influenza from which he did not fully recover. On the morning of January 23, 1890, he took a cab to his office, from which he planned to go to the law school for a recitation. When he attempted to alight, he was seen to be in difficulties, and James T. Moran, who happened to be near by, went with him in the cab to his home at 256 Bradley Street, where he died at one o'clock. Simple services were held there on January 25, President Timothy Dwight officiating, the pall bearers being Simeon E. Baldwin, John W. Alling, Thomas R. Lounsbury, Edward J. Phelps, Thomas R. Trowbridge, Francis Wayland, John F. Wier, and Arthur M. Wheeler. The remains were accompanied to Newtown for burial by Simeon E. Baldwin, Morris F. Tyler, James T. Moran, and James F. Colby. The local bar association, the law faculty, and the students passed resolutions of regret. The students said that "in their intercourse with him he impressed them as a most able, enthusiastic, and kind instructor. They feel that he was one who did much for them and for the success of the institution of which they

41

are members. They unite in paying a grateful tribute to his memory."

Despite his lameness, he was a constant walker, and was a lover of fields, woods, flowers, and birds. His wide cultural reading broadened his interests and made him a companionable person. His death was a great loss to the school, not only because of his learning but because of his personal influence. "As an instructor in the law school," wrote his partner, Morris F. Tyler, in a memorial (58 Conn. 603), "he left upon the hundreds of young men who in the twenty-one years of his instruction came under his care, the impression of a gentle, helpful, sympathetic, and thorough scholar. His sympathy with young men was very marked and very true. . . . He enjoyed his office of teaching, not only because the occupation was congenial to his taste as a scholar, but because it gave him so free an opportunity of expressing that active sympathy with others which was so individual a feature of his character, and which, in the ordinary work of his practice, he was so often called upon to restrain or disguise."

When William Callyhan Robinson began teaching in 1869, he was thirty-five years of age, six years older than Baldwin and ten years older than Platt. He had, however, little advantage over them in length of service at the bar, for he had back of him an entirely separate career in one of the other learned professions, the ministry. And he had fought out with himself an intellectual struggle which resulted in a change in his religious faith, and in his life work. This experience, together with his twenty-six years of law teaching at Yale, were eventually to place him in a post in the Academic world for which he was uniquely fitted.

42

Born at Norwich, Connecticut, on July 26, 1834, the eldest son of John A. and Mary Callyhan Robinson, he attended the Norwich public schools, Wesleyan University at Middletown, and Dartmouth College, from the last of which institutions he graduated in 1854. Thereafter, he studied at the General Theological Seminary in New York City, and on February 9, 1859, was ordained as a priest of the Protestant Episcopal Church. While he was Rector of the Episcopal Church at Scranton, Pennsylvania, he came in contact with the Paulist Fathers. This association caused him to re-examine his religious beliefs with the result that he became a member of the Roman Catholic Church. Being barred from the priesthood by his previous marriage to Anna E. Haviland of New York City (July 2, 1857), he found it necessary to adopt another vocation, and he chose the law. He began its study in 1862, and was admitted to the bar of Luzerne County, Pennsylvania, in 1864. In the next year, he moved to New Haven, and began practice. In 1869, when his association with the Yale Law School began, he had already built up a clientele, was Judge of the New Haven City Court, and was later to be Judge of the Court of Common Pleas. He served, first as Secretary and then as Dean of the law faculty from 1869 to 1873, when he gave up these administrative duties because of the demands of his practice. He had been promoted to a professorship on July 11, 1872, and had been assigned to teach Elementary law, Criminal law, and Real property. In his long career at Yale, he is listed as teaching at one time or another, the following subjects: Medical jurisprudence, Admiralty, Forensic oratory and rhetoric, Canon law, Origin of law, Nature of legal authority, Contracts, Patents, Pleading, Private corporations, Estates, Parliamentary law, Criminal procedure, Con-

43

veyancing, Domestic relations, and Evidence. Besides this, he carried his load of moot court work, and occasionally held extra classes for interested students. For example, beginning in February, 1874, he gave instruction in logic to a class which met every Thursday evening at a quarter before eight.

A course which he taught year after year, no matter what other courses he might be giving, was Elementary law. For this course, beginning in 1872, he prepared tabular outlines in leaflet form to aid the student. Three of these, published for the school and copyrighted by Charles Frederick Bollman, a senior then serving as librarian, have been preserved in the law library. They respectively outline the subjects, Rights, Wrongs, and Remedies.

Robinson's method, at first, was to read his lectures slowly so that students might take them down in class, and then require the students to commit them to memory. This having been done, and a certain amount of collateral reading having been required, there were recitations and discussions. Robinson never lost his belief that memory plays an essential part in law study, even though, as will later be shown, he recognized the necessity for the use of the logical and creative faculties. In 1875, urged by his students, he caused his well-tried lectures, under the title, *Notes on Elementary Law*, to be printed "for the Law Department of Yale College," by Hoggson & Robinson, of New Haven. The book contains 152 octavo pages and is the first book published under the auspices and at the expense of the school. At a cost of $550.84, 1,250 copies were printed, and copies, bound in black cloth, were sold to students at seventy-five cents each. Later, the price was raised to $1, $1.25, and finally to $1.50. In his preface, he says that the work is intended to serve three purposes:

44

(1) To be used as notes to the lectures on Elementary Law delivered by the author to the students in the Law Department of Yale College; (2) To guide the private student in his investigation of the rules and doctrines of the Common law; and (3) To familiarize the student, to some extent, with the leading text-books on the principal topics of the Common law.

We may be sure that he still required his own students to commit the book to memory, before he elaborated any of the topics, thus doing under his direction what he recommended, as follows, for the student working alone:

The text should first be thoroughly mastered, the rules and definitions being *committed to memory*, and the authorities referred to being examined as far as may be necessary to an understanding of the principle stated in the text. Then, beginning once more with the Introduction, the authorities referred to in connection with each succeeding paragraph of the text should be carefully studied, *in the order in which they are named.*

This italicized injunction, as was elsewhere explained, was in order that the historical development of topics down to "their present condition" might be traced. The references were given, not as citations in support of the text, but as readings presenting to the student a more extended view of the respective topics. The book is in fact an outline of part of Blackstone's *Commentaries*, with marginal references to sixty-six other books. Of these, all are treatises or digests, except eight which are law reports. In 1882, the work was enlarged by its author and published by Little, Brown & Company under the title, *Elementary Law.* The preface with its directions for study was reprinted unchanged, but the references to collateral readings were revised. In 1910, a second edition, revised and enlarged by the author, was published. In his preface, he briefly summarized his conclusions as to

45

the best method of training young men for law practice. The book is still recommended by those who used it as students, and it is still listed in the law book sales catalogues. With Robinson as the instructor, it was doubtless a useful tool. He was no truckler to convention and neither his book nor his method was for idlers. The effectiveness of neither can be evaluated without taking into account the author's own impressive personality in the class room.

In 1879, Dartmouth College conferred upon him the degree of Doctor of Laws, and in 1881, Yale University made him a Master of Arts. From 1884 to 1886, he was Chairman of a commission to revise the tax laws of Connecticut. Its report, signed by Robinson and eight others, of whom Simeon E. Baldwin was one, was published in 1886.

Meanwhile, he had been preparing his most voluminous work, *The Law of Patents for Useful Inventions*, three volumes, published by Little, Brown & Company, in 1890. How happily he had been working with his associates in New Haven, may be inferred from the paragraph printed at the beginning of volume one:

To my colleagues in the faculty of the Yale Law School, Francis Wayland, Simeon E. Baldwin, Johnson T. Platt, and William K. Townsend, I dedicate this treatise, in commemoration of the intimate personal friendship which, for so many years, has inspired and lightened our united efforts to advance the learning of the law.

His next published work, which appeared in 1893, was a volume entitled *Forensic Oratory*, a subject which for many years he had taught in the law school. Fluency and purity of style and diction were characteristics of his own speech and writing, shown particularly in his public addresses. The book deals not only with forms of expres-

46

sion, but with the art of persuasion in the court room including the collection of facts through the examination of witnesses, and their organization into addresses to the jury.

The year 1894–1895 was the last of Robinson's twenty-six as a professor in the Yale Law School. Next year, he took up his duties as Dean of the School of Social Sciences in the Catholic University of America, Washington, D.C. Even before leaving New Haven, he had begun to organize his new work. To state his theory of it, he prepared *A Study on Legal Education: its Purposes and Methods*, which was printed in the *Catholic University Bulletin*, for April, 1895. This, with his address on October 1, 1895, at the inauguration of the Schools of Philosophy and of the Social Sciences, and an earlier work, mention of which has been deferred to this time, together give the philosophical basis for his scheme of knowledge and education. So wholly different are these from his technical works on law that they might have been written by another man. The latter are rigid, stark, and didactic, somewhat pedestrian in style, giving no hint, except by a few prefatory words, of theory as opposed to precept. The former are the works of a thinker, whose philosophical position commands respect, whether or not assent is given to it. The earlier work referred to is *Clavis Rerum*, a book of 142 pages, published anonymously in 1883 (Norwich, Conn., F. A. Robinson & Co.), twenty-one years after he gave up the ministry for the bar. Intensely religious in its attitude and assumptions, it sets forth his conclusions concerning the relation of the natural sciences and man to Revelation as found in the Bible. The data from which the conclusions are drawn are the facts of physical science; the character and operations of the human mind; the political, social, and reli-

47

gious history of the human race; and the Revelation of God as given in the Scriptures. By this study he reconciled for himself the fundamentals of orthodoxy with the new ideas of science, particularly evolution. Thus he found justification not only for the investigations of the natural sciences, but for his own work in the realm of the social sciences, including law. God permits us to trace our origins and speculate upon the ways of Nature, through which the universe functions. "Never by the intellect, but only by the will, can man stray away from God."

The deanship, to which Robinson was called in 1895, was of a school of social sciences divided into four departments, Sociology, Economics, Political science, and Law, established in order to "furnish opportunities for instruction and research in the various sciences that treat of the reciprocal relations of mankind." Its scope was broad enough so that it could claim as an immediate purpose the training of lawyers, teachers, journalists, statesmen, and publicists. An elaborate system of interlocking courses was projected. It was just such a plan as would appeal to one who believed that the universe is made up of harmonious parts all of which are serving a common purpose. The natural sciences were being investigated to learn how their phenomena fit into the great scheme. He would now apply similar methods to the social sciences. The means by which he hoped to do this were set out in his inaugural address (October 1, 1895), and as regards law, in his *Study of Legal Education* (April, 1895). In the latter, he discussed law first, as an ethical and historical science, and second, as an intelligible and practicable art. The purposes of legal education he conceived to be (1) to aid the ordinary citizen in his daily life and in the functions of government, and (2) to qualify lawyers for their responsibilities and duties. The

48

lawyer class, he thought, was so important to society "that it might well be provided and maintained at public expense for the gratuitous service of individual citizens." This class, he thought, should be divided into two groups. The first would comprise those chiefly interested in law as a science, from whom would be drawn legislators, appeal judges, teachers, and writers. The second would comprise trial judges, practitioners, and ministerial officers. In the ideal school which he was trying to establish, he would adapt methods of legal education to the needs of the individual whether he were studying law to fit himself for citizenship, or to serve, as a lawyer, in one of the above two kinds of professional activities. There would be the utmost freedom in choice of subjects and in methods of study, using all available means of helping students to attain their respective objectives.

The catalogues of the school show that as time went on, Robinson more and more confined his attention to the law department, but up to the time of his death this department continued to be unorthodox in scope as compared to other law schools. He found time to publish in 1900, his *Elements of American Jurisprudence*, a book organized on the lines of his *Elementary Law*, but with a wider scope and purpose; and in 1903 was published his edition of Horne's *Mirrour of Justices*. In 1904, he came to New Haven to deliver, in commemoration of his former colleague, Dean Francis Wayland, an address which contains many frequently quoted paragraphs concerning the Yale Law School. He died on November 6, 1911, at the age of seventy-seven. As his portrait, reproduced herewith, shows, he had a grave and handsome face which was indicative of his character. His students and colleagues agree that he had extraordinary ability as a teacher, that he was actuated by ideals for which he

49

exhibited almost a religious loyalty, and that he possessed
an unusual intellectual versatility.

VII

ONE of the perennial problems of the law faculty was to
provide a library commensurate in scope and size with
the expanding needs of the school. In the preceding pages,
incidental mention has been made of library happenings,
but not consecutively or with any particularity. The
story begins with the appointment by the Corporation,
in 1869, of committees to raise funds for the school, including the library. No great success immediately followed these efforts. The library contained about 2,000
volumes and no money was available for its increase.
Donations of money came slowly and sometimes accompanied with discouraging comment. For example, William Walter Phelps (Yale 1860) of New York City,
replying to an appeal made by Simeon E. Baldwin, wrote
on February 10, 1870, "Dear Sim: Inter nos. I think very
little of the Yale Law School; but I think enough of you
to promise two hundred & fifty dollars next July. I can't
give more or earlier." The Prudential Committee and the
Corporation considered carefully whether the school
needed a new book case, and on July 19, 1870, the latter
formally voted twenty-five dollars to be used for that
purpose. The only other recorded donor was Henry C.
Kingsley, Treasurer of the College, who gave seventy-five
volumes of textbooks and law reports, including the six
volumes of Peters' Condensed United States Reports.

There were, however, encouraging signs, for the pamphlet by the Reverend Timothy Dwight (April, 1871),
the annual account of the needs of Yale College (July 10,
1871), and President Porter's inaugural address (October
11, 1871) all stressed the necessity for improving the law

50

library. All agreed that from five to ten thousand dollars should be spent to fill in gaps, and that a fund for upkeep was essential. Even with its existing meagre proportions, the prospect of using the library was considered by the bar of New Haven to be an important inducement for providing quarters for the school in the new court house. When this arrangement was agreed upon, the Corporation voted, on December 10, 1872, that ex-President Woolsey and the Honorable Henry B. Harrison be appointed a committee to confer with the law faculty "respecting proper measures for the care of the library of the Department after it has been removed to the new Court House." In January, 1873, the library was moved to its new home. Meanwhile, under the stimulus and largely by the personal efforts of Francis Wayland, money was being raised for immediate expenditure for books. An active worker and a contributor to the fund was the Honorable James E. English. It is much to be regretted that no list of contributors has been discovered, for these men deserve to be honored along with those who, in 1846, made the purchase of the Hitchcock library possible.[7] Apparently the gifts were made directly to the law faculty and were expended by it, since they are not listed in the reports of the College treasurer. A better collection of books now being assured, the Corporation on March 25, 1873, voted the thanks of the Board "to Hon. James E. English and the other donors to the Library of the Law Department and also to the Faculty of that Department (and especially to Hon. Mr. Wayland) for their exertions in procuring this Library." By June, 1873, $14,000 had been raised, and $12,000 had been spent for books. Their purchase and arrangement on the shelves were directed by Professor Platt. Contributions at

7. See *Yale Law Library Publications*, No. 3, p. 57.

51

this period eventually amounted to about $20,000, all for immediate expenditure. Still needed was a permanent fund, the income of which would be used for the upkeep of the library. There was great satisfaction, therefore, when on July 1, 1873, President Porter received the following letter from Governor English providing the sum of $10,000, which at that time was thought to be adequate. It was the largest single gift from one person thus far made to the school.

Dear Sir: Some time since I expressed an intention to provide a fund for the establishment of a law library in this city. Soon after my attention was called to the fact that earnest efforts were being made by the faculty of the Law Department of the College to secure the funds necessary for bringing the reports up to the present time, and the purchase of such treatises as were needed. The efforts of the faculty having been warmly seconded by the friends of the school the library is now substantially complete to date, and I am satisfied that anything I may give will serve a better purpose if reserved as a separate fund, the income to be applied towards the maintenance of the library.

I therefore enclose my cheque for ten thousand dollars the same to be held in trust by Yale College, the income to be applied towards maintaining the library of the Law Department in a suitable condition for the use of those engaged in the study and practice of the law.

Inasmuch as the members of the New Haven County Bar have shown a warm interest in the success of the school and have contributed liberally towards the completion of its library it is my wish that they may have the privilege of using the same under such regulations as may be necessary and proper for the safety and preservation of the books.

Everybody was elated at the situation. It was announced that the library contained "everything which is necessary for the uses of a law school," and the *New Haven City Year Book*, speaking for the legal fraternity,

52

said that "New Haven has at last, for the first time in its history, a law library adequate to all the wants of the Bar and the courts; and one which is already superior to the State Library at Hartford, where the lawyers from all parts of the State have hitherto been forced to resort in order to prepare themselves for the argument of important causes involving questions of legal difficulty."

When the contributed funds had all been spent, the library on October 28, 1874, contained 7,351 volumes, subdivided as follows: Law reports, 4,015 volumes, text-books, 1,345 volumes, statutes, 419 volumes, and Congressional documents, 1,572 volumes. Included in the above were 100 volumes on Roman law, and 1,300 volumes on political science and constitutional history. From time to time gifts of books came in. Frederick J. Betts, in 1874, gave 1,100 volumes from the library of the late Samuel R. Betts of New York City; the Supreme Court of Errors directed its clerk to send to the Law Library all Connecticut records and briefs; ex-President Woolsey gave a collection of books and pamphlets on the Alabama Claims and the Geneva Arbitration; and in 1875, books were received from Benjamin D. Silliman of Brooklyn and from Horatio G. Jones of Philadelphia. In 1878, alumni in St. Louis began giving the current volumes of Missouri Reports. Further gifts of money also came in. In 1876, Mason Young of New York gave $250; Mrs. John M. Davies of New Haven, $150; and Benjamin D. Silliman, $100. In 1879, four persons each gave $100, so that the Upper Canada Law Reports might be bought. The donors were Dr. John J. Crane of New York and Mrs. T. D. Wheeler, Miss E. W. Davenport, and Miss I. Hillhouse of New Haven.

The English Fund of $10,000 was being held in trust for the law library by the Treasurer of Yale College. Up to

53

January 1, 1875, he had paid the income semi-annually to Simeon E. Baldwin, Treasurer of the Law School. On that date, the College Treasurer announced that he could no longer turn over the income, but that bills would have to be submitted to him for payment. This decision immediately made difficulties because book bills to be paid from the income of the school could not be separated from those chargeable to the income of the English Fund. Therefore, on February 19, 1875, all four members of the law faculty signed a letter addressed to the Prudential Committee, asking that the former practice be restored. Part of that letter throws light on the workings of the school. "The income of this fund," it reads, "is largely spent in small sums, and in payments for special purchases or contracts. From it we pay for many annual subscriptions to legal periodicals, for binding pamphlets, and rebinding old books, and for odd volumes picked up here and there to fill up sets or replace vacancies. We furnish the students with their text-books at cost, paying for them ourselves from our receipts from tuition fees, and waiting for sales for our reimbursement. These orders amount every year to much more than the whole sum derived from the English fund. Our booksellers include in their accounts, which accompany their shipments to us, both these text-books, and such other works as we order for the Library, without discrimination. They cannot discriminate, for we frequently order several copies of a work, one of which is for the Library and the rest for sale. It is therefore extremely inconvenient for our Treasurer to go up to the College Treasurer's office, every time that it is necessary to pay a bill against the English fund, large or small, and equally inconvenient to leave the receipts or vouchers for such payments, with the College Treasurer, which prevents us from readily

54

comparing them with subsequent bills, as rendered, as is often necessary."

This letter was before the Prudential Committee on March 31, 1875, but action was deferred until a member of the law faculty might be present. On June 28, 1875, Professor Baldwin appeared before the Committee, and the subject was referred to Governor Ingersoll and the Honorable Henry B. Harrison, who were to confer with the Law Faculty and report. Finally, on December 9, 1875, they reported favorably upon the request, and it was directed that the income of the fund be paid over semi-annually, and that an account of expenditures with vouchers be rendered to the College Treasurer twice a year. Later on, the account books show that the income was transmitted quarterly. The annual income from the fund at the outset was $700. After five years, it dropped to $600, so remaining for many years.

Meanwhile, the inevitable result of enlarging the library had become apparent. The Fund's income was not sufficient for the annual purchase of continuations and new books. Therefore, on June 13, 1881, Dean Wayland and Professor Baldwin appeared before the Corporation to urge that a sum be appropriated to make up the deficiency. This request was finally granted, at a meeting on June 25, 1881, with the result that the sum of $135.83 was appropriated "from the income of the General Library Funds for books to be deposited in the Law Library." At a meeting of the Prudential Committee on October 31, 1881, a request of the Librarian of the College for a refund of this money was laid upon the table. Similar deficiency grants were made until 1884, when on April 18, the Corporation appropriated $300 from general university funds. A grant of this sum was made each year until 1894. Thus it is seen that, except when special gifts came

55

in, the total annual expenditure for books and binding during the ten years from 1884 to 1894 was about $900. When the library was moved into the completed section of Hendrie Hall, in the summer of 1895, it contained about 12,000 volumes.

Those who served as librarians of the law school from 1869 to 1894 were the following:

1869–1871. WILLIAM LYON BENNETT
1871–1872. FRANK ALLYN ROBINSON
1872–1873. CHARLES FREDERICK BOLLMAN
1873–1874. Rev. WILLIAM WOODRUFF ATWATER
1874.   DAVID DWIGHT BALDWIN
1874–1894. Dr. JOHN ADAMS ROBINSON

The first three of these, as was the case with their predecessors, held the office while they were students in the school. William Lyon Bennett graduated from Yale College in 1869, and from the law school in 1871. In 1876, he entered the partnership of Doolittle, Stoddard, and Bennett, later Doolittle and Bennett, and devoted himself to successful practice until July 1, 1905, when he became a judge of the New Haven County Court of Common Pleas. In September, 1908, he was elevated to the Superior Court Bench for a term of eight years. He now lives in well-earned retirement at his home at 357 Elm Street in New Haven. Besides being law librarian of the school, he served from 1895 to 1898 as instructor in insurance law and in contracts.

Frank Allyn Robinson, after being law librarian and graduating from the law school in 1872, practiced law for six years in the office of his brother, Professor William C. Robinson. Returning then to his birthplace, Norwich, Connecticut, he maintained a legal printing establishment. One of his publications was *Clavis Rerum*, already referred to. He died on December 25, 1915.

56

The last of the student librarians was Charles Frederick Bollman. Born in Prussia on April 19, 1847, he came to the United States in April, 1864, where he was placed under the guardianship of Heinrich Sinterness in New York City. In August of that year, he ran away to join the Union Army, and served in Company B, 1st Connecticut Volunteer Cavalry, until mustered out on August 2, 1865. He served as a teacher of music and languages at the Russell School in New Haven, and entered the Yale Law School in September, 1871, graduating in 1873. After eight years devoted exclusively to practice, he served from 1881 to 1885 as a member, and later as the President, of the New Haven Board of Police Commissioners. During this same period, he was successively New Haven City Coroner, and County Coroner. From 1885 to 1891, he was New Haven Chief of Police, and from 1893 to 1896, President of the Board of State Prison Directors. After 1891, he specialized in probate law. He died on June 3, 1920.

The extensive additions to the library made in 1872 and 1873 as the result of contributions for the purchase of books, emphasized the need of something more than student administration which necessarily had changed nearly every year. Any other arrangement, however, would involve the expenditure of money, instead of merely remitting a student's fees. The latter plan, of course, had been maintained at the expense of the law teachers, whose stipends were reduced by the amount of the uncollected tuition. Application was therefore made to the Corporation, which, on March 25, 1873, voted that an annual salary of $400 be appropriated for a law librarian. This was the first salaried position ever provided for the law school not directly supported by the income derived from tuition fees. To this post was appointed the

57

Reverend William Woodruff Atwater, a native of New Haven, who had graduated from Yale College in 1846, had studied for the ministry at Andover and in New Haven, and who had been pastor of various churches in Michigan, Indiana, and Connecticut. On account of ill health he resigned his last pastorate at South Killingly, Connecticut, and began his duties as law librarian in the summer of 1873. The change of work did not restore his health, and he died on March 15, 1874.

Atwater's successor was David Dwight Baldwin, the son of the Reverend Dwight Baldwin (Yale 1821), a missionary in Hawaii. He was born in Honolulu on November 26, 1831, studied in that city in the Punahou School, and entered Yale College. He won the first Clark Premium for work in practical astronomy, and supported himself partly by serving as organist of the First Congregational Church in Bridgeport, Connecticut. After his graduation in 1857, he married Lois G. Morris of Bridgeport, and returned to Hawaii. There he was engaged as Superintendent of government schools in the first section of Maui, was a member of the Hawaiian Parliament, and from 1865 to 1872, manager of the Kohala Sugar Company on the Island of Hawaii, where he introduced the "Lahaina" cane. Returning to the United States with his family in 1873, he registered for the M.A. degree at Yale, and received it in June, 1874. His salary as law librarian, beginning July 1, 1874, was $800, this amount having been fixed as the annual stipend of the law librarian, on June 25, 1874, by vote of the Corporation. His resignation, to take effect October 31, 1874, was the occasion for the following resolutions drawn up by a committee appointed at a meeting of the law students:

58

Whereas, our librarian, Mr. David Dwight Baldwin, is about to leave us for other lands, therefore be it

Resolved, that the thanks of the institution are due to Mr. Baldwin for the faithful and efficient manner in which he has performed the duties of his office, and especially for the catalogue which has been compiled by his labor and thoughtfulness.

Resolved, that his kindness and gentlemanly way of bearing towards the members of the Law School, have been highly appreciated by us, and that he carries with him our best wishes for his future happiness and prosperity.

Resolved, that a copy of these Resolutions be given to Mr. Baldwin, and printed in the college papers.

In behalf of the Law School, M. N. WHITMORE, ⎫
                                  W. FOSTER, ⎬ *Committee.*
Yale Law School, Oct. 31, 1874.

After his return to Hawaii, he served from 1878 to 1885 as Inspector-General of Schools, assistant principal of Lahainaluna Seminary, 1886 to 1890, and principal of the Hamakuapoke English School, 1891 to 1905. At the same time, he was vice-president and director of the Haiku Fruit and Packing Company, being a pioneer in the pineapple industry. In 1893, he published a *Catalogue of Land and Fresh-Water Shells of the Hawaiian Islands*, in which subject, as well as that of ferns, he was an authority. He died on June 16, 1912.

Neither Atwater nor Baldwin was a lawyer. Baldwin's successor was trained both in law and medicine. He was Dr. John Adams Robinson, a brother of Professor William C. Robinson, and of Frank Allyn Robinson, who had served as student librarian in 1871–1872. Born on October 18, 1837, he graduated from Dartmouth College in 1855, and from the College of Physicians and Surgeons in New York City in 1858. After practicing medicine in Pittston, Pennsylvania, and serving as assistant surgeon

59

in the 11th Indiana Cavalry of the Union Army during the Civil War, in 1868 he entered the Yale Law School, from which he graduated in 1871. He practiced law in New Haven until he succeeded Baldwin as law librarian in November, 1874. This position he held until December 31, 1894, when he resigned and became Professor of Law in the law school of the Catholic University of America, of which Professor Robinson had just become Dean. He died, while spending the summer in New Haven, on September 1, 1904. That he, as well as Dean Wayland, was viewed with awe by incoming students may be inferred from James E. Wheeler's account of his first visit to the Court House, written when he was a junior law student in 1894:

The first impression of our new home was indeed one never to be forgotten. If by chance, we happened to have any especial friend in the Senior class, he was sure to wish to show us the sights of the school. How proud he seemed as he pointed out the library, with its rows of ponderous legal tomes, and in a subdued whisper, designated the presiding deity of the spot, Dr. Robinson; then escorted us on tip-toe to the door of the *sanctum sanctorum*, where the Dean sat on his throne of state presiding over the destinies of the school. Finally he explained the beauties of the Yale system, and commenced the oft repeated discussion as to the respective merits of the text book and the case methods. (*Yale Shingle*, 1894, p. 48.)

Beginning in 1886, the rate of annual growth in the size of the student body began to accelerate. In the year 1885–1886, there were 62 students in attendance, and in 1894–1895, there were 199. In 1886, it was necessary to move the library into a larger room which had formerly been used by the Supreme Court of Errors. Until 1891, the library hours on week-days were 8 A.M. to 12:45 P.M., and 2 to 5:45 P.M., with the exception of Saturday afternoons. By vote of the Corporation, on November 10, 1891,

60

the school was authorized to keep the library open from 7 to 9:30 P.M., under the direct supervision of the Assistant Librarian. There had been Assistant Librarians since 1888, but some of them had served also as quiz masters. Usually the law faculty, at the opening of the fall term, installed a student in the post, and asked that the appointment be confirmed at the November meeting of the Corporation. The minutes show that the following persons were thus appointed:

1888–1889.   CLEMENT D. RINEHART
1889–1890.   GEORGE E. BEERS
1890–1891.   PORTER B. GODARD
1891–1892.   GEORGE W. ANDREW
1892–1893.   ALFRED W. CARTER
1893–1894.   HOWARD A. COUSE
1894–1895.   CHARLES V. HENRY

On the floor below that occupied by the law school was the New Haven County Bar Library, the organization of which on November 6, 1848, has already been described.[8] A list of books in this library on November 1, 1874, is appended to one of the early catalogues of the school library. Leonard M. Daggett, writing in June, 1889 (*Green Bag*, 1:246), said that it then contained a "complete set of standard English and American treatises. The two libraries are used in common by the students and the members of the association, and are managed in conjunction with each other so that there may be as little duplication as possible,—an arrangement which is mutually advantageous. The books are directly accessible to the students without the intervention of the Librarian, but cannot be taken from the rooms except for use in court." The record of books loaned from the two libraries from February 12, 1873 to July 2, 1885 is contained in the

8. See *Yale Law Library Publications*, No. 3, p. 61.

61

"Librarian's Register, Yale Law School," a large blank book (16 x 11 in.) ruled into columns with printed headings for Date of drawing, Name of person drawing, Books drawn, Books returned, and Date of return. The names of many prominent New Haven lawyers and judges are there recorded as borrowers.

The first catalogue of the Yale Law Library was the inventory of Samuel J. Hitchcock's books made by appraisers in 1845 in preparation for the sale of them, consummated on January 18, 1847, to the Yale Law Library.[9] No trace of any other catalogue has been found prior to one which bears on its fly leaf the words "Catalogue of the Library of the Law Department, Yale College. Commenced October, 1869." This is an ordinary ledger containing 408 ruled pages. The list of books is spread over 314 of these pages, leaving numerous gaps and blank pages. Pencil notes in these spaces indicate the number of volumes needed to complete sets. Short, one-line titles are given of the books in the library, divided into groups containing reports, digests, statutes, textbooks, serials, and miscellaneous material. The original listing is in one handwriting, with a few additions in other hands, bringing the record down to June 25, 1873. Probably Bennett, F. A. Robinson, and Bollman, librarians from 1869 to 1873, took part in its preparation. Ten years afterwards, and up to the year 1887, this ledger was used as a scrap book in which to paste notices, addressed to the librarian, advertising board and rooms for law students.

A more elaborate catalogue was made in 1874. The Reverend William W. Atwater did not prepare it for he served as librarian only part of a year, during most of

9. See *Yale Law Library Publications*, No. 1, frontispiece and p. 29; No. 3, p. 58.

which time he was ill, and just prior to his death a temporary assistant had been called in. "Mr. Tyler of the last class," says the *Yale Courant*, February 14, 1874, p. 227, "has been engaged in making systematic catalogues of the books in the library. These catalogues will be extremely valuable." This was Morris Franklin Tyler, a graduate of Yale College in the year 1870, and of the Law School in the year 1873. The catalogue of 1874 is contained in two elephant folios, 18 x 12 inches in size, made up of sheets of fine paper upon which are pasted the entries written on ruled paper. Between the pages are guards to which to attach new titles. The items are arranged in one alphabet, with individual volumes of reports, statutes, treatises, digests, and serials intermingled in the order in which their authors or titles bring them. This arrangement is highly impracticable for quick reference, but in another respect the catalogue is superior to its predecessor. Full titles are given, with publisher, place of publication, and date. Only a few additions were made to the original catalogue, and there is no evidence that it was extensively used. Its pages are as unsoiled as when they were first bound. Apparently it was a *de luxe* record of the library's contents, rather than a catalogue for use.

In the resolution presented to David Dwight Baldwin by the law students on October 31, 1874, special thanks are given him for "the catalogue which has been prepared by his labor and thoughtfulness." This catalogue is a book 12½ x 8 inches in dimensions, containing 124 pages. The cover title reads "Catalogue of the Books in Yale Law Library with Supplementary List of Books in the Bar Library." The items are beautifully printed by hand in ink, a line being given to each title. There are six groups containing respectively reports, textbooks,

63

digests, statutes, serials, and Congressional documents, and at the end there is a subject index. Where spaces had been left for missing volumes or for new titles, here and there, additions have been made in another hand. Baldwin started also another book entitled "Record of Books Received in Law School Library Since January 1, 1874," which he continued for a few pages to include additions up to October 28, 1874, three days before his resignation from the librarianship took effect.

Baldwin's catalogue shows the effect of constant use, the edges of the pages and the corners being discolored and worn thin. Except for printed leaflets such as the eight-page "List of English Reports in the Library of Yale Law School, Jan. 1, 1891," this catalogue served the students and faculty until the library was moved to Hendrie Hall in 1895.

VIII[10]

PRIOR to the year 1876, there seem to have been no law school student publications. Nor do we suspect, except in one instance, that students found means of self-expression through the college literary magazines. It is supposed that some of the law students coöperated with college students in editing *The Little Gentleman*, which, in six numbers, ran from January 1 to April 29, 1831. Numbers 4, 5, and 6 contain "Notes Taken in the Court Room," describing without using names, judges and lawyers as they appeared in the preceding term of court. It is possible that a note on the back cover of a copy of number 3, in the Yale University Library, discloses the names of the authors of these notes. It reads "J. H.

10. Sections VIII, IX, and X, relating respectively to student periodicals, the admission of women, and law school athletics, are not confined to the period covered by the foregoing sections.

64

Jones & J. M. Wilson, 10 o'c Wednesday morning called on *The Little Gentleman*." These two were law students, viz. Iverson H. Jones of Clinton, Georgia, and John M. Wilson of Amherst, New Hampshire. The authors, whoever they were, poked a little fun at their fellow students sitting in court, and at the learned works that they studied, when they wrote: "If we were to bring them into our gallery of portraits, we might find it convenient to divide them into two classes—those that have whiskers and those that have no whiskers; and this we maintain would be as legitimate a classification as some that are to be found in grave treatises."

The Yale Courant and its rival *The College Courant*, two college papers, both of which began publication in 1867, for a number of years contained news notes and editorial comment about the law school. One of these is the source of information concerning the first law student periodical. *The Yale Courant* of April 1, 1876, carried the following:

The first number of "L.S." (the new Law School paper,) made its appearance Thursday evening [March 30]. It was well received and reflects great credit on its board of editors.

No copy of "L. S." has been discovered, nor have we any further information concerning it.

From 1878 to 1891, the only student outlet for law school news was the *Yale Daily News*, which contained occasional law school notes.

Then came a major event in the history of the school— the establishment of the *Yale Law Journal*, the first number of which appeared in October, 1891. During the previous winter the idea of publishing a journal had been conceived in a Quiz Club, of which Edward G. Buckland (1889 L.) was instructor. The Club was composed of the following members of the class of 1892: William P.

65

Aiken, Arthur P. Day, Samuel H. Fisher, Lewis S. Haslam, William A. McQuaid, Robert T. Platt, William H. Smith, Samuel A. York, Jr., Thomas F. Bayard, Jr., and Horace F. Walker. On the initiative of this Quiz Club, a meeting of the School was called in the spring of 1891. Mr. Buckland was chosen chairman and John W. Roby, secretary. Speeches were made by York and by Aiken, and a committee was appointed to investigate and report on the project. At another meeting this committee recommended the publication of a journal six times a year. A nominating committee composed of George E. Hill, Paul R. Jarboe, and James M. Self, of the class of 1891, and Mr. Buckland, suggested the following seven men from the class of 1892 as editors of the first volume, and they were elected: William P. Aiken, Samuel A. York, Jr., John J. Healey, Francis W. Treadway, William H. Smith, Robert T. Platt, and William A. McQuaid. After the issuance of the first number, McQuaid resigned and Mr. Buckland was selected in his stead. This board elected Aiken to serve as chairman, and York as treasurer. Before these momentous decisions were made the investigating committee had been assured by several alumni and by Dean Wayland, and Professors Baldwin, Townsend, and Watrous, that any deficit at the end of the first year would be made up. It was not necessary to call upon them, for the *Journal* at the outset was a financial success. "The end of the year," wrote Harry G. Day (*Yale Shingle*, 1893, p. 87) "showed a substantial balance in the treasury, which was by the consent of the Editorial Board deposited as a fund, the income from which, when the same shall amount to $1,500, shall be used to pay for articles written for the *Journal*." This fund continued to grow, but was never, I believe, used to recompense authors. At the end of the third year, one of the editors,

66

William B. Bosley (*Yale Shingle*, 1894, p. 83) remarked on the great restraint of the board in husbanding the *Journal's* profits for the enlargement and improvement of future volumes instead of distributing them to the editors themselves. "Strange as it may appear," he wrote, "the *Law Journal* is the only publication at Yale which is not intended to confer pecuniary benefits upon its editors. It is hoped that this instance of unselfish devotion to the interests of the profession and the Law School of which we are members may be instrumental to some extent in destroying the popular impression that attorneys are mercenary rather than zealous servants of justice whose purpose it is to succor the oppressed."

Part of the *Journal's* income in its early years came from the sale of advertising space to local tradesmen. When the business manager could not collect money for this space, he accepted articles of trade in lieu thereof, whether the stock were composed of "books, clothes, coal, provisions, chalk, marbles, potatoes or corsets, and then tried to sell these things to the unwary at a discount." When he could not sell them, he turned them over to the trustees (See *post*, p. 70) at the end of the year. "An opinion by Professor Buckland, one of the trustees," says a writer in the *Shingle* for 1896, "as to how he administers a trust, the subject matter of which is one dozen pairs of golf stockings, two barrels of potatoes, and one hundred boxes of hairpins would be interesting."

The subscription price of the *Journal* for its first six volumes, each containing six numbers, was $2. Volumes seven and eight contained nine numbers. Thenceforth, beginning with volume nine, there have continued to be eight numbers to the volume. The subscription price for volumes nine to 28 was $2.50, of volume 29, $3.00, and from volume 30 to the present, $4.50.

67

Beginning with 278 pages in volume one, the volumes grew in size to an average of about 450 pages, when with volume sixteen there was a sudden increase to over 600. This number steadily increased until, for volume twenty-three, the number was 705. The volume for 1935–36, contains 1,544 pages.

The financial prosperity of the *Journal* has not always been stable. In 1893, its profits amounted to $247, in 1894, to $250, and in 1895, to $368. In the last of these years, the entire bank balance for an unexplained reason, was withdrawn. In 1899, the sum of $1,000 was redeposited. No deposits were made after 1902, but by 1914, there were in the trust fund, including accumulated interest, about $2,000. For a number of years prior to 1920, the *Journal* was operated at a loss. In December of that year, a new Yale Law Alumni Association was formed. It was provided in the by-laws that part of each member's dues should go to the *Journal* as a subscription payment in the name of that member. This plan was the beginning of renewed prosperity which has continued to the present.

College students at first found it difficult to understand what kind of a new magazine was being published. One of them asked if the *Journal* was a "funny paper," and the editors replied that it was not intentionally funny and that they had already "rejected a number of lyrics on that ground." As stated in its first number, the purpose of the *Journal* was conceived to be threefold: to provide a means of communication between graduates and students, to serve them both as a common arena for discussion of legal matters, and to aid in the education of student editors and contributors.

The news feature of the *Journal* has never been prominent, but an attempt was made to make good this portion

68

of its prospectus. Occasional editorials told about happenings in the school, and beginning with volume three (1893–1894) a supplement containing Memorabilia et Notabilia, later known as Alumni and School Notes, was published for each volume through the twenty-second volume. These notes related chiefly to events in the lives of recent graduates—notes similar to those which now appear in the *Yale Alumni Weekly*. For many years, the *Journal* was somewhat more receptive than its rivals in other law schools to articles not intended for practitioners. For example, in the first volume, one number is devoted to a symposium on methods of legal education in which the case method is argued pro and contra, and in another number a place was found for Frederick J. Kingsbury's reminiscences of the New Haven Bar. Volume ten gave a full account of the John Marshall Day exercises, and volume seventeen gave a good deal of space to Macgrane Coxe's illustrated article on Chancellor Kent at Yale.

Since the first sixteen volumes are not always available for consultation in law libraries, it may come as a surprise to some readers to know how varied are the interests represented in those volumes. Problems of the day having a bearing on public law were discussed by such men as Mr. Justice David J. Brewer, David Jayne Hill, Charles J. Bonaparte, John W. Foster, Jacob G. Schurman, Daniel Coit Gilman, Whitelaw Reid, Frederic R. Coudert, Elihu Root, and William H. Taft. Technical questions and those relating to the organization of the bar were treated, for example, by William A. Keener, John C. Gray, Roger Foster, Samuel Williston, Emlin McClain, James Bradley Thayer, George Wharton Pepper, Charles C. Hyde, William Wirt Howe, Henry T. Terry (notably his Legal Rights and Duties), John H. Wigmore, and

69

Joseph H. Beale. Similar contributions were made by members of the Faculty, beginning with Baldwin, Robinson, Buckland, John A. Hoober, George D. Watrous, Theodore S. Woolsey; continuing with Leonard Daggett, John Wurts, William K. Townsend, George E. Beers, Theodore D. Woolsey, and Philip P. Wells, as they were successively recruited to the teaching staff; and ending, for the period, with articles by Arthur L. Corbin and Henry Wade Rogers. Throughout the whole series of volumes, with few exceptions, there continued to appear articles by Simeon E. Baldwin.

Although the *Journal* has always been a student publication and its importance as an educational instrument for the students who edit it was well-recognized by the Faculty which authorized its establishment, it is a curious fact that no mention is made of it in the law school catalogues until that issued for the years 1906–1907. This belated recognition was given during the administration of Dean Henry Wade Rogers. The fact is that the *Journal's* official connection with the school was not well-defined until the year 1914. When it was organized, as has been said, the editors were chosen at a meeting of the student body. It is said that in 1892 or 1893 (*Yale Shingle*, 1893, p. 87), "the management of the Journal" was "incorporated as the Yale Law Journal Company under the statutes of Connecticut," in order to give it a continuous existence, but the articles of incorporation have thus far not been found. It is certain, however, that there were trustees of the funds of the *Journal* and that the first incumbents were Edward G. Buckland and Samuel A. York, Jr. When Mr. Buckland withdrew, Mr. York continued to serve with Harry G. Day and William B. Bosley as associates. In the year 1914, Professors John Wurts and Arthur L. Corbin were the

70

trustees. Writing about these events in his annual report for 1914–1915, Dean Rogers said that diligent search had failed to produce the documents in accordance with which trustees were appointed to hold the funds of the Law Journal Company. "The trust appears to have been oral in its inception. . . . There is an idea that the original trustees were to hold the fund in accordance with the by-laws of the *Journal* board. But it has been so far impossible to find any by-laws, or that any ever existed." He then referred to the fact that the *Journal*, disregarding its supposed former incorporation, had just been incorporated as the Yale Law Journal Company. The articles are dated October 30, 1914, and the incorporators were Henry Wade Rogers, Arthur L. Corbin, and Wesley N. Hohfeld. At its first meeting, the incorporators adopted by-laws, according to which, as later amended, members of the Faculty "who give full time to the School and are in active service shall be members of this Company."

It has never been the policy of the Company to lay a heavy hand on the editorial board, or to restrict it in the normal development of its policies.

The personal and lighter side of the school was represented for twenty years by *The Yale Shingle* and during three of those years also by *The Yale Law School Mirror*. In accordance with the custom of the time, the graduating classes felt called upon to issue class books. It was the class of 1893 that first yielded to this urge, producing a book for which Professor William K. Townsend suggested the name, *The Yale Shingle*. Twenty volumes were issued carrying it through the year 1912. When the *Shingle* was abandoned, the school doubtless thought that it had come of age, but thenceforth there was lacking a useful source of information concerning the life of the

71

school. These books not only contain records of student life and activity for the years 1893 to 1912, but they preserve for us something of the spirit of the school. In them, one finds pictures of the members of the successive senior classes and of the faculty, with biographical sketches of both groups, class odes, lists of class officers and committee members, pictures and lists of members of the debating clubs, of prize winners, of members of fraternities, and "slams" on the graduates. There are occasional historical articles, and many pictures of buildings.

The Yale Law School Mirror, published in 1898, 1899, and 1900, was much less pretentious than the *Shingle*, and although intended to represent the whole school rather than the senior class, did not make a place for itself. It contained little that was not to be found also in the *Shingle*.

IX

THE question of admitting women to the law school was first raised in the year 1872. It was a novel point which the faculty found it necessary to submit to the University Corporation. The following letter addressed to Professor Baldwin, written by George G. Sill, a graduate of Yale College, 1852, and from 1873 to 1877, lieutenant-governor of Connecticut, called for a definite answer.

Hartford, Conn. March 9th 1872

Dr. Sir.

A young lady has applied to me for permission to become a student of law in my office. I advised her to seek admission into Yale Law School for one year and then enter my office. Are you far advanced enough to admit young women to your school? In theory I am in favor of their studying & practising law, provided they are *ugly*, but I should fear a handsome woman before a jury. Please let me know whether she could be

72

admitted if she should desire to do so, also send me your circular or catalogue.

The Corporation, however, when this letter was placed before it on March 13, did not feel equal to putting its decision into words. The minutes merely record that "an informal application from a woman for admission to the Law Department was laid upon the table."

The next woman who aspired to enter the school took a more effective method of accomplishing her purpose. She came on from her home in Coldwater, Michigan, and presented herself for registration. According to a newspaper writer who later interviewed Professor Baldwin on the event (*New Haven Register*, October 28, 1923), the moment when the applicant reached the registrar's desk was tense. The writer in question probably drew upon his imagination to a considerable extent, but nevertheless he presented a picture which ought not to be lost.

In the fall of 1885, there was a long snake-line of students which wound into the registrar's office. At the very end of the line stood a lone woman. She had a firm jaw and clear, cool eyes that stared straight ahead. The craning necks, the inquisitive eyes, the audible "who is she" left her passive and uninterested. The wild call of "fire" with which the presence of a woman on the campus has ever been hailed, would have failed to ruffle the calm exterior of this well-poised woman. At last her turn came. With that instrument mightier than the sword, she wrote "Alice Rufie Jordan, B.S. University of Michigan, 1885,—Registered in Department of Law, Yale University."

The startled registrar cleared his throat, "I'm sorry, but women are not admitted."

"Why not?", the cool eyes rested upon him.

"Why—er—they never have been."

"You'll have to admit me," the young woman put in grimly, "there isn't a thing in your catalogue that bars women."

It was true that no reference to the sex of students was

73

made in the printed admission requirements. Moreover, Miss Jordan not only was a Bachelor of Science, but after spending one year in the law school of the University of Michigan she had been, in June 1885, admitted to the Michigan bar. She could not be peremptorily refused admission and she was allowed to enroll. She paid the preliminary fee, and began to attend classes. Dean Wayland thought this to be the best solution of the problem, but President Porter was unconvinced. Therefore the matter was laid before the University Corporation. Dean Wayland asked whether Miss Jordan might be enrolled in the Annual Catalogue of the College, either as a candidate for a degree or as a special student. On October 29, 1885, it was "Resolved, that the name of the young woman in whose behalf the Dean of the Law Department has addressed the Corporation, is not to appear in the Annual Catalogue." She was not expressly forbidden to remain in the school, but it was probably expected that she would withdraw, since the Treasurer was authorized "to repay the fee which she has already paid, if she desires to cease her attendance on the exercises of the School." With the consent of the law faculty she continued her work, and passed her examinations with credit. Thus it came about that on June 28, 1886, Dean Wayland and Professor Robinson, as a committee of the law faculty, personally presented her name to the Corporation along with those of other candidates for the law degree. After discussion, it was voted to confer degrees on the entire list of candidates, but a special minute was entered concerning Miss Jordan. It specifically granted her the degree of LL.B., but added that "in order to avoid any misunderstanding in future, the Corporation hereby direct the following to be inserted as a note in future annual Catalogues or Statements of the

74

Course of Instruction in this College, viz.:—It is to be understood that the courses of instruction are open to persons of the male sex only, except where both sexes are specifically included."

Only by perseverance and courage had Miss Jordan won her victory, and become the first woman to receive a degree from the Yale Law School. After her graduation she married George D. Blake, a University of Michigan law graduate, travelled extensively with him, and for a time lived in Seattle, Washington. She died in Chicago, on November 29, 1893.

The warning statement which the Corporation drew up for insertion in the annual announcement of courses never appeared in the special Law School Bulletin, but it was printed regularly in the general University Catalogue until that for the Academic year 1918–1919. Next year, there was substituted for it the announcement that "properly qualified women are admitted as candidates for the degrees of Bachelor of Laws," and other named degrees.

This complete reversal of the former decision was precipitated by the application of Miss Isabelle Bridge for admittance to the law school. She had in the summer of 1918 taken a course at a western university which was conducted by a law professor of the Yale Law School. At her request, he promised to exert what influence he had to induce the faculty to open the school to women. When she made formal application, the law faculty, on September 25, 1918, voted to recommend her admission. The Corporation on October 21, 1918, approved the recommendation and requested the Governing Board of the school to draft a statement of the conditions under which other women might be admitted as candidates for law degrees. At its meeting of November 18, 1918, the Cor-

75

poration voted that women who are graduates of recognized colleges be admitted as candidates for law degrees.

Ill health prevented Miss Bridge from entering the school, but "it was she who caught sight of the promised land and opened the way for others." The first to be accepted was Josephine H. Powers, of New Haven, who applied in the summer of 1919. Because she was a teacher in the New Haven High School and could attend courses only after hours, she did not receive her degree until 1923. Five others registered in 1919. The first of these to graduate was Mrs. Shirley M. Moore, who received her degree in 1920, and thus, though second to Miss Jordan in point of time, she was the first to graduate after the school was officially opened to women.

From the year 1919 to June, 1936, a total of ninety-three women have been registered in the school. Thirty-two of these for one reason or another did not receive a degree, leaving sixty-one who completed their courses. Fifty-six of these received the LL.B. degree, one the degree of Doctor of Jurisprudence, and four that of Doctor of Juridical Science.

X

In view of the fact that to-day the only athletic contest sponsored by the law school is the annual baseball game (soft ball) played between the faculty and the *Law Journal* Board, it is worth recalling that in 1874 and for many years thereafter, the school had its own athletic teams, and that for a much longer period, members of the school played on the University teams. Although members of the school showed prowess in wrestling, fencing, lawn tennis, swimming, and bicycling, the athletic history of the school centers about rowing, football, the track, and baseball.

76

The first boat race between Harvard and Yale was rowed in 1852. In the following year the Yale Navy was formed. This organization for boating was superseded in 1870 by the Yale University Boat Club, and in 1872, the Rowing Association of American Colleges was organized. Law men, as members of a University department, could belong to the Boat Club by payment of a fee, and they individually developed such skill that in 1874, the school had its own crew. The members of the law faculty from their own pockets contributed $50.00 to support it. In 1875, the school owned a barge, purchased with the aid of further subscriptions. For a number of years, an annual spring regatta was held on Lake Saltonstall. In October, 1875, there was a shell race there between the Junior class (1877) in Yale College and the law crew. The latter rowed in a shell borrowed from Columbia College, and won the race handily. "The Law School had a splendid set of men, far superior in physique to any other crew on the lake. They made a very fine appearance and it is a matter of great regret that none of them are available for University regattas" (*Yale Courant*, October 23, 1875, p. 53). Something of the atmosphere of the race can be gathered from the following description of it:

The shell race between '77 and the Law School was called at 3:05, with the Law School on the outside. At this thrilling moment a boat containing three Micks and a dog, must needs get in the way, so that the word *go* was delayed until the intruders, accelerated as to their movements with stones from the crowd on shore, and a few pithy observations from the other side of the lake, had pulled out of the course. The referee now pulled the trigger of his pistol as a signal for the boats to start, but the cap snapped; the weapon missed fire a second time, the referee yelled go! and they went, the Law School taking the best start, while the occupants of the judges' boat sat down in pious and reflective meditation over the un-

77

certainty of pistols in general. At the stake the Law crew turned first, gaining a lead which they held to the finish; spurting by the point amid the yells of the Law students and their friends. Time:—Law School, 19:37; '77, 20:00. No. of strokes to the minute.—Law School, 38; '77, 39. Course.—Three miles turn about. Prize.—Six silver oars. (*Yale Courant*, October 23, 1875, p. 58.)

On May 27, 1876, there was a barge race between the College Freshmen and the law crew, which the former won by two seconds. The law crew was composed of Richard H. Johnston (stroke), John B. Ward, Charles Ives, Jr., John W. Wescott, Austin A. Canavan, Victor H. Metcalf (bow), and Sterne Wheeler, coxswain. These men called forth the plaudits of the spectators by their "large muscle and browned complexion." Richard Johnston, on September 9, 1876, in a single scull race on the Alleghany river course won from James Hutchinson, "champion single sculler," by a boat's length. Elected captain of the law crew for 1877, he found no other man in the school who had ever pulled in a race. Undaunted, he formed a crew and entered them in the May regatta of 1877 in a barge race with the Medical School. The stroke of the latter crew was Mr. Dudley A. Sargent, teacher of gymnastics and former stroke of the Bowdoin University crew. Johnston's crew won by half a length. Referring to the inexperience of his own men, he said before the race, "If my crew will only keep their oars well out of the water and not catch any crabs, I will guarantee to beat the Medics myself."

The next year, in May, 1878, the Medics challenged the lawyers to a return race. The invitation was declined because it came too late to make arrangements to accept it. This declination was the occasion for some sarcastic comment printed in the *Yale News* (May 8, 1878). An-

78

other verbal wrangle involving the law school crew enlivened the *News* in June, 1879, when a rebuke was administered to some of its members for taking a plunge in Mill River from the float in front of the boat house near Chapel Street. In the exchange of pleasantries it appeared that the law crew had only been recently given equal rights with college crews at the boat house, and that the offending members were ignorant of the rules forbidding swimming there. A side light is cast on Yale college life, when it is admitted by the *News* that law students have cause to complain at "allusions to their being tucked away in the attic of the City Hall, never crossing the campus, and contributing not so much as a car fare to our athletic interests."

There was surely error in this statement, for law students were then taking and continued to take their parts regularly as members of the University crew and as players on other University teams. The following are some of the law students who rowed in the annual race with Harvard: John W. Wescott, in the crew of 1876, Terah H. Patterson (1879), George B. Rogers (1881), Nathaniel T. Guernsey (1882, 1883), Joseph R. Parrott (1884, 1885), Percy Hagerman (1891), Philip H. Kunzig (1900, 1901, 1902), Cameron B. Waterman (1901, 1902, 1903), and Thorpe Babcock (1906, 1907).

The Yale Football Association was formed in 1872, and this University stimulus soon resulted in a series of inter-class and inter-departmental games. In October, 1874, there was a game between the Senior and Junior classes in the law school. They played, as did the University team, what was called the American game, similar to Association football in which a round rubber ball was used, and in which players could not pick up, pass or carry the ball. The Rugby game was adopted in 1875.

79

The law school seems to have had no regularly organized team until 1893. In that year the school's team went on a trip, on which it lost to the Syracuse Athletic Club and to the Orange Athletic Club, and played a 6 to 6 tie game with Colgate University. It played games in the roundabout towns in 1895, 1896, 1898, 1899, and 1900, and in the two latter years it journeyed also to New York, Newark, Detroit, and Chicago to play games with athletic clubs. In 1901, the team was beaten at Cambridge by the Harvard Law School team. The Faculty soon thereafter ruled that there should be no trips outside the state, and thenceforth the school's team was eligible to play only in inter-departmental games. Beginning in 1877, its individual members, when they could qualify under the rules, played on the University team. Some of those who were members of that team in the years given, are the following: David Trumbull (1877), Howard H. Knapp (1882, 1883), Louis K. Hull (1883), Harmon S. Graves (1892), Charles Chadwick (1897), Morris U. Ely (1898), Albert R. Cunha (1899), Perry Keifer (1899), William J. McConnell (1899), Claude W. Shattuck (1899), Albion L. Gile (1900), Philip H. Kunzig (1900), Joseph C. Roraback (1903), Harry S. Batchelder (1903), Francis J. McCoy (1905), Carl S. Flanders (1905), and Graham Foster (1907).

On the track also, law men won many points for the University team. A few of the men who participated in these events are the following: George F. Sanford (1894), 440-yard race, and member of the Yale team which competed in the Oxford meet, John H. Morgan (1895), who ran in the mile race at Cambridge, England, Charles Chadwick (1897), 16-lb. hammer throw, John S. Spraker (1902), broad jump, Samuel G. Camp (1902), dashes, Fay R. Moulton (1902), quarter-mile race and dashes,

80

John M. Cates (1903, 1904), hurdles and relay team, Clarence A. Alexander (1904), high jump, and Lester B. Stevens (1907), dashes.

Baseball was the sport in which the school's team earned most reputation. There were games between teams representing the law Seniors and Juniors in June, 1876, and in the same year, a school nine played the Sheffield Scientific School, the Post Graduates and the College classes of 1877 and 1880. The best of the men developed by these inter-class and inter-departmental contests were sometimes drafted for the University team, and this arrangement seemed then to be satisfactory to the sporting interests of the school. The new "one-year residence" rule limiting graduate and freshman participation in University sports brought out protest in the form of a law school team. "Red-hot meetings for permanent organization of a Law School Base Ball Association" were held, and the following members of the class of 1894 were elected officers: "Black" Roger S. Baldwin, President, Howard A. Couse, Secretary, Harold R. Durant, Manager, and Herbert O. Bowers, Captain. The sum of $400 was collected forthwith. Thus the Law School baseball team of 1893 was organized. The team began practice in March, and boldly challenged the University team to a series of games. The invitation was declined. The season began, just after the Easter vacation, with a defeat of Wesleyan at Middletown. Defeat was administered to the New York Athletic Club, just after it had won from the Yale University team, and these victories were followed by others over Brown, Fordham, Dartmouth, Georgetown, and Johns Hopkins. Harvard won by a score of 4 to 3, and the game with Amherst ended in a tie. The team played thirty-two games and won twenty of them.

81

[197]

In the following summer, on the invitation of Amos Alonzo Stagg, the nine went to Chicago to take part in the World's Fair Intercollegiate Base Ball Tournament. They played five games, won four of them, and were awarded the championship, in token whereof A. G. Spalding & Brothers gave them a silver and gold trophy which is still preserved in the law school. The teams with which they played were those of the University of Vermont, the University of Virginia, and Amherst College. According to Captain Bowers (*Yale Shingle*, 1894, p. 107) the contest was of a kind which tries men's souls. "Losing two games meant disqualification from the tournament. We lost the first one. It was a bad outlook, but just here we developed the historic 'Yale sand,' sometimes called 'Yale luck.' Our second game was with Vermont, who had been our opponents in the first game. It was in the ninth inning that we proved our right to live. With the score 1 to 0 against us, and with our last turn at the bat, we batted and ran out two tallies, all done so quickly as to leave the poor Vermonters dazed and limp. . . . Virginia fell an easy victim and Amherst alone stood between us and victory. She made a stubborn fight, but at the close of game number one we had one score to her nothing, while in the decisive game we were better stayers, making nine runs toward the end of the game and again shutting her out." So Yale Law School's most successful baseball season ended. The team had collected nearly $5,000 in guarantees, and had travelled over 7,000 miles.

There were no baseball trips in 1894 and 1895, but in 1896 a luxurious but disastrous southern trip was taken. Remembering the great advertising value for Yale of the team of 1893, "Chauncey Depew gave the team his private car, his two car attendants, and $200 toward

82

getting the nine South. 'It will be the greatest advertisement that ever was!' was the way he was approached. They guaranteed to give him back whatever they made on the trip and off they started. They lost every game and came home. They had some small degree of thankfulness, so they returned the private car and the two colored 'gemmen.' Slavery days are over so the two men were safe, and nobody would buy the car. The fellows sent Chauncey a picture of the team and $17. They say he has the picture in his office now. Underneath it is written, 'This picture cost me $183.' " (Edgar Atkin in *Yale Shingle*, 1902, p. 122.)

After this experience, it is no wonder that in 1897, the law school nine had no support and that law students were urged (*Yale Shingle*, 1897, p. 113) to "find scope for their capabilities in the regular university organizations without resort to picked-up aggregations from the professional departments, which are at once unsatisfactory to the individual men and a blot upon the fair name of their alma mater." Next year, however, due to the enthusiastic management of John Knox Blake, 1898 L., there was a team which took a southern trip despite the observation of the faculty that "ignorance of the law excuseth no man." The team won three out of five games, but came home encumbered by unpaid bills which continued to plague the manager. On this team was Arthur L. Corbin, 1899 L., who still in the year 1936 represents the school at first base in the annual game between the faculty and the *Law Journal* Board. Permission to arrange for a similar trip in 1899 under the management of Samuel E. Hoyt, 1899 L., was obtained largely on the assurance that Corbin would be a member of the team and would serve as tutor in law during the trip. In the final examinations of 1898, he had won the Betts Prize,

83

and on the trip which began on March 29, 1899, besides playing a good game of baseball, he did what else was expected of him. "Owing to the fact that an examination was to be held on the morning of their return" wrote Hoyt (*Yale Shingle*, 1899, p. 85), "Corbin, the 'shark,' held daily quiz clubs until information on the statute of uses and other legal matter issued from their brains with great readiness." They won four out of six games and came back without a deficit. There were southern trips and local games in 1900 and 1901, but thereafter excursions out of town were banned by the faculty. For ten years, interest was kept up by games with other departments of the University, and then the game as a law school activity became a thing of the past. In 1902, the school's nine won the inter-departmental championship, and in 1904, the University Athletic Committee awarded an L.S.B.B. to law men who played in all of the local games.

Law men who played on the University team in the years indicated are the following: Daniel A. Carpenter (1883), James F. Hunt (1887, 1888), William Norton (1892), George O. Redington (1894, 1895), George B. Ward (1900, 1901), Frederick A. Robertson (1901), Albert R. Cunha (1901), James S. O'Rourke (1901, 1902), Henry J. Patton (1902), John L. DeSaulles (1902), Clarence A. Barnes (1905), Paul A. Schlafly (1906, 1907, 1908).

𝔜ale Law Library 𝔓ublications

No. 7   September 1938

Yale Law School:
1895–1915
Twenty Years of Hendrie Hall

By

Frederick C. Hicks

PUBLISHED FOR THE YALE LAW LIBRARY

BY THE YALE UNIVERSITY PRESS

1938

[201]

Simeon Eben Baldwin

Yale Law School:

1895–1915

Twenty Years of Hendrie Hall

FREDERICK C. HICKS

I

IN THE YEAR 1891, Timothy Dwight was President of Yale University; Francis Wayland was Dean of the Law School; one former student, Henry B. Brown, was a Justice of the United States Supreme Court, and another, George Shiras, was in the following year to join him on the same bench; one of the professors, Edward J. Phelps, had recently been on leave to serve as Minister to Great Britain; the school had a registration of 118 students; and the rooms in the county court house, where the school had been since January, 1873, were found to be no longer adequate. Simeon E. Baldwin's prediction, made in 1871, that the school would eventually need a building of its own, was about to come true. (*Yale Law Library Publications*, No. 4, p. 7.)

On April 27, 1891, the Prudential Committee of the Corporation considered a request from the Faculty of Law that an appropriate site for a law building be provided, but took no action beyond a general encouragement of the plan. On May 12, however, when a committee of the Faculty, consisting of Dean Wayland and Professors Phelps and Robinson, appeared before the Corporation, it was voted "that the President, the Treasurer

3

(William W. Farnam), Lieutenant Governor Merwin, Mr. Kingsbury and Mr. Bennett be a Committee to confer with a Committee of the Law Faculty in regard to a site for a law building, with power to make a purchase if they see fit." The result of these conferences was the purchase, in June, 1891, of the property at 83 (now 165) Elm Street, owned by Edward A. Anketell, and consisting of a lot having a frontage of 93 feet, and a depth of 307 feet, and on which stood an eighteenth-century house. The purchase was made, but the property was not formally allotted to the Law School; and so on October 24, 1891, the Governing Board of the school asked that this be done, reinforcing its request by proposing the erection of two buildings, "one in front and one in the rear, with an open campus between," for which they agreed to raise subscriptions, and hopefully guaranteed "to commence the erection of at least one of said buildings during the year 1892." Their expectations were not immediately realized, but on April 1, 1893, we find them considering what rooms would be needed in a new building, and instructing Dean Wayland to obtain floor plans from an architect, so that they might be submitted to the Faculty for approval. These plans, prepared by Cady, Berg and See, of Union Square, New York, abandoned the idea of an open campus, but provided for erecting the building in two sections, front and rear. Meanwhile, Dean Wayland had begun his campaign for a building fund, and with sufficient success to cause the Corporation to vote, on June 26, 1893, "that the President, the Treasurer, and Professor Wayland be appointed a Committee, with power to erect a building for the Law Department, according to such plans as may be approved, and to proceed with the same as fast as the necessary funds are collected and placed in the hands of the Treas-

4

urer." By June, 1894, enough money was assured so that work could be begun on the rear section of the building, leaving the Anketell house still standing facing the street. The records show that in 1893 and 1894, the sum of $41,986.66 was on hand, of which amount $29,896.66 had been collected by Dean Wayland personally. The subscribers during these two years included Henry F. English, Simeon E. Baldwin, and John W. Hendrie, whose names were to recur regularly in the list until the fund was completed.[1]

The rear section was completed early in 1895, and classes were transferred to it from the court house at the beginning of the spring term, April 11, when according to Herbert Knox Smith (*Yale Shingle*, 1895, p. 70), students rejoiced that they were "passing beyond the fear of judges and sheriffs." The formal opening of the building occurred on Friday evening, April 26, when a reception, attended by members of the Corporation, the University faculties, and the Connecticut bar, was tendered to the donors of the building fund. Later in the evening, Dean Wayland introduced President Dwight, who expressed his satisfaction at the prosperity of the school. Professor Phelps spoke of the "refreshing simplicity" of the earlier days, leaving it to be inferred that the present generation must be on its guard against the debilitating effects of its new luxurious surroundings. He congratulated Dean Wayland on his success in raising funds and suggested that the building be named Wayland Hall. "The building has now progressed so far," he said, "that any very rich man, who should contribute handsomely to the fund for its completion, would, with the modesty which goes with great wealth, hesitate to accept the honor of a memorial. If Dean Wayland carries out his threat of

1. For a summary of subscriptions to this fund, see *post*, p 13.

5

dying when the building is finished, he will leave us soon. I hope he will reconsider that threat. Perhaps he will stay with us longer if we name the building after him." Dean Wayland objected to this proposal and said that he still hoped to find someone who would like to make the Law School a memorial to his name and would furnish the funds to complete it. "The height of my ambition," said he, "has been to have the old Anketell house, which has now been painted red and changed into a temporary dormitory, called Wayland Hall. But this ambition has been denied me. It is already known as Buckland Hall, after the youngest member of the Faculty." Remarks were made also by Judge Dwight Loomis, ex-Governor Luzon B. Morris, and by Professors Baldwin and Robinson.

The part then occupied—more than half of what was to be the completed building—was externally without beauty, lacking a façade and being obviously unfinished. Its ground dimensions were 73 by 88 feet, and it stood, like a box, three stories high, rearing its brick walls above the surrounding buildings. In the basement were a lounging room for general discussions and recreation, a locker room containing separate lockers for each student (a novel idea in those days), a washroom, coal bunkers, furnaces for hot-water and hot-air heating, and a dynamo to run a ventilating fan. Provision of light and air was made much of in descriptions of the building—not only the ventilating scheme which "sends a constant stream of air to all the rooms," but the size and number of the windows—"there is not a dark room in the entire building." Thomas H. Breeze, LL.B. 1895, remarked (*Yale Shingle*, 1895, p. 38) that "it is impossible for classes of the present day, installed in that monument of architectural beauty, the new school, to realize how we climbed

6

Hendrie Hall Stairway

up to the Alpine heights of our old quarters and battled against the foul miasmas of the recitation room." The first and second floors each contained two large recitation rooms, and there were also nine smaller rooms for the use of professors, quiz clubs, and the *Yale Law Journal* board. The Dean's office was at the southeast corner of the first floor, a small room jutting out from the building, a temporary addition which was removed when the front section was constructed. The third floor contained a study room, 70 by 30 feet in size, "one of the largest in the University," fitted with large oak tables. Next to it was a stack room fitted with iron Library Bureau book shelves to hold the collection of about 12,000 volumes, "one of the most complete working law libraries in the country." "Access to the shelves is perfectly free, and the resulting familiarity with the reports is of much benefit to the student."

The only entrance to the building was on the east side, approached by a passageway from the street alongside the Anketell house. From the vestibule, a broad staircase led to the third floor. Those who have trod those now well-worn steps, have stood on the landings of mosaic tile, and looked at the engraved portraits of lawyers and judges hanging on the adjacent walls of mottled brick, may find interest in what a representative of the *Yale Alumni Weekly* wrote about them on May 1, 1895 (vol. 4, p. 1). "An architect may be pardoned for an extravagance once in a while, especially if he err in favor of the aesthetic. That is what Messrs. Cady, Berg & See must plead guilty to in the Law School staircase. Architecturally it is a masterpiece. Imposing, graceful, and yet in perfect taste, it forms a splendid companion piece to Mr. Gandolfo's staircase in the new Gymnasium. The Gymnasium staircase, with its white marble banisters, steps and posts,

7

always impresses one with a certain degree of something akin to awe. In the presence of that structure one always takes off his hat, makes sure that his shoes are not muddy, and feels like begging the pardon of each separate step for setting his foot upon it. The Law School staircase cannot claim any such aristocracy, yet its bronze and gold balustrades, vaulting and tracery, its Romanesque windows hexagonal-paned and massive, and its dark substantial stone steps, suggest the luxuriousness of a metropolitan business block. And so one will not only pardon the architects for this distinct addition to Yale's architecture, but will in the same breath express the hope that architects who come after will err in the same way."

The school settled down in its more ample quarters to a routine broken only by term receptions tendered to students by the Faculty and their wives, the first of which was held on May 17, 1895. By formal vote (February 13, 1896), the Law Faculty agreed to wear academic gowns at these receptions, as well as at Commencement exercises. The class which entered in September, 1895, was the largest up to that time in the history of the school. The Faculty was busy with its regular duties, but ever-present in their minds, and particularly in the mind of Dean Wayland, was the necessity for raising money to erect the front section of the building.

In this campaign, the same men who had liberally contributed before again set the example, and they were joined by Professor William K. Townsend and Pierce N. Welch as donors of substantial amounts, and by many unlisted persons whose subscriptions, collected by Dean Wayland, amounted to $7,500. John W. Hendrie was the largest donor. Nevertheless the gifts did not come in fast enough. On November 8, 1897, the Law Faculty represented to the Prudential Committee that the sum of

8

$35,000 was still needed, and the University was asked to lend the money to complete the building. The President and the Treasurer were made a committee to consider the request. Nothing came of this, and the Dean redoubled his efforts, with considerable success, to raise the money by subscriptions. By May, 1899, the goal was in sight, but $12,000 still were needed. The Faculty could wait no longer. On May 19, 1899, it proposed to the Prudential Committee that it would itself be responsible for the sum of $12,000, if it were not raised, and on that basis it induced the Committee to recommend to the Corporation that the erection of the front section of the building be authorized. On May 25, 1899, the Corporation accepted the offer, and gave its consent that work should begin. The first step, begun on June 29, 1899, was to tear down the Anketell house.

Since this house was of considerable importance in connection with the Law School and with New Haven, it ought here, when its physical disappearance is being noted, to be given passing attention.

In 1892, a year after the University purchased the house and the lot on which it stood, the group which afterwards formed the Graduates Club obtained the privilege of occupying the house. At that time there was a kitchen in the rear with a large fireplace, and the group used to gather there for social events, using the rest of the house as living rooms. The legal organization of the Graduates Club was perfected on March 30, 1894, at a meeting held at 954 Chapel Street, to which it had moved. On June 25, 1894, the Corporation of the University voted "to allow the Faculty of the Law School the use of the house, No. 83 Elm Street, until otherwise ordered." In that same month, work on the rear section of the new law building was begun, and this necessitated the re-

9

moval of the kitchen and the fireplace. This left the front of the house, similar in many respects to the front of the present Graduates Club, with four large bedrooms upstairs and four rooms downstairs. It is this section of the house which law students saw from 1894 to July, 1899. In 1894, Edward G. Buckland, then an instructor in law, rented the house from Dean Wayland and occupied it jointly with students and other recent graduates, among whom were Harry G. Day, Wendell G. Bronson, Herbert Knox Smith, Herbert S. Bullard, John Hill Morgan, Origen S. Seymour, William Lloyd Kitchel, and Francis Parsons. Similar groups occupied the house until it was taken over by Corbey Court, the last occupant before it was torn down.

When the Class of 1899 entered the school, says Custis S. Bacon (*Yale Shingle*, 1902, p. 106–7), and saw the rear section of the building, "we found the front door on the side. A shapeless brick construction met our view, to which since then the beautiful frontage has been added. . . . During the first year, in the progress of building, we were reminded of the temple of Solomon, which rose 'without sound of axe or hammer,' like the silent growth of a tree, or the airy fabric of a dream—because it was so different." After the completion of the building and its occupancy in September, 1900, Herbert Wescott Fisher, LL.B. 1901, remarked (*Yale Shingle*, 1901, p. 28) that "our ungainly old building has taken to itself a spouse, gladly sacrificing more than one of his iron ribs for the sake of that comely addition." The building, although neither a thing of beauty nor appropriate to its surroundings, was in fact much admired because it was such an improvement over the rear section, which its three stories, finished in Indiana limestone, now hid from view. The front door was now where it belonged, and a

10

Hendrie Hall

hallway led from it to the stairway, already described. On the west side of this hallway was a lecture room seating 200, and on the east side were offices for the Dean, Secretary, and Registrar. Outside, a covered passageway led to the rear. The second story, occupying the entire width of the lot, about 93 feet, provided an auditorium seating more than 400. The third floor was given up to a reading room and offices. Since electric lights were not installed in classrooms until 1916, students recited in the late afternoons, according to an anonymous writer (*Yale Shingle*, 1901, p. 31), "by the lurid light of the gas-jets."

Within two months after the occupancy of the front section of the building, John William Hendrie, largest individual contributor to the building fund, died on November 25, 1900, at Sound Beach, Connecticut. On November 23, 1899, the Corporation had voted that as a tribute to his generous interest, the new building should be named after him, and the inscription HENDRIE HALL was placed over the main entrance. He began giving in 1894, and increased his contributions each year until they amounted to $65,000. "I well recall the day," wrote Dean Wayland (*Yale Shingle*, 1903, p. 17), "when, accompanied by his classmate, the Rev. Dr. Munger, I called upon him to solicit his aid. He heard our presentation of our case without comment or question, and replied: 'I will give you $5,000; you shall have my check for that sum before you go.'" He also, on August 4, 1900, established in the University a fund of $14,933.28, the income of which is used to encourage debating. Born at Sound Beach, Connecticut, November 18, 1821, he was the son of a sea captain. He worked on a farm until he was of age, studied when he could, taught school, and finished his preparation for college at the Hopkins Grammar School. At this time and during his years at Yale he

11

carried on a lobster and fish business, canvassed for books, and did odd jobs, by means of which he graduated from Yale College in 1851 with money in his pocket. He received the M.A. degree from Yale in 1861. For three years following his graduation, he taught at the Stamford Academy. Then with a capital of $1,000 which he had saved, he took passage for Panama, went overland to the Pacific, and sailed to San Francisco. There, with H. M. Lockwood, he became a merchant and later dealt largely in real estate. In the spring of 1863, he sold out to his partner, and having already accumulated a considerable fortune, returned to Sound Beach. Here he became a gentleman farmer on the place where he was born. He spent his winters in California, where he continued occasionally to buy and sell real estate. Since he never married, he disposed of much of his fortune during his lifetime, making generous gifts to his church, to the cities of Stamford, Connecticut, and San Francisco, California, as well as to Yale University. His portrait is printed in the *Yale Shingle*, 1903, and in the *History of the Yale Class of 1851*, which latter also contains an autobiographical sketch. A memorial, written by Dean Wayland, was published in the *Yale Law Journal*, February, 1901.

The Law Faculty was never called upon as a group to make up a deficit in the building fund, but several of them individually added substantially to the sums that they had already given. The total sum needed was not completed until the year 1902, and even then some of the donations came by way of transfer from the University Bicentennial Fund. Unfortunately, the records do not contain the names of all who contributed. The missing names include those who together gave $37,986 through Dean Wayland, members of the law class of 1871 who made up a fund of $1,000, and members of the Kent Club

12

who gave $100. Of those listed, the chief donors were the following:

JOHN W. HENDRIE	$65,000	LYNDE HARRISON	$500
HENRY F ENGLISH	15,000	THEODORE S. WOOLSEY	500
PIERCE N. WELCH	5,025	M. DWIGHT COLLIER	300
SIMEON E. BALDWIN	3,500	JOHN F. DILLON	250
PHELPS MONTGOMERY	1,500	HENRY A. JAMES	250
WILLIAM K. TOWNSEND	1,500	GEORGE D. WATROUS	250
FREDERICK J. KINGSBURY	1,000	C. LA RUE MUNSON	200
FRANCIS WAYLAND	1,000	W. W. FREAR	200
MORRIS F. TYLER	1,000	HENRY W. FARNAM	150
JOHN H. PERRY	1,000	EDWARD G. BUCKLAND	125
LEROY MAYER	1,000		

Other persons who contributed sums of $100 or less were: Dr. W. L. Bradley, Thomas N. North, Henry C. White, Livingston W. Cleaveland, Winthrop Turney, Samuel S. Doroff, John G. Tod, Robert C. Fergus, Frederick L. Averill, James H. Brewster, Roger S. Baldwin, John H. Morgan, Allan W. Paige, S. L. Whipple, E. B. Gager, Arthur A. Wilder, Louis H. Bristol, J. H. O'Rourke, E. D. Robbins, Justus S. Hotchkiss, Henry L. Hotchkiss, H. A. Hull, William W. Hyde, F. H. Parker, S. O. Prentice, Harry Goodyear Day, Howard H. Knapp, Frank D. Pavey, Louis E. Stanton, Robert C. Morris, E. H. Trowbridge, W. F. Day, W. E. Miller, Max Adler, S. E. Merwin, E. G. Stoddard, W. R. Tyler, Eli Whitney, G. H. Ford, E. B. Bowditch, H. C. Warren, R. A. Brown, Joseph Parker, William E. Downs, D. Cady Eaton, Joseph Porter, Burton Mansfield, Thomas Hooker, William W. Farnam, Charles H. Peterson, E. A. Bowers, C. S. White, S. J. Elder, Francis Parsons, E. Henry Barnes, J. D. Dewell, T. Attwater Barnes, S. W. Kellogg, H. B. B. Stapler, and John M. Hall.

Including $2,490.88, representing interest on the fund when it was being held, the total amount raised, of which a record has been found, was $147,572.24.

13

The first public exercises held in the auditorium of the completed building were those of John Marshall Day, February 4, 1901. The occasion was the one hundredth anniversary of the inauguration of John Marshall as Chief Justice of the United States, which was celebrated throughout the United States by Congress, the Supreme Court, bar associations, and law schools.

In New Haven, a February storm was raging, but nevertheless a large audience assembled at the school. The state bar association was represented on the platform by Charles E. Perkins, President of the association, and by His Excellency, Governor George P. McLean; the Federal courts were represented by Judge Nathaniel Shipman of the United States Circuit Court, and by Judge William K. Townsend of the District Court. For Yale University, there were present President Hadley and many members of the Faculty. Simeon E. Baldwin represented the National Committee on John Marshall Day. After brief welcoming remarks by Dean Wayland and President Hadley, Governor McLean, as presiding officer, thrilled his audience by the following stirring words: "I do not agree with McCullom or Sarah Dobney or Herbert that the mill will never grind again with the water that is past; the lines fascinate in their hopelessness only; they are not true; the mill may grind again and again with the water that is ever journeying from sky to earth and from earth to sky. And I do not agree with Shakespeare that it is the evil rather than the good that men do that lives after them. When a great man loves and labors and passes by the living, his life returns ever to help and elevate succeeding generations, and the influence of that life gathers rather than loses energy with the years. Washington is dearer and Lincoln comes closer to the hearts of the people with every passing February;

14

and we, to-day, have met to welcome, with renewed interest, the spirit of the man who stood with Washington and Hamilton and kept the bridge so valiantly in the brave days of old; defended and saved the Constitution from the assaults of error and envy, and laid the base of the pyramid of the great Union in stuff that can never be moved or broken." The formal addresses of the day by Charles E. Perkins, Judge Shipman, and Simeon E. Baldwin are printed in full in the *Yale Law Journal*, March, 1901. Following the addresses, there was an inspection of the building, and a refection was served in the large library room on the third floor.

The Law School took an active part in the celebration of the two hundredth anniversary of the founding of Yale University, held from October 20 to 23, 1901. On its committees of arrangement served Dean Wayland, William K. Townsend, Thomas Thacher, and Theodore S. Woolsey of the Faculty. An undergraduate committee from the Law School consisted of Osborne A. Day, Thomas G. Gaylord, Lucius P. Fuller, Charles T. Lark, Frank W. Tully, and Eliot Watrous, all of the Class of 1902; and of the Class of 1903, Morgan B. Brainard, Robert S. Binkerd, Franklin Carter, Jr., John F. Malley, Charles D. Lockwood, and Henry J. Patton.

In the football game on the afternoon of October 22 between Yale University and Bates College, resulting in a victory of 21 to 0 for Yale, the Law School was represented by John L. de Saulles, 1904, quarterback, and Clarence A. Weymouth, 1903, fullback. Apparently the students of law took a formal part in everything except the torchlight procession, which with twenty-five bands stretched its line over a mile and a half of New Haven's streets on the night of October 21. Five thousand students and graduates, headed by the chief marshal and

15

aides, "on Locomobiles," were arrayed in costumes symbolic of periods in the history of the University. Medicine was in green, and Divinity in red.

In the serious exercises of the celebration the school was represented by Thomas Thacher, of New York, since 1887 lecturer on corporate trusts, who gave an address at Battell Chapel on October 21. Introduced by Simeon E. Baldwin, he spoke on "Yale in its Relation to Law," tracing the activities of Yale graduates, both of the College and Law School, as lawyers, judges, teachers of law, as statesmen and as diplomats. This address took its appropriate place in the elaborate volume, *Record of the Celebration*, and it was reprinted in pamphlet form. In connection with the celebration there was issued a series of twenty-five Bicentennial Publications, to which the Law Faculty contributed a volume entitled *Two Centuries' Growth of American Law, 1701–1901*, copyrighted by Yale University, and published in September, 1901, by Charles Scribner's Sons. It contains eighteen articles of which Simeon E. Baldwin and William K. Townsend each wrote four, Edwin B. Gager two, and of which one each was written by George E. Beers, William F. Foster, George D. Watrous, Leonard M. Daggett, Henry Wade Rogers, David Torrance, James H. Webb, and Theodore S. Woolsey. The subjects of which these men traced the American historical development were constitutional law, real property, contracts, torts, equity, mortgages of real property, wills, municipal corporations, private corporations, pleadings in civil actions, evidence, criminal law and procedure, patents, copyrights, trade-marks and unfair trade, admiralty, and international law.

Between 1901 and 1903 there were important developments in the school which will be treated in other sections. From the point of view of physical development, the

16

latter year marks the end of a Law School period. On March 9, 1903, Dean Wayland presented his resignation to take effect at the end of the academic year, and on January 9, 1904, he died. His joking prophecy that as soon as the new building was finished, he would probably die, came near to being fulfilled, for he survived the event only a little more than three years, and during the last two of them he had been ill.

II

ALL of the predecessors of Dean Wayland had been men who could give only part of their time to the school, and that part they preferred to devote to teaching. They had been forced to parcel out among themselves the routine tasks of administration, and the more delicate ones of promotion and representation of the school in public. Baldwin, Robinson, and Platt had been doing their share of such duties, but they gladly relinquished most of them to Wayland, when he became Dean. As Robinson put it (*Francis Wayland: Commemorative Address*, p. 23), the school needed and found in him "a leader who could multiply its resources, extend its fame, and be an acceptable medium of communication between it and the outside world." He was uniquely fitted for his new work, and he performed an indispensable function in promoting the growth of the school. Much has already been said about him in these pages, but it is fitting to gather up some of the scattered threads and weave them into a pattern that will more adequately represent him.

Francis Wayland was born on August 23, 1826, in Boston, Massachusetts, the son of Lucy Lane Lincoln Wayland, and Francis Wayland, President of Brown University from 1827 to 1855. The son attended the Providence public schools and Phillips Academy, An-

17

dover, Massachusetts, and when sixteen years old, in 1842, entered Brown University. On his graduation in 1846, he read law in the office of W. H. Potter in Providence, and then spent one year, 1849–1850, in the Harvard Law School. After his admission to the Massachusetts bar, and a brief association with the firm of Chapman and Ashmun, in Springfield, Massachusetts, he began the practice of law in Worcester. Here he maintained an office until 1858. In the previous year he had married Martha Waite Read, of New Haven. Miss Read was an only child and her father's health was poor. At the latter's request Wayland transferred his practice to New Haven. For fourteen years, until 1872, he was ostensibly a practicing lawyer there, but it is said that he gave more time to public affairs and official engagements than to legal practice. He served two terms, 1864–1865, as Probate Judge, and in 1869 was elected Lieutenant Governor, with Marshall Jewell as Chief Executive. In this capacity he was for two years, 1869–1870, an ex-officio member of the Yale Corporation. He was a life-long member of the Republican party. On his return from Europe in 1871, he was, on the recommendation of Robinson, Baldwin, and Platt, July 11, 1871, appointed a lecturer in the Law School, and on October 11, following, he was authorized by the Corporation to solicit funds for the school. Thus began what was to be a major objective for him until his retirement. He was promoted to a professorship on July 11, 1872, and a year later, July, 1873, his colleagues put him officially in a position of leadership by electing him their Dean.

The school was the chief interest of his life, but he had others which combined effectively with it, since they made him widely known as a representative of the school. He was an ardent student of the social sciences and

18

Dean Francis Wayland

identified himself both with their practical and theoretical aspects. He was president of the American Baptist Union, and, with his wife, built and largely maintained a Baptist church in the outskirts of New Haven. He was for three years president of the American Social Science Association, and for twenty-four years chairman of its Jurisprudence Department. He was the founder and continuous secretary of the New Haven Social Science Club. He was the organizer and, for twenty-five years, the president of the Board of Organized Charities of New Haven. He was for fourteen years president of the Board of Directors of the Connecticut State Prison, and a member of the Board of Pardons. He was a member of the National Prison Reform Association, president of the Connecticut Prison Aid Association, and president of the Connecticut General Hospital. In 1880, he was president of the Board of Visitors to the United States Naval Academy. For years he was a member of the Corporation of Brown University. His *Alma Mater* conferred upon him the doctorate of laws, in 1880. The year previous he had received the same honor from the University of Rochester.

The catalogue of his formal activities and honors inside and outside of the school, however, does not tell much about him as his colleagues, students, and associates remember him. He was well over six feet in height, wore a full beard, and had a commanding presence described by his friends as dignified, and by some others as pompous. He was an early riser and spent an hour or more in the saddle before going to his office. On these rides he was fond of talking with people whom he met on the roads in the environs of New Haven. Nearly everyone who knew him remembers the picture which he presented as he solidly and securely sat on his mount. He

19

needed a good horse and he had one. "He rode a great black horse even upon the football field, to the horror of the greenskeeper," wrote Theodore S. Woolsey. "How many of us," exclaimed William C. Robinson, "can recall that once familiar scene when, sauntering near his home, we saw him riding toward us on his favorite steed beneath the arching elms of Whitney Avenue—a picture worthy of the pencil of the artist in whose fame this institution shares." He looked and acted like a strong man, but he suffered from recurring ailments which occasionally required a change of climate, and therefore both before and after he joined the Law School Faculty, he and Mrs. Wayland travelled widely. These trips and some of his experiences were the subjects of informal talks in clubs to which he belonged, and of a few periodical articles.

As administrator, he bore the brunt of complaints and misunderstandings, and because he did not meet the students often as teacher, sometimes they, without knowing what constructive work he was doing for the school, thought that he was indolent. With the cruelty of youth, one mock court jury, in a trial over which he presided, played a trick on him. The case was heard at the last hour before lunch time. It was planned that "when the evidence was all in and the case went to the jury, the jury would disagree for so long a time that the Dean could not get out for his lunch, and this was put over to the great amusement of the students and the annoyance of the Dean." He interviewed all applicants for admission to the school, and like his successors today, sometimes found this work trying. His skepticism, when fulsome letters of recommendation were presented, showed itself in an occasional sarcastic phrase. There is no doubt, however, that he had the welfare of his charges

20

sincerely at heart. His niece, Mrs. Frederick Wells Williams, remembers assisting him at Law School receptions, and says that his "personal interest in every single student was both touching and amusing." "The students," wrote Judge Baldwin (*Yale Shingle*, 1904, p. 31), "felt his kindness of heart, and that with him justice would always be tempered with mercy. Not but what he could be firm, on occasion. A friend of a student who had been dropped for hopelessly poor scholarship, came to the Dean once to ask for his re-instatement, and found that he could make no impression. 'Now, Professor Wayland,' said he, at last, remembering the church connection of the man whom he was addressing, 'don't forget that the poor fellow is a good Baptist.' 'My dear sir,' was the reply, 'it would make no difference with the Faculty, even if he were a Buddhist.' "

He was successful also in handling his Faculty and in his dealings with the University authorities. Professor Robinson's *Commemorative Address* delivered before the Law School on April 22, 1904, might be considered to be exaggerated praise if one did not know what manner of man Robinson himself was. The latter was a gifted writer with strong loyalties, but he was also notable for his accuracy and the care with which he sifted his facts. Simeon E. Baldwin paid Wayland tributes in print at the time of his retirement and after his death. (*Yale Shingle*, 1903: 22–24; 1904: 29–31.) "His zeal and energy in promoting the interests of the school were untiring," wrote Baldwin. "Many of the qualities for executive office which had distinguished his father, when President of Brown University, he had inherited. While a man of marked dignity of bearing, he joined with it that quick sense of humor which is so helpful in getting over rough places in life. He was always looking forward, rather than back-

21

ward, for light; but still showed a wise moderation in matters of policy as well as of discipline. He saw through shams. He was equally quick to recognize merit. There was a very close association between the members of the early Faculty of four under his presidency. Our meetings were informal, and the line between business discussion and social chat and chaffing not very much regarded. He could say a caustic thing, if he chose, but it was more easy for him to commend than to condemn." The informality of some of the Faculty meetings may be inferred from the minutes kept for many years by Wayland. Frequently they ended with some such comment as the following: "After much informal but, let us hope, not unprofitable discussion of various topics, more or less connected with the interests of the Law School, voted to adjourn."

On his retirement from active duties the Corporation, on March 9, 1903, adopted a minute, prepared by Theodore T. Munger and Charles R. Palmer, which is full of appreciation for his services to the University and of his qualities as an executive officer. After referring particularly to his achievements in raising money, the minute says that his administration "was characterized by conscientious devotion to the welfare of the school; great kindness and tact in dealing with students; sound judgment as to methods of instruction; keen perception of character; outspoken sincerity in dealing with questions at issue, and a broad and sympathetic spirit towards his fellow officers that kept relations free from mistrust and irritation, and created a unity of which he was the inspiring center."

His contemporaries were impressed with the persistency of his purpose, and his devotion to any cause which he espoused. Theodore S. Woolsey (*Historical Address*,

22

June 16, 1924, p. 11) says that he "gave the school what it most needed, a real head. Day by day in every way he pushed its interests. No one could withstand him. Once only did he meet his match. He had begged from Steinert, the music dealer, and inadvertently let him off with $500 when he was prepared to give $1,000. Steinert boasted of what he had saved and it came to Wayland's mortified ears, so he sought another donation. 'You made $500 off me,' said the one. 'Judge, what I makes I keeps,' said the other." Mortified he was at such fiascoes, but not retarded in his pace or deterred from further effort. "That my uncle was more devoted to the Law School than to almost anything in life, I very well know," wrote Mrs. Williams in a recent letter. "His efforts to collect money for the new building, his charm in extracting contributions from unwilling victims, his perfect serenity when he failed to extract them, and his loyal pride in the Law School—these recollections are stamped upon my mind." Professor Robinson was fully conscious of the truth of the above when he said in Hendrie Hall (*Commemorative Address*, April 22, 1904, p. 25): "The college treasurer and the architect can tell you what this building cost in money, but what it cost to him [Wayland] in care and thought and correspondence, in travel far and near, in disappointed hopes and new resolves, appears in no account book and never will be reckoned. You call it Hendrie Hall, and fitly so, from its chief benefactor; but the name of Wayland is written in invisible characters on every brick, and lurks in all the silent echoes of its lordly rooms."

Emphasis on the persistent money-collecting side of his character is apt to give the impression that he was a man whose approach eventually would be avoided. The opposite apparently was the case. This fact is brought

23

out clearly in a charming tribute paid to him by his friend Frederick John Kingsbury (*Journal of the American Social Science Association*, No. 43, 1905, p. 25–29). With all his dignity and his masterfulness, he was a companionable man. Kingsbury draws a choice picture of him attending meetings of the American Social Science Association, arriving ahead of time to make arrangements, reading papers and taking part in the discussions, but best of all spending long hours on the porch and in the reading room of the United States Hotel at Saratoga, conversing with other delegates, among whom were Andrew D. White, Daniel Coit Gilman, Judge John F. Dillon, Edward Atkinson, and many others whose names are equally familiar. He kept in touch with his large circle of friends through constant correspondence. Although he wrote all letters to prospective students in his own hand, and for years wrote his brother, Reverend Herman Lincoln Wayland, every day, he dashed off short and humorous notes to his intimates whenever the spirit moved him. He loved nonsense rhymes and passed them on to others with the comment, "How's this?" He wrote to Baldwin from London, April 26, 1881, saying that he was still ill and would probably not be able to do much for the school on his return; and then he added, "I presume that you and W.C.R [obinson] are squandering our funds in expensive and abundant advertising." Kingsbury says that "if he wanted to make a word very emphatic, he would write in large letters, stretching it across the whole page," and "if he despised a man,—and there were some such,—he would write his name in the smallest of letters without capitals."

Such a life left little time for writing books, but he did, with his brother, edit in 1867 a two-volume set of the memoirs of his father, and he wrote some popular maga-

24

zine articles as well as addresses on penology and the social sciences. He could have had a career in public life following up his term as Connecticut Lieutenant Governor. Once, at least, he allowed his name to be used for political purposes when, on the night of October 27, 1880, the "Wayland Escort," with uniforms and torchlights furnished by the Republican party, marched in a procession in the Garfield–Hancock presidential campaign. (*Yale News*, October 25, 1880, p. 2.) He could have been a successful businessman, devoting himself to acquiring a personal fortune. He did neither of these, but gave himself to the Law School. At the outset he served without salary; later he received his meager share of "dividends" with the others; but for the last fifteen years of his professorship he accepted, as Dean and Professor of English Constitutional Law, a fixed salary of only $500 a year.

III

WHEN Francis Wayland joined the Law Faculty, he had only three colleagues, Robinson, Platt, and Baldwin. During the thirty-two years which elapsed before his retirement on June 30, 1903, there was a long succession of lecturers, who in many ways left their impress on the school; and a notable group of men who attained to the rank of professor or assistant professor. These, arranged in the order of their accession to the Faculty, were:

1876	THEODORE S. WOOLSEY	1892	EDWIN B. GAGER
1881	WILLIAM K. TOWNSEND	1893	DAVID TORRANCE
1881	EDWARD J. PHELPS	1895	SAMUEL O. PRENTICE
1887	EDWARD V. RAYNOLDS	1895	JOHN WURTS
1889	GEORGE D. WATROUS	1895	WILLIAM F. FOSTER
1892	GEORGE E. BEERS	1896	EDWARD D. ROBBINS
1892	EDWARD G. BUCKLAND	1900	HENRY W. ROGERS
1892	MORRIS F. TYLER	1902	JOHN K. BEACH

At the end of Wayland's term as Dean, Townsend had

25

given up teaching and there had been lost from the Faculty by resignation, Robinson (1895), Buckland (1898), Tyler (1900), Foster (1903), Robbins (1903); and by death, Platt (1890), as already noted, and Phelps (1900).

Edward John Phelps was a man of distinction whose presence had added to the prestige of the school. His death was said by Dean Wayland to have been the severest blow that the school had received since its renaissance. That this could be truthfully said of a man in his seventy-eighth year argues much for the strength of his personality. He was born in Middlebury, Vermont, on July 11, 1822, the son of Samuel S. Phelps, who graduated from Yale College in the Class of 1811. The son received his A.B. from Middlebury College in 1840, and attended the Yale Law School in the year 1841–1842. He finished his preparation for the bar in the office of Horatio Seymour, in Middlebury, and began law practice there. In 1845, August 13, he married Mary L. Haight, and moved to Burlington, Vermont, where he maintained his legal residence until his death. He became a leader of the bar, and in 1880 was President of the American Bar Association. He was active in politics, first as a Whig and then as a Democrat. Under President Fillmore he was Second Comptroller of the United States Treasury from 1851 to 1853. In 1870, he was a delegate to the Vermont Constitutional Convention, and he was Democratic candidate for the governorship of Vermont in 1880, and for the senatorship from the same state in 1890 and in 1892. He began his career as a law teacher by lecturing at the University of Vermont, 1880 to 1883, on medical jurisprudence; and in 1882 he lectured on constitutional law at Boston University. He was orator at the Yale Law School Commencement exercises in June,

26

Edward John Phelps

Theodore Salisbury Woolsey

William Kneeland Townsend

1880, his subject being "The True Dignity of the Legal Profession." On June 29, 1881, he was called to fill the Kent Professorship of Law in Yale College, a post which had been vacant since the death of Henry Dutton in 1869.[2] The Corporation also conferred the degree of Master of Arts upon him. He was then nearly fifty-nine years of age. For the rest of his life, he spent half the year, January to June, in New Haven, and the other half in Burlington; but twice this routine was broken by duties of international importance. From 1885 to 1889, he was Minister to Great Britain, having been appointed by President Cleveland as successor to James Russell Lowell; and in 1893, together with Frederic R. Coudert and James C. Carter, he was counsel for the United States in the Fur-seal Arbitration. While Minister to Great Britain, he was instrumental in establishing the Morgan Fund (see *Yale Law Library Publications*, No. 4, p. 38), which partially supports the Edward J. Phelps Professorship of Law. Middlebury College in 1870, the University of Vermont in 1887, and Harvard University in 1889, conferred upon him the degree of Doctor of Laws.

Following his election to the Kent professorship, he sent to President Porter an outline of the work in law that he proposed to give in the College. This having come to the attention of Simeon E. Baldwin, the latter wrote Phelps calling attention to the courses given in the Law School and inviting him to participate in them. Phelps replied from Burlington, July 8, 1881, as follows: "It had not at all occurred to me that I could be of any use in the Law Department. Your organization there seems to me already so excellent and complete, and the instruction so satisfactory, that I do not think you ought to be 'in-

2 For the origin of the Kent Professorship, see *Yale Law Library Publications*, No. 1, p. 39–42.

27

cumbered with help.' " Baldwin's persuasion prevailed, however, and next year, 1881–1882, his name appeared in the Law School bulletin as special lecturer in evidence. For a brief period, in deference to his Kent professorship, he was listed among the professors, as distinguished from lecturers; but thereafter he was listed only among the special lecturers. Subjects which he gave from time to time were evidence, equity, equity pleading, conflict of laws, international law, mortgages, and constitutional limitations. Toward the end of his life, he lectured only on equity and international law. He performed a great service to the school by fostering a movement then much discussed of integrating law work with that of other departments of the University. He lectured not only in the College and in the Law School, but also in the Divinity School, where his subject was the "Relation of the Clergy to Municipal Law."

In the Law School, he did not carry on class discussions, but lectured in a formal way. His performances, however, were eminently successful, so that students were eager to hear him. He was a fine public speaker, with faultless diction, and he supplemented his prepared lectures by examples from his own experience. He had the winning and gracious manner of the gentleman of the old school, and the effect of dignity was enhanced by his side whiskers and clean-shaven chin and lips. During his last illness students came daily to his residence to inquire about him, and alumni wrote from far and near. He was well known to the alumni because of his interest in the Law School Alumni Association, of which he was president for several years. In 1897, his friends had presented to the school a portrait of him, painted by John F. Weir. It now has an honored place in the Sterling Law Buildings. He died in New Haven on May 9, 1900, and on

28

May 16, the Corporation adopted a memorial resolution prepared by Charles Ray Palmer, Theodore T. Munger, and Anson Phelps Stokes, Jr., in which he is characterized as "an admirable illustration, in conspicuous spheres, of what the scholar, the citizen, the lawyer, the Christian gentleman, ought to be in the manifold exigencies and opportunities of modern life."

Two years after Phelps' death, William Kneeland Townsend found it necessary to give up teaching, but he remained on the Governing Board of the Law School in an advisory capacity. He had been since 1881 a teacher on whom the school relied heavily to carry on a substantial part of its regular work; and in other important ways, intangible but real, he had made classroom and office, places to which students liked to come.

His associations by ancestry and by environment were with Yale University. His granduncle, Isaac H. Townsend, who was a professor in the Law School from 1840 to 1847 (see *Yale Law Library Publications*, No. 3, p. 8–13), established in 1843 the Isaac H. Townsend Prize in Yale College. His father, James Mulford Townsend, established in 1874 the Townsend Prize in the Law School; and his brother, James Mulford Townsend, B.A. 1874, lectured in the Law School from 1887 to 1914, on the "Transfer of Monetary Securities."

Born in New Haven, June 12, 1848, William K. Townsend graduated from Yale College in 1871, and spent a year in Europe before entering the Law School in 1872. On June 24, 1874, he received his LL.B. degree and at the same time was awarded the Jewell Prize for the best dissertation on the Cy Pres doctrine in the United States, and the Civil Law Prize for his essay on "The Roman Advocate as Compared with the English Barrister." The latter was later published by request. Admitted to the

29

bar in the same year, he entered the office of Simeon E. Baldwin. Two years later, he joined the newly established course leading to the degree of Master of Laws, receiving the degree on June 27, 1878. (See *Yale Law Library Publications*, No. 4, p. 27.) He continued his studies for another year and became a Doctor of Civil Law, June 30, 1880. On July 1, 1874, he had married Mary Leavenworth Trowbridge, of New Haven, and he established himself further in the community by accepting election in 1878 to membership in the New Haven Common Council. For two years, 1880–1882, he was a member of the Board of Aldermen. Later, 1889–1891, he was to serve as corporation counsel. On May 1, 1885, he formed a law partnership with George D. Watrous, which lasted until 1892, when he became a Federal judge. In 1881, he edited and largely rewrote the Connecticut practice manual for lawyers, justices of the peace, constables, and selectmen, which had already run to thirteen editions, and which with the title, *The New Connecticut Civil Officer*, survived in new editions until 1923. The first sixty-one pages of this book, relating to pleading, were reprinted for use in the Law School.

When, on June 29, 1881, the Yale Corporation appointed him Professor of Pleading in the Law School, he had all of the qualities necessary for a successful teaching career—an unusual academic and professional education, practical experience both in municipal government and at the bar, a winning personality, habits of industry, and a scholarly attitude toward his profession. He justified expectations in every way, even though he continued his practice for a decade and then went on the Federal bench. He was the first Edward J. Phelps Professor in the Law School, a title which he retained from 1887 to 1907. His schedule of subjects from 1881 to 1902, varying some-

30

what from year to year, included pleading, code pleading, contracts, admiralty, torts, patents, trade-marks, and copyright. His abilities as an instructor were unusual. President Hadley said that students "were quite carried away by the enthusiasm of his teaching. They praised his clearness, his close establishment of the relation between case and principle, and above all things, the concrete way in which he showed them how the law was an active agent in the ordering of human affairs."

His first service on the judicial bench began on March 28, 1892, when President Harrison appointed him United States District Judge for the District of Connecticut. Ten years later, March 23, 1902, President Theodore Roosevelt appointed him Judge of the United States Circuit Court, Second Circuit, by designation from which he usually sat in the Circuit Court of Appeals. These new duties, necessitating his continued presence in New York City, caused him to retire from teaching, but it is significant that the Law Faculty prevailed upon him to retain his professorial title and his seat on the Governing Board. He did not lose interest in the school, and in many ways continued to contribute to its welfare. He was affectionately known by his associates and generations of students as "Billy" Townsend. During his active professorship, he supported the student body in many of its enterprises. He was a financial sponsor for the *Yale Law Journal* (see *Yale Law Library Publications*, No. 4, p. 66), and wrote articles for it. He was responsible for the name of the class-book series, the *Yale Shingle*, and wrote three articles for it. These are full of practical advice, illustrated by examples from his own experience, but couched in such terms as to delight the reader. The first, 1893, is in the form of an after-dinner speech; the second, 1896, is a judge's charge to a jury; and the third, 1903, relates to

31

the handling of clients. He was a substantial contributor to the Hendrie Hall building fund, and in 1898, he established in the College, in memory of a son who died while a member of the Class of 1901, the Winston Trowbridge Townsend Prize for excellence in English composition.

During the last few years of his life he was afflicted with pulmonary tuberculosis, from which, in his fifty-ninth year, on June 2, 1907, he died in New Haven. He had chosen to continue his work rather than to seek relief in a more beneficial climate, and he presided in his court until two weeks before his death. On June 7, 1907, in the Circuit Court room in the Post Office Builidng, New York, where he had heard his last case, proceedings were held in his memory. Judges E. Henry Lacombe and Henry G. Ward presided, and addresses were made by Thomas Thacher, Judge William J. Wallace, and Edmund Wetmore. The tributes were of an unusual character since they stressed not only his professional ability, his patience, industry, skill, and knowledge, but the personal characteristics which had endeared him to both bench and bar. These were courage, a joyous spirit, generosity, sympathy, steadfast loyalty, and capacity for friendship. It was these same qualities which had made him the friend, and not merely the formal associate, of his colleagues and students in the Law School. Commemorative exercises were held in Hendrie Hall on June 18, 1907, and the addresses then delivered were published in pamphlet form. President Hadley presided, and the other speakers were Simeon E. Baldwin, Thomas Thacher, and George D. Watrous. They all dwelt upon his ability, scholarship, and strength of character, but the keynote of every address was his lovable qualities, and the feeling of personal loss that was experienced at the announcement of his death. Mr. Justice David J.

32

Brewer, in a letter read at the meeting, described Townsend as the "light of every gathering . . . the noblest type of Yale graduates. A Yale Commencement without him will seem like a rose bush without a bloom." In New Haven he was loved by all who knew him, was in great demand as a toastmaster, told stories well, was known as an amusing and vivacious conversationalist, and withal was respected for his knowledge and judgment. The tradition still lives in the city and in the Law School, where there is a portrait of him presented by his widow. Mrs. Townsend also gave to the Law Library 1,007 volumes of his law books. His only surviving son, George H. Townsend, B.A. 1908, on July 7, 1925, established in the Law School in his memory the William K. Townsend Professorship of Law.

When, in the autumn of 1901, Dean Wayland became ill, Professor Theodore S. Woolsey acted as Secretary *pro tempore*, keeping the minutes of the Governing Board meetings, some of which were held at Dean Wayland's house, with him in bed. When it became evident that Wayland's illness would be prolonged, the Governing Board, on November 26, 1901, requested Woolsey to act as Dean, and for a salary at the rate of $250 a year, spend a morning hour at the Dean's desk. He held this temporary office until July, 1903. Although he later gave himself no credit for his services as acting Dean, his influence was of considerable importance. He immediately set about studying the needs of the school, and on February 8, 1902, following suggestions made by Maurice Dwight Collier, a former lecturer in the school, presented to the Governing Board a memorandum setting forth the need for two professorships at $100,000 each, and for additional library funds of $30,000. He brought about closer relations between the Law School and the College,

33

later to be told in detail, and he instilled a friendly spirit into Law School life. In his "Historical Address," June 16, 1924, it is the last of these only to which he referred when he said: "I think my only contribution to the life of the school during that time, was the creation of what the students called the 'midway plaisance.' For years the Faculty had given the students a party once or twice in the winter. My idea was that the students should return the favor. We contributed a mild punch and cigars and our willing pupils did the rest. An Hawaiian, wreathed in flowers, sang his native airs. A Japanese told us how much easier his language was than ours. A Chinaman made one of the best speeches given in any language. Song and jest abounded and we were all young together."

Another of his projects was the beautifying of the lot back of Hendrie Hall. On March 15, 1902, he induced the Governing Board to vote $400 for laying out and planting it as a garden. In 1924, he wrote (*Historical Address*, p. 13), "there was a deep garden which I planted and watered. Flowering shrubs enclosed it; hedges bordered its lawn. This was the center of the school's Commencement festivity. But alas, in the war it was commandeered as a coal dump by the University with a promise of restoration which has never been redeemed."

"Midway plaisances" and such informalities were, as Woolsey said, things "too good to last." Important changes were impending. Chief among them was the election to the Deanship of Henry Wade Rogers. "He had been a professor of law and president of Northwestern University," wrote Woolsey. "He ruled us by law and ordinance, not by rule of thumb as our tendency was. He did us good but sometimes we resented the process."

Rogers had been at the school since the fall of 1900. On June 24, 1900, the Governing Board of the Law School

34

discussed the desirability of calling him, and on June 27, 1900, it voted to invite him to become an instructor for one year at a salary of $3,500. His appointment as "Lecturer in the Law School" was voted by the University Corporation on November 13, 1900. In the year 1901, the Governing Board twice, that is on February 19 and February 21, voted to lay on the table a motion of Simeon E. Baldwin that Rogers be promoted to a full professorship. Baldwin had become well acquainted with Rogers while they served together in the Section on Legal Education of the American Bar Association. Thereafter, on April 20, 1901, the Governing Board recommended to the Corporation that he be appointed professor of law, that he be required to teach not to exceed twelve hours a week, and that he be "requested to deliver a public inaugural address . . . before the Law School, the Faculty of the University and invited guests, in the auditorium of Hendrie Hall." The Corporation elected him professor of law on May 14, 1901, but no record has been found that he delivered an inaugural lecture. When Wayland's resignation from the Deanship became effective, June 30, 1903, President Hadley announced that Professor Rogers would succeed him. During the summer, William F. Foster resigned his post as Secretary of the Law School, and on November 29, 1903, John W. Edgerton was elected to serve in his place. The Corporation, on June 22, 1903, had already elected George Zahm instructor in law, and Arthur Linton Corbin, instructor in contracts. The latter had graduated from the Law School in 1899, and after four years of practice, at the age of twenty-nine, was then at the outset of a career as teacher, writer, and loyal supporter of the school, which was to have a permanently beneficial effect upon its destinies.

35

IV

SINCE the school was already well settled in Hendrie Hall when Rogers became Dean, the obvious next step was to improve the educational status of the institution. One notable advance in this direction had recently been made on the initiative and through the perseverance of Simeon E. Baldwin. On July 1, 1896, a new rule had gone into effect lengthening the regular course from two to three years. This change was one of Baldwin's pet projects. He began to advocate it as early as 1885, when he wrote in the *Columbia Jurist* (1:67, March 31) on "The Time Necessary to Get a Legal Education." He first formally presented the plan to the Governing Board of the Law School on June 13, 1888. Again on June 25, he brought up the subject, and procured the appointment of a committee to consider it, composed of Professors Robinson and Wayland and himself. The committee met at the Dean's residence on September 15, 1888, and as a result, in accordance with previous authorization, the scheme was printed and placed in the hands of members of the Law Faculty for examination. This leaflet, printed on the two inside pages of a folded sheet, bears the heading: "Confidential: for Members of the Law Faculty only. Heads of S.E.B.'s Scheme, as revised by the Committee, for 3 years course for LL.B. degree."

Read today, the proposals do not seem to be revolutionary, but in 1888, no law school insisted upon three years of resident study as a prerequisite for a degree. It required eight years to put the plan through, and then it was only in a modified form. The stumbling block was Head No. 1, "No LL.B. degree to be given, except on three years previous study." It did not propose that all three years must be in residence in the Yale Law School,

36

but it said that time was of the essence. There could be no doubling up of years. On this point the project stuck, and "Professor Baldwin's Scheme" was laid on the table at Governing Board meetings of November 30, 1888 and May 13, 1889. Nothing further appears to have transpired until March 27, 1893, when the Kent Club debated the subject, "Resolved that a law school course ought to cover three years" (*Yale Daily News*, March 27, 1893). Next year, October 10, 1894, the Governing Board "voted that Professor Baldwin and Professor Robinson be a committee to present for our consideration a modification of the plan, looking to the provision by which students might take the 3 year course in 2 years." The report, presented at a meeting held November 3, 1894, was recommitted with instructions to report on November 6. At that time agreement was reached; but on November 9, another meeting was held at which President Dwight was present. After prolonged discussion, it was "voted that the Governing Board recommend to the Corporation that the regular Law School course . . . be so arranged as to make the undergraduate course extend over three years and the graduate course over one additional year, reserving to the Faculty of the school the right to allow Bachelors of Arts and others who give satisfactory evidence of possessing the necessary ability and attainments to complete the undergraduate course in two years of study and be admitted to graduation upon passing satisfactory examinations upon all the required studies of the three years: this change not to affect students in attendance before that time." This recommendation was approved by the Corporation on November 13, 1894, the rule to become effective with the year 1896–1897. The announcement in the Law School bulletin for that year and thereafter was so worded as to discourage

37

attempts to graduate in the shorter time. "Bachelors of Arts of approved colleges," it reads, "will be permitted to complete the three years' course in two years, if they are able to do so; and the same privilege will be accorded to any others who in the judgment of the Faculty are qualified by their natural abilities or previous training to undertake so arduous a labor."

At last "S.E.B.'s Scheme," in part at least, was a reality. Beginning in 1897–1898, students in three undergraduate classes are listed in the bulletins as Junior, Middle, and Senior. These class names were dropped in 1903–1904, when they began to be known as the First, Second, and Third Year classes. We suspect, however, that Baldwin was not yet satisfied. At any rate, on February 4, 1902, the Governing Board voted "that from and after October, 1902, no one shall be allowed to endeavor to take all the studies of the undergraduate course in two years." The resolution then went on to provide for admittance to partial advanced standing of those graduates of approved colleges who had taken in their college courses the equivalent of five hours a week of strictly legal studies and had passed a creditable examination upon these studies. Examinations were required to be passed on all Law School undergraduate subjects not included in the credits accepted. This resolution, differently phrased, appeared first in the bulletin for 1902–1903, and marks the adoption of a full-fledged three-year course.

The lengthening of the undergraduate course from two to three years necessarily brought changes in the regulations for the graduate courses. The development of the courses to July 27, 1892, has been traced in a previous pamphlet. (*Yale Law Library Publications*, No. 4, p. 23–28.) The most striking change brought about by the

38

three-year-course regulation was the reduction to one year of the residence requirement for a graduate degree. This new arrangement came into effect on July 1, 1898. Both the M.L. and the D.C.L. degrees were provided for, the degree conferred being dependent upon the grade of excellence of the work done during the year, except that all candidates for a D.C.L. were required to take Roman law as a major study. Grading was by means of examinations and the submission of theses. The latter might be completed, *in absentia*, during the second year. To register for a graduate degree, a candidate must have received an LL.B., a B.C.L., or an M.L., after not less than three years of law study, but one year of practice could be presented by attorneys in lieu of one year of study, and properly recommended attorneys having five years of practice were exempt from the requirement of a law degree. The latter, however, could not receive the D.C.L. degree unless they were Bachelors of Arts, Philosophy, or Philology.

These regulations remained in force until the year 1907–1908, although candidates were regularly warned in the Annual Bulletin that two years of study would generally be found necessary in order to complete the work for the degree of D.C.L. On November 18, 1907, the Corporation approved a new set of rules, which differed from the foregoing chiefly in that candidates for the D.C.L. were required to possess both an academic bachelor's degree and a law-school degree; but an exception was made in favor of Yale Law School graduates, who, while lacking an academic degree, had obtained the Yale LL.B., *cum laude, magna cum laude*, or *summa cum laude*. Beginning in 1910–1911, by virtue of action by the Corporation on June 20, 1910, the exception in favor of Yale Law School graduates was rescinded, and thereafter

39

all candidates for the D.C.L. were required to possess both an academic degree and a law degree. On the same date the Corporation established the degree of Jur.Dr. (Doctor of Law) which might be taken under similar conditions by those who were not qualified in Roman law.

These rather involved regulations for the three graduate degrees were modified gradually, always in the direction of simplicity and the elimination of exceptions, so that in the first year of the deanship of Thomas W. Swan, an academic degree and a law degree were both prerequisites to admission to any graduate degree and two years of study were required for the D.C.L. The regulation, as it appears in the Annual Bulletin for 1916–1917, follows: "Admission to the graduate curriculum in law leading, after one year of advanced study, either to the degree of Master of Laws (LL.M.) or to that of Doctor of Law (Jur.Dr.) and, after two years of advanced study, to the degree of Doctor of Civil Law (D.C.L.) is granted, without examination, to persons holding a degree from an approved college or scientific school and also a degree from a law school belonging to the Association of American Law Schools or one having an equal standing."

Another educational problem that had been partially solved before Rogers became Dean was that of the relation of the Law School to the College. Educationally the two had been operating as though they were not parts of the same institution. Yale College students seemed unaware of the advantages offered by the Yale Law School. So much was this so, that on June 21, 1898, the Governing Board of the Law School appointed Dean Wayland and Professor Townsend to confer with the President and the College Faculty "with reference to ways and means to control the increasing annual exodus of Yale graduates to Harvard Law School." One way to accomplish this

40

would be to get students interested in the school before they graduated, and quite aside from the desire to meet competition, it was thought that such a plan would be educationally sound. November 17, 1898, Dean Wayland presented to the Corporation a memorial from the Law Faculty asking leave for "Seniors in College to count a part of their work for the LL.B. degree." This request was referred to a committee. On March 10, 1900, the Governing Board, having invited Professor John C. Schwab of the College Faculty to meet with them, discussed the subject of law electives for academic Seniors. Professors Baldwin and Woolsey were appointed a committee to confer with a similar College Faculty committee. May 19, 1900, the Governing Board received and accepted the report of this committee, to the effect that academic Seniors would be permitted to elect five hours of law work to count toward the B.A. degree. This was a recognition of the cultural value of law study, and it was referred to by Professor Townsend as "the Law School extension of the University principle." (*Yale Law Journal*, 10: 211–213, March, 1901.) Under this arrangement, from 1901 to 1904, an average of eighty-seven academic Seniors annually took a five-hour course covering parts of elementary law, evidence, contracts, and wills. In February, 1903, the Law Faculty urged the Prudential Committee to arrange for a further adjustment of courses between the Law School and the College, and as a consequence, after various committee conferences, reports, and recommendations, there was established what was known as the "combined course." In the year 1903–1904, academic Seniors were allowed to elect six hours of law courses to count toward a B.A. and also toward the LL.B. degree. Next year, 1904–1905, Seniors were allowed to elect eleven hours, and Juniors, three hours,

41

making in all fourteen hours which might give credits in both schools, so that a student might get both degrees in six years. This arrangement lasted until 1911. There followed various adjustments culminating in the requirement that Seniors who wished to count their last College year toward a law degree must give the whole year to law study. This was the status of the "combined course" until it was abandoned in 1930.

A question closely connected with the length of the law course and with the "combined course" was that of educational qualifications for entrance to the school. No important change in this respect was made between the years 1875 and 1901 (see *Yale Law Library Publications*, No. 4, p. 29–30), and in the latter year, the regulation which went into effect after adoption by the Governing Board on May 19, 1900, merely put the requirement on a par with those specified for entrance to the Sheffield Scientific School. President Hadley, in his report for 1901–1902 (p. 13–20), discussed at length the question whether it would be wise to require a B.A. degree for entrance to law and medical courses. He doubted the wisdom of such a requirement. On November 27, 1905, the Law Faculty decided that the time was still not ripe for a change; but in the next year, June 18, 1906, both the Governing Board and the Law Faculty, in their separate official capacities, recommended that entering students be required to have had the equivalent of two full years of college work, fifteen hours per week. The Corporation on June 25, 1906, approved this plan to become effective with the year 1909–1910. The impending change having been announced, there was a marked increase in the size of the first-year classes before September, 1909, and a marked decrease in them immediately after that date. Before it could be known what the ultimate effect of the

42

change would have been, the Corporation, February 20, 1911, approved further regulations recommended by the Governing Board, which went into effect with the year 1911–1912. These regulations raised the entrance requirements to four years of college work, except in the case of Yale College Seniors who had taken the "combined course." Since there had been no notice of this further change, the Dean was given special authority to admit students who satisfied him that their preparation had been made with a view to entering under the old rule. The school had not adjusted itself to this new regulation when the World War intervened. It was not until the year 1919 that the beneficial effects of the new rule could be observed under normal conditions. The final step in arriving at the present standard of entrance requirement was the abolition in 1930 of the "combined course," so that the four-year rule thereafter applied to Yale College students as well as to those of all other approved colleges.

The "Yale System" of instruction, and its modifications down to the year 1895, have been described in a previous pamphlet (*Yale Law Library Publications*, No. 4, p. 28–35). The minutes of the Law School Governing Board show that steadily from 1891 to 1901, the plan of printing individual cases was pursued, and that these cases, assembled into loose-leaf volumes, were sold to students to be used to supplement their textbooks. Cases and casebooks were used in the second and third years for intensified study of subjects which students had already taken as textbook and lecture courses in the first year. In 1903–1904, the case system first was used in third-year courses for subjects to which students had not previously been introduced. The final victory for the case method of instruction must be observed in the first-year courses. It was assumed that however well it might be adapted to

43

third-, and perhaps to second-year classes, it was too cumbersome a method to be used for first-year men. The older members of the Faculty were firmly convinced of this, yet they countenanced the use of the separately printed "Yale Cases," and Professor Watrous in his first-year course in torts used Chase's *Cases* along with Cooley's text. The tendency to use casebooks for first-year men was quickened when Arthur L. Corbin and John W. Edgerton joined the Faculty in 1903. Along with a textbook, at first Clark on Contracts and later Huffcut's Anson, Corbin used Hopkins' and later Williston's *Cases on Contracts*. Edgerton, beginning in 1907–1908, used both Mechem's *Cases* and Mechem's *Agency*, and in 1909–1910, he used both Goddard's *Cases* and his text on bailments. Professor Vance, in 1911–1912, used both of Mechem's books on agency. Although up to this year there was always a text assigned along with a casebook, the tendency had grown, especially in Corbin's classes, to teach by the study of cases. Formally, the rule still stood that the first-year courses were conducted by a modified form of the "Yale System." Each new text or casebook had to be specifically approved by the Faculty, and no outright adoption of the case method had been made. This finally came when the Law Faculty, on April 27, 1912, "*Resolved*, That in case the instructor in charge of any course shall prefer to make use of the case system of instruction in such course, he shall be permitted to do so, with the consent of the Dean." This resolution, it will be observed, applied to the first year, as well as to the two upper years. In the year 1912–1913, nearly every course in all three years was taught by casebooks only. Dean Rogers, in his report for 1911–1912 (p. 226–230), traced the stages by which the transition to the case method had come about at Yale, and gave his personal

44

endorsement of it. Some faculty members were not yet convinced, yet they bowed to the will of the majority. Theodore S. Woolsey was one of these. As late as June 16, 1924, in his *Historical Address*, p. 16, he held to his doubts on this reform. "The old way bred great lawyers," he said, "but like the caste mark of the Brahmin, the case system is the cachet of the crack law school of today."

Dean Rogers' report for 1911–1912, above referred to, ends with a summary of important events. "Since 1900," he wrote, "three great changes have been accomplished in the Law School, each of which is epoch-making in the history of the school, and each has been attained by gradual transition rather than by sudden and revolutionary methods. That these changes had to come will not be questioned by those who are familiar with the best thought concerning legal education. That it was best that they should come by gradual transition, and that they could not very well have been brought about in any other way under conditions as they exist here, will also not be questioned by those who have been familiar with the situation. The changes now accomplished are:

"1. A degree from a recognized college or scientific school is required as a condition of admission, except in the case of Yale College Seniors.

"2. The case system of instruction has displaced the former method of text-book instruction.

"3. The instruction is now given almost exclusively by resident professors who devote their entire time to the work of the School and who are withdrawn from the active practice of law."

The third and last of the above objectives was not one which could be said to have been accomplished on a given date, or to have been approved as a policy by formal

45

resolution. As early as 1871, the Reverend Timothy Dwight, afterwards President of Yale University, and Simeon E. Baldwin had urged that the school be staffed chiefly with full-time teachers. (*Yale Law Library Publications*, No. 4, p. 6–7.) Wayland was the first person to devote himself wholly to the school, and Theodore S. Woolsey, appointed three years later, 1876, was also a full-time man, in the sense that he had no other business or profession. For a few years prior to 1895, William C. Robinson gave most of his time to teaching. John Wurts and William Frederic Foster, appointed in 1895, came in as "resident" instructors, as did also Henry Wade Rogers in 1900. In 1902, Acting Dean Woolsey wrote that "it is the policy of the school to rely for instruction more and more upon its permanent staff." This policy was strengthened in 1903, as has already been noted, by the appointment of three full-time teachers, Arthur Linton Corbin, George Zahm, and John W. Edgerton. Charles Phineas Sherman joined them in 1905, and William Reynolds Vance (for three years only, but to return later) in 1909. Woolsey retired in 1911, ending a notable career in the school exceeded in length of service only by Baldwin's. Besides the full-time teachers above mentioned there were listed in 1911 as part-time teachers, Professors Baldwin, Prentice, Gager, Beach, Watrous, Beers, and Gordon E. Sherman; and there were also thirteen special lecturers.

The emphasis given the subject by Dean Rogers was, however, beneficial to the school, and new appointments, when older men retired, were on the basis of a full schedule of teaching. Thus in 1917–1918, it was announced that "there are ten resident professors who devote all of their time to the work of the school and are accessible from day to day in their offices at the law

46

building." A paragraph similar to this appeared regularly in the Law School Bulletin until 1927–1928, when it was omitted, doubtless because the fact was already too well known to require repetition.

Woolsey's withdrawal from the list of full-time teachers, mentioned above, and his appointment as Professor *Emeritus*, was an event worthy of notice in the history of the school. The Corporation, in regretfully accepting his resignation, laid emphasis on his loyalty to the University and the Law School and upon the important part which his wise counsel had played in many emergencies. An equally appreciative resolution was passed by the Law Faculty. Born on October 22, 1852, the son of President Theodore Dwight Woolsey, his whole life was connected with Yale University. He graduated from Yale College in 1872, and from the Law School in 1876. Immediately, he was made an instructor in public law, and two years later, April 1, 1878, he was elected Professor of International Law. (See *Yale Law Library Publications*, No. 4, p. 38–39.) He held this office continuously, with the exception of the years 1886 to 1890, when he resided in California for the benefit of his wife's health. As has been said, he was acting Dean of the Law School for two years, 1901 to 1903. His contributions to the subject of international law were important, but he did not seek to make them widely known. He was a modest, scholarly gentleman, who loved his work, but did not become excited about it. He would have been an ideal Oxford don, for he let his studies, his leisurely writing, his teaching, and his other duties to the school, fill his life. After his death in New Haven, on April 24, 1929, it became known that he had bequeathed to the University his collection of books on international law, as well as a fund to be used in maintaining it.

47

V

THE story of the origin, history, and growth of the Law Library down to the year 1894 has been told in some detail in previous pamphlets of this series, numbers 1, 3, and 4. Although the collection amounted during its last year in the court house only to about 12,000 volumes, it had long outgrown the library space allotted to it and had been spread about in other Law School rooms. Supervision was therefore difficult, and books were disappearing—leading one student to cast his vote, in the *Yale Shingle*, 1894, p. 69, for "replacement of confiscated books in the library." The Faculty recognized that such complaints were not fanciful, for it voted on November 3, 1894, that beginning with the next term there should be two student Assistant Librarians instead of one, and that the library hours, under supervision, should be 8:30 A.M. to 1 P.M., 2 to 5:15 P.M., and 7:30 to 10 P.M., Sundays excepted. Herbert J. Wyckoff was appointed to serve for the rest of the academic year 1894–1895, along with Charles V. Henry; and in subsequent years regular appointments were made by the Faculty and confirmed by the Prudential Committee. The following students served as Assistant Librarians down through the year 1902–1903,[3] the last in which such formal student appointments were made:

1895–1896	EDWARD T. BUCKINGHAM
	ROBERT S. ALEXANDER
1896–1897	EDWARD T. BUCKINGHAM
	LORING V. STEWART
1897–1898	PHILIP Z. HANKEY
	HUGH B. CHACE

3. For a list of Assistant Librarians, 1888–1895, see *Yale Law Library Publications*, No. 4, p. 61.

48

1898–1899 ERNEST H. WELLS
           CHARLES H. STUDINSKI
1899–1900 ERNEST H. WELLS
           HORACE G. EASTBURN
1900–1901 HORACE G. EASTBURN
           JAMES T. ADAMS
1901–1902 EDWARD H. KELLY
           GEORGE T. BICKLEY
1902–1903 HOWARD B. SNOW
           RALPH C. BENEDICT

The office of Law Librarian, from 1895 to the present, has been occupied by six persons, as indicated by the following list:[4]

1895–1896 WILLIAM TRUMBULL
1896–1906 PHILIP PATTERSON WELLS
1906–1909 CHARLES PHINEAS SHERMAN
1909   EDWIN RUTHVEN KELSEY, Acting Librarian
1909–1917 HENRY WESTBROOK WINFIELD
1917–1928 EDWIN MONTEFIORE BORCHARD
1928–   FREDERICK CHARLES HICKS

William Trumbull served as Law Librarian from January 1, 1895 to February 1, 1896. His appointment was the occasion for increasing the emolument of the office from $800 to $1,000. He was given extra funds to spend for books, enabling him to purchase the National Reporter System, and it fell to his lot to arrange for the removal of the library, in the spring vacation (March 28 to April 11, 1895), from the county court house to the rear section of Hendrie Hall. For this task he employed students, who made the transfer at first by means of push-carts, and later with the assistance of an open two-horse truck. When the books were displayed on the new shelves in the reading room and stacks, on the third floor

4 For a list of Law Librarians, 1845–1868, see *Yale Law Library Publications*, No 3, p 62; for those from 1869–1894, see *Yale Law Library Publications*, No 4, p. 56

49

of the building, surprise was shown that the school possessed such a good library, especially in the way of English Reports, some of which students had had no access to in the court house. This job done, Trumbull resigned. Born on December 25, 1861, in Valparaiso, Chile, he was a direct descendant of Governor Jonathan Trumbull, of Connecticut. In Yale College, from which he graduated in 1883, he was an editor both of the *Yale News* and the *Yale Literary Magazine*. From 1883 to 1887 he taught school and engaged in business, and then entered Yale Law School from which he graduated *magna cum laude* in 1889. On March 30, 1891 he married Anne Leavenworth Train of Albany, New York. From 1890 to 1896, he practiced law in the office of Simeon E. Baldwin, doubtless through whose influence he was induced to become Yale Law Librarian. After his resignation, he resided in Litchfield, Connecticut, but made many trips abroad. He devoted himself chiefly to writing, and was the author of books relating to social problems. He died on January 11, 1933, and was buried in Milford, Connecticut.

Philip Patterson Wells, who followed Trumbull, was the first incumbent who brought to the place special qualifications, and who paid attention to the professional side of librarianship. He was a native of Grand Rapids, Michigan, where he was born February 5, 1868. He entered Yale College in 1885, won honors as a student and acclaim as an athlete, and graduated in 1889. In the Graduate School, he was Macy Fellow in the social sciences from 1889 to 1891, a connection through which in the year 1900 he earned the Doctorate of Philosophy. He studied law in the Yale Law School, 1891–1892, and the following year, 1892–1893, in the Columbian Law School, in Washington, D.C., where he had gone to join

50

Hendrie Hall Reading Room

the staff of the West Publishing Company and serve as an editor of the *Supreme Court Reporter*, the *Federal Reporter*, and *Federal Cases*. On May 22, 1893, he married Eleanor Duncan Munger, of New Haven, and in 1894, he returned to New Haven to practice law in partnership with Henry G. Newton (LL.B. 1872). This professional relationship was continued even after he became Law Librarian on February 1, 1896, and while he served also as an instructor in evidence, 1898–1899, and as a College lecturer in history, 1902 to 1906. In February, 1906, he resigned his various offices, gave up his law practice, and joined the law department of the United States Forestry Service, Washington, D.C. From 1907 to 1910 he was chief law officer of that service, under Gifford Pinchot; in 1910–1911, he was counsel for the National Conservation Association; from 1911 to 1913, he was chief law officer of the United States Reclamation Service, and special adviser to the Secretary of the Interior; from 1913 to 1923, he practiced law, first in Washington, D.C., and later in Middletown, Connecticut; and from 1923 to 1927, he was Deputy Attorney-General of Pennsylvania. He died in San Francisco, on March 12, 1929, mourned by a host of friends and former associates who respected his ability and treasured the memory of his friendship.[5]

The ten years of his connection with the Law School as officer were of great importance to the Law Library. He was the first to use an accession book here, and he devised and put into effect a scheme of classification in which symbols placed on the books indicated their location in relation to each other, and he and his assistants prepared a shelf-list in loose-leaf form which listed every item in the library in the order of the arrangement on the shelves. The notation adopted by Wells continued to be used by

5 See tribute by Lewis S. Welch in *Yale Alumni Weekly*, April 26, 1929.

51

his successors until the year 1917. It was Wells also who made the first card catalogue of the Law Library. One of his first acts, February 13, 1896, was to induce the Governing Board to authorize the purchase of "a suitable outfit for a card catalogue." Up to that time the only catalogues had been in the form of ledgers in which the titles of books were written. (See *Yale Law Library Publications*, No. 4, p. 62–64.) In his report for 1899–1900, which was the first printed annual report of the Law Library, he said that since 1896, a "short-title card index" of 11,000 volumes had been made and that 4,000 volumes yet remained to be catalogued. In 1901, the library began to use printed catalogue cards procured from the Library of Congress, but progress was slow because of frequent changes in assistants. There were no longer student Assistant Librarians formally appointed by the Prudential Committee, but there were student assistants. In 1903–1904, four were employed in this way.[6] The library was growing, had now expanded into the front section of Hendrie Hall, and constant use was being made of it. Stimulated by the example of Maurice Dwight Collier, B.A. 1866, who was providing the library annually with the reports and statutes of the state of Missouri, Wells urged law alumni to assume a like responsibility for other states. This plan was difficult to put into operation, but eventually proved to be a very effective method of enriching the library. The Governing Board authorized the Librarian from time to time to order state digests and compilations of statutes, and to keep the continuing sets down to date. Students began to ask that the reading room be kept open on Sunday. With longer hours and more active use, emphasis had to be placed on

6. No professionally trained Assistant Librarian was appointed until 1918, when Miss Elizabeth Forgeus began her present term of service.

52

regulations which to some students seemed like useless "red-tape." A new conception of what a law school library should be was forming. In 1902, Acting Dean Woolsey included in a list of needs of the school an additional library fund of $30,000; and students began to ask for systematic instruction in the use of law books. On April 20, 1901, the Governing Board invited Mr. Wells to give five lectures on that subject. Eventually two series of exercises were given, one by Mr. Wells on "the use of the library," and one by Mr. James E. Wheeler on "looking up the law."

An event of great importance for the school happened during Mr. Wells' librarianship. This was the deposit in the Law School Library of Albert Sproull Wheeler's private collection of books on Roman law. From 1872 to 1897, when he retired on a pension, Mr. Wheeler was an instructor in German in the Sheffield Scientific School. When graduate courses were established in the Law School in 1876, Mr. Wheeler, who was a profound student of classical history and institutions, had been made an instructor in Roman law. At the time of his retirement from work in the Sheffield Scientific School, he did not resign from his instructorship in the Law School, but the change in his circumstances made the upkeep of his large library more burdensome. At this juncture, October 29, 1897, the Governing Board offered him "the sum of $250 to be expended in the purchase of books for his library," and this amount was paid to him on November 1 (Law School Treasurer's Account Book, p. 275). Four years later, 1901, at Mr. Wheeler's suggestion, the school fitted up a room in the law building to receive the collection. The terms of the arrangement were given by Mr. Wells in his report for 1901–1902 as follows: "Mr. Wheeler retains the custody of the books and will admit his stu-

53

dents and other investigators to the use of them as he may see fit. The librarian has had the books arranged in order and a card list of them made. The collection contains about 1,000 volumes." He prepared also a list on sheets which has been preserved. Mr. Wheeler died on January 30, 1905, and on that day the Law Faculty adopted appropriate memorial minutes, announced the suspension of school exercises on the afternoon of his funeral, and arranged for commemorative exercises to be held in Hendrie Hall on May 9. The addresses then delivered were published in a separate pamphlet. By his will, Mr. Wheeler gave to the University his collection of books, and a fund of $17,858.07, the income of which is used to purchase additions to it. Thus began the present Roman law and foreign law collections, which have been much enlarged by gifts and by purchases with Law Library funds, as well as with the income of the Wheeler Fund.

Constant reminders of Mr. Wells' work in the school as Librarian and as instructor are 200 volumes from his personal library, presented to the school in 1936 by his widow, Mrs. Eleanor D. Wells.

For three years beginning February 1, 1906, the post of Law Librarian was filled by Charles Phineas Sherman. Mr. Sherman graduated from Yale College in 1896, from the Law School in 1898, and became a Doctor of Civil Law in 1899. During the last illness of Professor Wheeler, Dr. Sherman, beginning January 26, 1905, was engaged to carry on the work in Roman law, and in the following June he was made an instructor. To these duties were added those of Law Librarian, and also those of Curator of the Wheeler Collection. In 1907, he was promoted to be an Assistant Professor, and he continued in this capacity, as well as in his curatorship, until the year 1917.

54

Since then, he has been called to teach his chosen subject in several institutions, and has written extensively upon Roman law. On February 15, 1909, the Corporation regretfully accepted Dr. Sherman's resignation as Law Librarian, to take effect March 23. Dean Rogers, in his annual report for 1908–1909, highly commended Dr. Sherman's administration of the library. He had efficiently organized the work of his student assistants, had provided equal opportunities for all to use the books, had made progress toward completing the card catalogue, had brought about the installation of electric lights in the reading room and bookstacks, and more important still, had substantially enriched the collection itself. He was fortunate in being Librarian at a time when large accessions could be made of British colonial law reports, when the Cole Collection of American statute law was purchased, and when the Blackstone Collection was presented to the school. The last of these, a gift from the Honorable Macgrane Coxe, has been briefly described in the *Yale Law Library Manual*, 1937, p. 22–26 (*Yale Law Library Publications*, No. 5); and is the subject of a bibliographical catalogue prepared by Mrs. Catherine S. Eller, a Senior Cataloguer in the Yale Law Library (*Yale Law Library Publications*, No. 6).

The Cole Collection, as purchased from Theodore L. Cole in 1907, consisting of 3,364 volumes of American session laws and revisions of statutes, was the nucleus of the present very much larger collection now in the Law Library. In order to make possible the purchase of this collection at a cost of $15,000, the Governing Board appropriated $4,000, the University advanced $6,000 out of Law School funds, and the balance needed was made up by the following gifts to the Wayland Memorial Fund, specifically for that purpose: Cyrus La Rue Munson and

55

Henry F. English each gave $1,000; Simeon E. Baldwin and Thomas Thacher each gave $500; Theodore S. Woolsey, Henry W. Farnam, John W. Alling, and James B. Dill each gave $250; John H. Perry gave $120; Walter F. Frear, John K. Beach, George D. Watrous, Henry Stoddard, Burton Mansfield, Leonard M. Daggett, Edwin B. Gager, James H. Webb, and Samuel O. Prentice each gave $100; and David E. Fitzgerald, Howard C. Webb, Benjamin Slade, and John W. Bristol each gave $25.

On October 26, 1908, the Law Faculty approved the action of Dr. Sherman in appointing as Deputy Librarian, Mr. Edwin Ruthven Kelsey, B.A. 1897, LL.B. 1899, to serve during the serious illness which led to his decision to give up the office. After Dr. Sherman's resignation, Mr. Kelsey served as Acting Librarian from April, 1909 until August. On August 6, 1909, the Prudential Committee confirmed the appointment of Henry Westbrook Winfield as Law Librarian, at an annual salary of $1,250.

Mr. Winfield was born in Jersey City, New Jersey, on January 4, 1857. He graduated from Rutgers College in 1876, received the degree of Master of Arts from his *Alma Mater* in 1879, and in the same year graduated from the Columbia University Law School. For ten years, 1889 to 1899, he was counsel for the Board of Health of Hudson County, New Jersey. At the time of his appointment as Law Librarian, he was practicing law in Jersey City. There is little evidence that he took interest in law library technique or in the details of administration, but he was an enthusiastic bibliographer, and he made himself an authority on American session laws. He had a profound respect for well-made volumes and he disliked to see them neglected. His annual reports contain detailed accounts of the methods by which he brought life back into old leather bindings, and of his efforts to rebind

56

Dean Henry Wade Rogers

volumes in an appropriate manner. He contrasted cheap modern "edition" bindings with those of earlier days, and in his report for 1912–1913 gave the following eloquent description of a volume after his own heart: "Here," said he, "is a volume published in Virginia in 1845, the first of Grattan's Reports; it is bound in good sheep, sumac tanned and still of its original fine bistre-buff color; it is stretched over boards as dense as ivory as flat and sharp at the corners as when made; it is stitched with the best linen thread that shows no sign of wear; the wove paper is thick and smooth and not made ponderous with whiting and paste, the printing clear and without blemish from cover to cover—in short, a book gotten up on honor for men of honor willing to pay its value."

His reports abound with statistics of the growth of the library, and beginning in 1910–1911, he began to prophesy that soon there would be no room in Hendrie Hall for the annual accessions, because of the "ultra-Malthusian ratio of increase in the number of State reports." The library was indeed growing faster than had been anticipated when Hendrie Hall was planned, and this was so despite decreased expenditures when the income of the school was reduced in 1909 following the change in entrance requirements. Winfield hammered away year after year on this problem of space, until Dean Rogers was convinced. The latter's annual reports, beginning with the year 1912–1913, urged first, that there should be built near at hand a separate law library building with shelving for at least 100,000 volumes, or secondly, that a new Law School building should be provided large enough for all needs of the school including its library. This insistence of Winfield, supported by Dean Rogers, that the library and the school had "passed the day of small things," and that the problem of growth must be faced, was the begin-

57

ning of the agitation which culminated in the erection of the Sterling Law Buildings. Mr. Winfield resigned his position in July, 1917, and he died in London, England, on May 23, 1926.

The subsequent history of the Law Library under Professor Edwin M. Borchard and the present incumbent lies beyond the scope of the present pamphlet. As an indication that library growth is scarcely predictable, it should, however, be noted that in the period of Professor Borchard's stewardship the library grew from 42,551 volumes to 100,508 volumes, and that on July 1, 1938, the total was 233,103 volumes.[7]

VI

THE creative period of Henry Wade Rogers' deanship came to an end when on September 28, 1913, the United States Senate confirmed his nomination as a Judge of the United States Circuit Court of Appeals for the Second Circuit. After that time his chief interest was elsewhere. It is true that while he was still Dean, that is, until 1916, three notable teachers joined the Faculty—William Howard Taft, Ralph Waldo Gifford, and Wesley Newcomb Hohfeld—but their work and influence in the school tie up best with the administration of Dean Thomas Walter Swan. Under Rogers, in 1913, the Yale Law School had already become a graduate professional school, the case method of instruction had been officially approved and adopted, the superiority of instruction by a "resident" faculty had been conceded, and a library had been assembled large enough to raise the question of a new building, either for the library alone or for all of the purposes of the school.

7 For a description of the arrangement, classification, catalogue, and scope of the library in 1937, see *Yale Law Library Publications*, No. 5.

58

When Dean Rogers joined the Law Faculty in November, 1900, he had already had a distinguished career. He was born in Holland Patent, near Utica, New York, on October 10, 1853. He was reared by an uncle after whom he was named, and who lived at first in Buffalo, New York, and later in Ann Arbor, Michigan. He attended Hamilton College, Clinton, New York, for one year, but took his arts degree (1874) and his law degree (1877) at the University of Michigan. On June 22, 1876, he married Emma Ferndon Winner, of Pennington, New Jersey, and in 1877 he was admitted to the Michigan bar. From 1877 to 1880, he was engaged in general law practice in Minneapolis, Minnesota, and in New Jersey; but, returning to Ann Arbor in 1882, he was appointed Tappan Professor of Law at the University. In 1885, he succeeded Judge Thomas M. Cooley as Dean of the Law School. As professor and Dean he was so successful, that in 1890, he was called to the Presidency of Northwestern University, at Evanston, Illinois. In the same year he received the degree of Doctor of Laws from Wesleyan University. He maintained his interest in legal education, and in 1893, served as chairman of the Chicago World's Congress on Jurisprudence and Law Reform. He had been, since 1889, a member of the American Bar Association's standing Committee on Legal Education and Admission to the Bar, and he was later, 1905–1907, to be chairman of it. The Association's Section on Legal Education, initiated at Saratoga in August, 1892, and organized under the temporary chairmanship of Simeon E. Baldwin at Milwaukee, August 30, 1893, chose him to be its first permanent chairman. He presided at the meeting held in Saratoga, August 22–24, 1894, and read an address on the state of legal education in the United States. In 1898, he was chairman of the Saratoga Conference on the

59

Foreign Policy of the United States. The circumstances under which he joined the Yale Law Faculty and his work as professor and Dean from 1900 to September, 1913, have already been described in detail. (See Sections III, IV, V.) During this period he remained active in bar association affairs, and in 1906, he was president of the Association of American Law Schools. In 1910, he was a delegate to the Conference on Uniform State Laws, and to the International Prison Conference, held in Washington, D.C.

In 1913, when he became a judge, he resigned his position as Dean, but was requested by the Governing Board of the Law School to continue to act until his successor was appointed. The Corporation, on January 17, 1916, elected Thomas W. Swan to be Dean of the Law School and Hotchkiss Professor of Law, the duties of the deanship to be assumed on July 1, 1916. In the school's Annual Bulletin for 1915–1916, Rogers is listed as Dean, and Swan as Dean-elect. Thereafter Rogers' name appears only in the list of professors. He had been obliged in November, 1913, to give up most of his teaching, and an adjustment of salary had been made accordingly. From 1916 to 1921, when he became Professor *Emeritus*, he did less and less teaching, because his judicial duties filled all of his time. The subjects that he is listed as having taught from 1900 to 1921 are equity, insurance, trusts, private corporations, and municipal corporations. Although he was progressive in educational administration, as has been shown, he was himself a teacher of the old school who taught by the textbook and recitation method, and he was one of the last in the institution to change to the case method of instruction. He demanded of his classes almost literal memorization of assignments of text, and the unprepared student was suavely held up

60

to scorn. After putting a question to a student standing before him, he would say, "Tell me all you know about it"; and when no answer had been given, and a second student had arisen, Rogers would say, "Do you agree with all that Mr. X has told us?" Woolsey described him as a good disciplinarian and an intensive teacher.

Throughout his life Dean Rogers was an active churchman. In 1890, he was a member of the Ecumenical Conference of the Methodist Episcopal Church, held in Washington, D.C., and from 1908 to 1926, he was chairman of the Judiciary Committee of the General Conference of that church, of which for twenty-five years he was recognized as the leading layman. In 1910, he was President of the Peace Congress of New England states; from 1914 to 1926, he was a trustee of the Church Peace Union; and from 1922 until his death, he was President of the National Council of Religion in Higher Education.

The qualities which made him successful in church government fitted him also for politics, for which he had a taste. He was effective as a political speaker and was in demand as a convention orator. At the Connecticut Democratic State Convention in 1910, when Simeon E. Baldwin became the party's candidate for Governor, Rogers made the nominating speech; and two years later in Baltimore he presented Governor Baldwin to the Democratic National Convention as Connecticut's candidate for the Presidential nomination. It was on Baldwin's recommendation that President Wilson appointed Rogers to the Federal judicial bench, in succession to Judge Walter C. Noyes. In political life as well as in legal education, there was effective coöperation between Rogers and Baldwin.

His colleague on the bench, Judge Charles M. Hough, said of him that he was most at home in equity cases, and

61

those "that had or might have a social and even a political effect." Though he had always been conspicuous for his ability as an administrator, the administrative work of the court, while he was presiding judge from 1921 to 1926, was distasteful to him. Since he had had little experience as an attorney, and had learned his law as a teacher, he frankly sought help from his associates in matters of procedure, and, said Hough, "needed to be told what tricks of the trade were only half concealed in some fairly printed pages of motions and supporting affidavits." He was apt to disregard the technicalities in an appeal brief, and serenely to inquire "whether the result below was first consonant with sound morals, and second, agreeable to the law as taught in the books." There was need for a judge of this caliber and point of view, and undoubtedly he acquitted himself well in the new career to which he devoted thirteen years of his life. He suffered a slight paralytic stroke in May, 1926, apparently recovered his health, and then died suddenly at his summer home, Pennington, New Jersey, on August 16, 1926. His funeral was held on August 19 at the Madison Avenue Methodist Episcopal Church, New York City, where also was held a memorial service on November 21. The addresses delivered at this service, and the other tributes which were printed in a commemorative volume, illustrate the four phases of his life. Judge Hough spoke of him as a jurist; Professor Irving Fisher, as an educator; Dr. David G. Downey, as a churchman; and editorials from Connecticut newspapers dealt with his political affiliations. The *New York Times* reviewed his many-sided career, but concluded that "the Yale Law School is his sufficient and lasting monument."

A year and a half later, March 19, 1928, his portrait, painted by Eben F. Comins, at the request and expense

62

of Mrs. William M. Thompson, a sister of Judge Rogers, was presented to the court over which he had presided.[8] The presentation, under the auspices of a committee of the Connecticut State Bar Association, was made by Terence F. Carmody, President of that Association, and a response was made by Presiding Judge Martin T. Manton. Mr. Carmody described Judge Rogers as "aristocratic in appearance, well poised, with head and eyes of a thinker, and a nose and mouth indicative of strength and determination. His manner was reserved and refined. He had a dignified and commanding presence; and was an eloquent speaker, gifted with an agreeable voice."

In a funeral address, the Reverend Ralph W. Sockman, minister of his church, spoke of Rogers' attractive personality, his humor, tireless energy, and "shrewdly instinctive knowledge of men." "His was a brilliant, but not a meteoric career." Undoubtedly it was a career lived at a high level. He was not a natural student, and he did not become a great legal scholar. But he was a builder, an organizer, who saw things in the large, and never immersed himself in details. There was something of the statesman in everything that he did. He looked always for broad trends and large results, but, curiously enough, as shown by the long series of his annual reports while he was Dean, he had a taste for recording meticulously the details of progress made toward achieving those results.

VII

FOR fifty-nine years, Simeon E. Baldwin was an official of the Yale Law School, fifty-one years as instructor and professor, and eight years as professor *emeritus*. Between

8 On June 15, 1936, a replica of this picture, also painted by Mr Comins, was presented to the Yale Law School by William Dean Embree, on behalf of the Class of 1905 L, and it now hangs in the reading room

63

his entrance to college and his death stretched a period of seventy years, during only five of which his name was absent from the rolls either as student or teacher. He came of a distinguished Yale family. His great-grandfather, Roger Sherman, signer of the Declaration of Independence, was an Honorary Master of Arts, 1768, and Treasurer of the College, 1765–1776. His grandfather, Simeon Baldwin, graduated from Yale College in 1781, and was a tutor from 1783 to 1786. His father, Roger Sherman Baldwin, Governor of Connecticut, 1844–1846, United States Senator, 1847–1851, graduated from Yale College in 1811, as Governor was an *ex officio* Fellow, and received an LL.D. from Yale in 1845.

Simeon Eben Baldwin lived up to these great traditions both as a Yale man and as a citizen. It is of his Yale connections and of his life as an educator that this sketch must chiefly deal. To write of all phases of his career with equal particularity would here be inappropriate, even if it were possible. What is now said about him as lawyer, judge, writer, and public man, provides only a screen against which his life at Yale may be projected.

After his admission to the bar in 1863, he gave full thirty years to general law practice, with emphasis on railroad law. The next seventeen years he served as Judge of the Connecticut Supreme Court of Errors, from 1908 to 1910 as Chief Justice. Retired because he had reached the constitutional age limitation of seventy, he again opened his law office which he maintained until nearly the end of his life. He was an outstanding success as a lawyer, being in "the front rank of a State bar distinguished for its ability." Ceaseless industry, attention to details, patience, wide reading, unfailing if rather formal courtesy were attributes which served him well both as a lawyer and judge. He gave to each written

64

opinion the care usually accorded to a formal essay. His meaning was never in doubt. While he signed his name to no epoch-making decisions, he was conceded to be a learned and just judge. Governor McLean, at the John Marshall Day exercises, February 4, 1901, called him "the John Marshall of Connecticut."

It was the wonder of his contemporaries, as it is now of their successors, that while living the full life of lawyer and judge he could, as Judge J. K. Beach put it (106 Conn. 735), find "time to acquire an international reputation as scholar and author in the outlying fields of jurisprudence, comparative law, social science and colonial history, as well as in the field of substantive law." The list of his writings fills many closely printed pages. Many of his addresses were before learned societies of which he was a member, and of some of which he was President. He was one of the founders of the American Bar Association, served on its Executive Committee from 1878 to 1888, was its President in 1890, and was a director of its Bureau of Comparative Law for twelve years. A few of the other associations of which he was President, and before which he spoke, were the International Law Association, the Association of American Law Schools, the American Historical Association, the American Political Science Association, the Social Science Association, the Connecticut Academy of Arts and Sciences, and the Connecticut Society of the Archaeological Institute of America. A little-known fact about him is that in the year 1888, with Clarence Deming and Professor Henry W. Farnam, he purchased the *New Haven Morning News*, which he edited until 1894. He had an intense pride in New Haven, served on its Common Council and on its Public Parks Commission, and was President for long periods of its Young Men's Christian Association, the

65

New Haven Congregational Club, the New Haven Hospital, and the New Haven Colony Historical Society. He was assiduous in attention to the duties and privileges of any organization with which he became associated. For example, in 1872 he joined "The Club," an informal group of New Haven intellectuals which met in the members' houses. In the period from 1872 to 1913, he attended most of its meetings and led the discussions once and often twice each year. The breadth of his interest is illustrated by the wide range of topics chosen.

His personality was the direct opposite of the popular politician's, but his great ability and his profound sense of civic obligation brought him into political life. In 1867, he was a Republican candidate for state senator, but was defeated. In 1884, although he was President of the Republican organization in Connecticut, he was one of the independents who refused to support James G. Blaine for the Presidency. From that time on he was a member of the Democratic party. Incidental mention has already been made of his service as Governor of Connecticut from 1910 to 1914, and of his presentation as Connecticut's candidate for the Democratic Presidential nomination in 1912. He received twenty votes from Connecticut and Vermont. In 1914, he was the unsuccessful Democratic candidate for United States Senator. Regardless of his political affiliations, he was constantly called upon by his state to help in governmental reorganization. He was a member of commissions to revise educational laws in 1872, to revise all state statutes, 1873, to simplify legal procedure, 1878, and to revise the *Connecticut Statutes*, 1875. In 1885, he was a member of a commission to report to the General Assembly on methods of taxation, and he wrote a report proposing a better system. In 1915–1917, he was chairman of a commission to revise the tax laws.

66

All of these activities redounded to the credit of the Yale Law School, with which during the whole time he was intimately connected.

Simeon E. Baldwin's first public appearance at Yale College was at the Commencement exercises on August 20, 1846. Elizur Goodrich, first Professor of Law in Yale College (see *Yale Law Library Publications*, No. 1, p. 3–4) was then eighty-five years old, but was still serving as Secretary of the Corporation. "At Commencement exercises," he wrote Frederick J. Kingsbury (*Yale Law Journal*, 1:238, June, 1892), "he sat at the President's left hand at a table containing the degrees, six in a roll, and handed them to a page, generally a lad of eight or ten, selected for his presentable appearance and courteous manner, who in turn handed them to the President as the candidates came forward, six at a time, to receive them. The last page under Mr. Goodrich's administration was Master Simeon E. Baldwin."

At that time the young Baldwin was in his seventh year of age. He was born in New Haven on February 5, 1840, and he prepared for college in the Hopkins Grammar School, of which throughout his life he was a devoted supporter. For many years, he was President of its board of trustees, and he took pride in referring to it as the fourth oldest institution of learning in the United States. He entered Yale College in September, 1857, being then in his eighteenth year. He took part in the extra-curricular activities of the College, being a member of the Baseball Club, the Cymothoe Boat Club, and the Chess Club. Of the last of these he was President, and in 1860, he was Vice-president of the Republican Club. He was a member of Brothers in Unity, Alpha Sigma Phi, Psi Upsilon, and Skull and Bones. In 1860–1861, he was one of the editors of the *University Quarterly*, a periodical issued by students

67

from several American and European colleges, and he contributed three signed articles to it. Not until his Junior year did his name appear among those who distinguished themselves for scholarship, a fact perhaps not unconnected with the regulation which excluded Freshmen and Sophomores from using the College library. He was the English Philosophical Orator at the Junior Exhibition of his class, received one of the Berkeley Premiums for excellence in Latin composition, and was in two successive terms a prize winner in English composition. In his Senior year, he was elected to Phi Beta Kappa, and won a Townsend Premium in English composition, as well as the Berkeley Scholarship of $46.00 awarded each year to the student "who passes the best examination in the Greek Testament (Pauline Epistles), the first book of Thucydides, and the first six books of Homer's Iliad, Cicero's Tusculan Questions, Tacitus (except the Annals) and Horace; provided he remains in New Haven as a graduate one, two or three years." He delivered the Salutatory oration at his Commencement exercises.

As a Senior, he listened to fourteen lectures on the Constitution of the United States delivered by Henry Dutton, Kent Professor of Law in the College, and head of the Law School. These lectures, and his Berkeley Scholarship, made natural the transition to the Law School, where he spent the year 1861–1862, while working also in his father's law office. Being "liberally educated," he could have received his law degree after eighteen months of attendance, but he chose rather to spend one term, beginning in September, 1862, in the Harvard Law School. Thus he did not receive the LL.B. degree from either school. After further study in his father's office, he was admitted to the Connecticut bar on September 4, 1863.

68

The circumstances under which, after only five years of law practice, he substituted for Henry Dutton as teacher in the Law School and thus began his long career as an educator, have already been told in detail. (See *Yale Law Library Publications*, No. 4, p. 1–8.) He taught in Yale College as well as in the Law School. On March 25, 1873, the Corporation invited him to lecture to College Seniors on the Constitution of the United States, his compensation to be the income of the Kent Professorship Fund. After Henry Dutton's death in 1869, that professorship was vacant until 1881. Baldwin was only thirty-three years of age, and had not yet acquired the prestige required of a successor to Daggett, Bissell, and Dutton; and so he was listed in the College catalogue as lecturer on the elements of jurisprudence and American constitutional law. An incident leading up to this appointment may have been his invitation to the College Seniors to spend Friday evening, June 7, 1872, at his home, to meet the Law Faculty. The class, in the *Yale Courant* for June 12, 1872, thanked him for his hospitality but added, "We hope he will not think that the small attendance was from lack of appreciation. The class had all been out late the night before and had not recovered from the fatigue." From time to time he lectured at other institutions, for example, at Howard University, on wills, for several years beginning in 1895, and at Vassar College, on American law, in 1917. He was the Dodge lecturer on the Responsibilities of Citizenship, at Yale University in 1911.

The record of the long list of subjects that he taught at various times in the Yale Law School is remarkable for the versatility which it displays. These subjects, as described in the annual announcements, and roughly in the order in which he took them up, are the following:

69

constitutional law, commercial law, wills, contracts, Roman law, comparative jurisprudence, nature and history of American law, United States courts, railroad law, American constitutional history, study of modern European legislation, political history, conflict of laws, administration of estates, practice, private corporations, Code Napoléon, mercantile law, agency, partnership, bills and notes, bankruptcy and insolvency, American law, public corporations, criminal law, trusts, and legal ethics. The subjects that he taught for the longest uninterrupted periods were constitutional law, American law (variously designated from time to time), conflict of laws, and corporations. At the time of his retirement he was lecturing on legal ethics, and conducting an auxiliary course in required readings. Fifty-one years of such day-to-day teaching would have become boresome to anyone imbued with a less inflexible sense of duty than was Baldwin. It was said of him that "he considered it his duty to do his best in all things he attempted, whatever the task, small or great." He carried on with unflagging interest to the end. Students voted him the "most difficult to recite to," and "the hardest to bluff," nevertheless they named him second only to William K. Townsend as "favorite teacher," and second only to John Wurts as "best teacher."

He reached the age of sixty-eight on February 5, 1908, and therefore ordinarily would not have taught in the next year. On June 22, 1908, however, the Corporation voted "that the rule requiring retirement at sixty-eight shall not apply in the case of Chief Justice Baldwin at the close of the present year, and that he be requested to continue his instruction in the Law School until further action by the Corporation." A year later, February 6, 1909, the Prudential Committee voted "that persons

70

asked to continue instruction beyond retiring age be appointed from year to year," and therefore, from then on until his retirement, his appointment was renewed annually. After his term as Chief Justice was ended, and while he was Governor of Connecticut, he wrote, on November 18, 1911, the following letter to President Hadley, who presented it to the Prudential Committee two days later: "I do not care to continue my present teaching work in the Law School after June, 1912, which will complete the forty-fourth year in which I have given instruction there. I would be willing, if it were desired, to continue my lectures on legal ethics to third year men, and on the Outlines of American law to first year men, at a salary of $200, retaining my present titular position as Professor (not Professor *Emeritus*). I should not accept a retiring pension." Under this arrangement, he continued his active Law School connection for seven years until, on April 21, 1919, the Corporation accepted his resignation to take effect July 1, 1919. He held the title of Professor *Emeritus* until his death on January 30, 1927.

Baldwin was much more than a patient, industrious, and learned teacher. He was an educator in a larger sense. There were intimations of this in an article which he contributed to the *University Quarterly*, April, 1860, when he was only twenty years of age. "Nowhere is it more important that reform should enter," wrote this college Junior, "than into our colleges, where the leaders of the next generation are being trained to use the power that they are to wield. . . . There is much in the way of reform to be accomplished, and agitation is the only way to effect it." Agitation is not precisely the word to describe his methods in later life. Rather was he persistent in the quiet presentation of well-laid plans the intrinsic worth of which would commend them to his associates. He always

71

took the long view of educational policy. Theodore S. Woolsey said that "he was the brains and the conscience of the faculty. Always he strove for a higher scholastic standard." It was he, said William C. Robinson, who controlled the school's "academic progress, and directed its development—the man who has done more to elevate the general standard of legal education than any other person in this country." Judge John K. Beach said that "unquestionably Professor Baldwin was, and continued to be, the leading spirit" in the school. Dean Wayland called him the "wheel-horse of the Law School," and Arthur L. Corbin wrote that "as an educator, he contributed so much that any weakness or limitations of the product must be charged to his colleagues and assistants rather than to him." The educational ideals of such a man are worthy of careful examination if the history of the Yale Law School is to be understood.

His *Young Man and the Law*, first published in 1920, is an elementary work; but coming just after the close of his active professorship, it probably sums up accurately, though in a popular manner, his ideas concerning preparation for the practice of law. In it he discussed the attractions of the legal profession, the charges that have been made against it, the ideals of the profession, and the personal qualities and the education requisite for success in it. He was perfectly confident that the chief aim of law study was preparation to pass bar examinations and be ready to give skilled advice to clients. That was the essential first course; but the second was equally important. Three years of the student's "early manhood should be devoted to legal study from the standpoint of one who hopes to be a lawyer; the rest of his time on earth to legal study from the standpoint of one who is a lawyer." On the aims of law schools, he paraphrased a statement made

72

by him many years before (*Yale Law Journal*, 13:1, October, 1903), that they have "for their main office the imparting of such a knowledge of the legal principles and rules prevailing in some one particular community as will justify the learner in professing his ability to expound and apply these in practice, against all comers, as occasion may arise." By "one particular community" he did not mean one particular American state, but rather any state where the Common Law was in vogue.

Reading this book alone, one would come to the conclusion that he had a narrow notion of law and of its function. This would seem strange and inconsistent if one then learned of the great catholicity of his own interests and learning, and particularly of his pioneer work for graduate law study. He was perfectly in accord with President Woolsey when, in 1874 (see *Yale Law Library Publications*, No. 4, p. 18), the latter said that the Yale Law School should "be regarded no longer as simply the place for training men to plead causes, to give advice to clients, to defend criminals." The apparent inconsistency is cleared when it is known that both men believed in adding to the strictly professional course supplementary years devoted to further study of law and to the study of subjects which were elsewhere being organized into graduate courses in political science. Baldwin was then, as have been all subsequent teachers, bothered by the element of time. But for this, his scheme of legal study would not have been divided into the professional and the graduate. Related subjects would have been taken up side by side, instead of tandem. Even as it was, in the first few of his teaching years, he introduced Roman and comparative law into the undergraduate curriculum, and he never lost faith in their value for the practicing lawyer. The evolution of the graduate course in the Yale Law

73

School, already described (see *Yale Law Library Publications*, No. 4, p. 23–28), illustrates this point. In explaining Yale's experiment to the American Social Science Association, at Saratoga, September 6, 1877 (*Journal of Social Science*, No. 11, p. 123–137), he discussed the need for more time for regular law courses and the difficulty of arranging for it. The plan, then one year old, was first of all a device for lengthening the professional course for those who could afford to take it, and secondly a means of providing a basis upon which to build genuine advanced work in legal and related subjects. As we have seen (*ante*, p. 38), the first objective, lying dormant until 1888, and then revived as "S.E.B.'s Scheme," was finally attained in 1902. What the regular course gained in time, the graduate course lost, and so began again the task of organizing graduate study from a new starting point, and for the benefit of better-educated students. There was no project looking toward the improvement of the Yale Law School in which Baldwin failed to take an active interest. The part that he played in promoting the "combined course," stiffened entrance requirements, and provision for employing full-time professors does not appear often in public records. On the latter point, his belief was that there should be both full-time professors and part-time lecturers (see *Yale Law Library Publications*, No. 4, p. 7). To see his influence at work it is necessary to read the minutes of the Corporation and Prudential Committee of Yale University, and those of the Faculty and Governing Board of the Law School. But he took a public part in organizing the law-teaching profession and in setting up standards to guide American law schools. He was a member of the American Bar Association committee of five appointed at Saratoga, August, 1892, to plan for a meeting of those interested in legal education and admis-

74

sion to the bar. In the following August, at Milwaukee, he was temporary chairman of the meeting at which was organized the Section of Legal Education. When the first annual meeting of the Association of American Law Schools was held in August, 1901, he was present as a delegate from the Yale Law School, and he served as President of the Association in the year 1902–1903.

On only one subject did he find himself unsympathetic with educational trends. This was the movement toward the case method of instruction. He was one of the staunchest supporters of the "Yale System" (see *Yale Law Library Publications*, No. 4, p. 32–35), and he never lost his faith in it. I suspect that he wrote the explanations of the "Yale System," contained in the Law School's announcements, 1885–1895, and he published in several places his views on the subject. He had refrained from taking part in the symposium on methods of legal education published in the *Yale Law Journal*, in March, 1892 (Vol. 1, p. 139–161), leaving to Edward J. Phelps the task of representing the ideas then prevailing in the school. This the latter could not well do, because he was of a generation earlier than Baldwin's, and was in fact an advocate of an unadulterated lecture-textbook system. John Chipman Gray's account of the method employed at Harvard will give us the means of making clear the plan which Baldwin favored. "In all law schools, I suppose," wrote Gray, "the students learn from textbooks, cases and oral instruction. At any rate, they do so here. Each teacher is free to use these means as he pleases. The different professors do actually use them in different ways and proportions, and so does each professor, as he is dealing with different topics. But, while in most law schools, the textbook is the basis of instruction, and the lecture and sometimes a reported case is employed to

75

explain or illustrate (or it may be, contradict) the text-book, with us the *predominant* mode of study is to make reported cases the basis of instruction and to use oral instruction and the consultation of textbooks as aids in drawing out, formulating and classifying the principles involved in the decisions." Even at that time Baldwin would have denied that the Yale Law School could properly have been lumped with the other textbook schools. He would have said that in Yale the *predominant* mode of study was the textbook, but that cases were *extensively* used, many of them being specially reprinted for that purpose. In 1896, he published his *Cases on Railroad Law*, to supplement a text. He differed from Langdell, Keener, and Gray in his ideas of the best *approach* to a subject for the student, and as to *emphasis* in the use of texts as opposed to cases considered as instructional material. His opening sentence, in 1900, on "Teaching Law by Cases" (*Harvard Law Review*, 14: 258–261, December, 1900) is reminiscent of the first sentence by Gray. "No American law school," wrote Baldwin, "has ever existed in which the course of instruction, however narrow and poor it may have been, failed to include the study, in some sort, of reported cases. But how far should this study be carried? Here the views of law teachers diverge." In his own view, any system of instruction wholly from compilations of cases would necessarily be partial and imperfect unless supplemented by lectures. The latter he believed to be unsuited to beginners, and so the question came down to the relation in instruction between cases and texts. "Hence it is that the modern casebook is often partly a textbook," complete neither as a text nor as a collection of cases. Is it not better, perhaps necessary, to begin with a complete text and pass from it to the cases? "No science can be learned purely from

76

particulars. The universals must be studied to discover what the particulars mean and whence they sprang." This idea he illustrated by an analogy. "A statue is a work of art. Every art has its rules and principles. These have been formulated by men of skill and experience. They are expressed in words. They are also expressed in marble. But the marble speaks all that is in it only to the initiated, the instructed. To gaze upon it brings to all men pleasure, elevation of thought, perhaps a realization of history, an impulse towards the ideal in life. But that one may feel thus and think thus does not make him an artist. A study of a thousand statues could not make him even a good stonecutter. He needs the direction of a master, the light of books, the dry mathematics of anatomy." Passing then through intervening phases of his argument, he comes to an optimistic appraisal of the value of "good textbooks," ending with the general conclusion that "no general method of studying law is likely ever to be discovered which is better than that of requiring the scholar to read daily and read with care a chapter or two from such a book, and then to be ready to explain the principles of decision applicable to states of fact slightly variant from those given in the examples put by the author. As supplementary to this, the study of reported cases is of high value. Without it, I believe that it is worth far less." The study of subjects chiefly by cases, instead of secondarily, he would leave to the third year and to a fourth, or graduate, year.

In the year when he wrote this (1900), his own casebook on railroad law was being used in Yale's third year, and each year saw the introduction there of new casebooks. Three years later, Corbin and Edgerton began to extend the use of cases in the first year. Progressively the case system gained ascendency until its formal victory

77

in 1912. Baldwin was not present at the Faculty meeting when this action was taken. He was then Governor of the state, and had already given up most of his teaching. He remained unconvinced. As long as he wrote on legal education, he argued the point. The best statement of his position is in his "Study of Elementary Law, the Proper Beginning of a Legal Education," which was his presidential address before the Association of American Law Schools, August 26, 1903. (*Yale Law Journal*, 13: 1–15, October, 1903.) In 1915, we find him still unchanged, when he discussed "Education for the Bar in the United States" (*American Political Science Review*, 9: 437–448), taking Redlich's report on the case method as a text. And finally, in 1920, in his "Education Requisite for Success in the Legal Profession" (Chapter V, *The Young Man and the Law*), we find him repeating some of the paragraphs of his article of December, 1900. His insistence did not come from a failure to understand what the case method was, for he was surrounded by it, and probably knew its theory better than did many of its advocates. He believed the theory to be wrong. His own success in applying the "Yale System" tended to strengthen his resistance; and his former students often gave him support. A. S. Vande Graaf, one of his pupils in 1882, wrote him ten years later that his method of teaching had made an indelible impression upon the class. The technique referred to was the conduct of recitations "by putting cases to the men as they were successively called, requiring an application of the doctrines of the text to actual facts."

The adoption of the case method in the Yale Law School was the only instance in which Baldwin failed to attain his educational objective. It was a major defeat for him, and yet he did not lose his interest in the school, or despair of its success. Busy as he was at all times with

78

matters outside the school, he served through his whole professorship on numberless committees, wrote reports on all sorts of administrative problems, and personally undertook tasks which he thought might help the school. It was he who prepared the Alumni Record which appeared in the school announcements for 1881–1882, 1884–1885, and 1887–1888. The last of these contained a record of students and graduates from 1824 to 1886. On May 18, 1887, the Law Faculty formally thanked him for preparing it, and for giving $100 toward the expense of publication. In the period for which the minutes of Governing Board and Faculty meetings are available, beginning in 1883, it appears that he was absent from not more than a score of meetings up to the end of 1916. The last meeting that he attended was on November 5, 1918.

The most remarkable of the extraneous services that he performed was that of Treasurer of the Law School. He acted in that capacity from 1874 to 1910. His account book, written almost wholly by his own hand, is now preserved in the Law Library. The first entry is dated August 1, 1874, and the last, February 1, 1910. Below the totals is written, "Account as above, rendered and approved by Governing Board, Feb. 22, 1910. Simeon E. Baldwin, Treas." Until that time, although Baldwin rendered an annual account to the Treasurer of the University, a portion of the funds of the school had been on deposit in the New Haven Bank, to the credit of the Law School as distinguished from the University. To close out this account, it was voted that the balance on hand, $1,350.80, was "to be used for buying or paying for books for Law School library as a donation from the Governing Board."

What has already been said is confirmation enough of the remark of George D. Watrous that the school "was

79

nearer to his heart than any other institution with which he was connected." But there is further evidence. His monetary gifts to the school amounted to over $700,000. He founded two professorships, one of them in Roman and comparative law, and he gave over $500,000, the income of which is used for general Law School purposes. He was a liberal contributor to the Wayland Fund, and to the Hendrie Hall building fund. He left most of his law books to the Law Library, and in 1926, he gave to the University a collection of South Arabian antiquities.

Professor Baldwin died in New Haven, on January 30, 1927, six days before he would have reached the age of eighty-seven. He had been ill for two years, but confined to his house for only a month. He was buried in Grove Street Cemetery, across the street from the present Sterling Law Buildings. On the day of his funeral, February 1, the Connecticut Assembly adjourned, and the state offices in Hartford were closed, in tribute to his memory. Delegations appointed by Governor John H. Trumbull of Connecticut, and by President Charles S. Whitman of the American Bar Association, attended the funeral. The New Haven County Bar Association held a memorial meeting, and a volume entitled *Records & Addresses in Memory of Simeon E. Baldwin, 1840–1927*, was privately printed in 1928. It contains the local bar association resolution, addresses and articles by Judge John K. Beach, George D. Watrous, Henry H. Townsend, Chief Justice George W. Wheeler, and the Reverend Richard H. Clapp, and memorial minutes by the Connecticut General Assembly and by the Trustees of the Hopkins Grammar School. From these and other published statements a few excerpts only need be gleaned in order to show the esteem in which he was held. "He was beyond question the greatest man Connecticut has

80

produced" in the last fifty years. "As commentator, educator, reformer, historian, and judge, no member of the Connecticut Bar has rendered greater service to the profession, to the public and to the law." He gave to the Yale Law School "its greatest prestige through the classes that he taught." "The Yale Law School owes more to Simeon E. Baldwin than to any other person," wrote Arthur L. Corbin. "This is not the debt of an abstraction to a name; it is the debt of several thousands of law students and teachers to a strong and steadfast human personality."

A tradition has grown up about Baldwin that has made him an Olympian figure, distant, cold, forbidding, perfect in self-control, benign but inflexible, someone to esteem but not to love. He has been described as grave, dignified, austere, self-reliant, unemotional. His pastor, the Reverend Richard H. Clapp, said that "an austere and utter integrity marked every action. . . . His mind was alert, penetrating, incisive and capacious, keen in analysis, creative and constructive throughout, with a prophetic look toward possible new developments. He regarded truth and only truth as tolerable, no matter where the search for it might lead. . . . Under the sovereign compulsion of duty he moved, preoccupied with serious concerns, austere and grave with the 'antique Roman' in his manner." It was well-nigh impossible for him to drop the mask of his "hard New England exterior."

That this mask covered a far different inner man was never doubted by those who were observant. Underneath, he was a kindly, sympathetic gentleman. His extensive charitable gifts during his life were so simply made that few knew about them. He was tolerant in religious matters, although he held himself up to a rigid standard of personal responsibility to his own faith. As senior pro-

81

fessor and Law School treasurer, he was considerate of the feelings and needs of his associates. "Young and struggling instructors," wrote Arthur L. Corbin, "discovered that he appreciated their difficulties and recognized their merits long before they realized that such recognition was their due." Any earnest student in need of help could go to him with the assurance that aid of a practical kind would be forthcoming. Many of them served apprenticeships in his law office. He did not like to be thanked, and would ward off the ordeal by a seeming brusqueness of speech. This effect was accentuated by the fact that he believed in clarity and directness, and never embroidered or ornamented any statement. In classroom he was serious, grave, dignified. He was not of the story-telling kind, but he had a sense of humor. His eye lighted with merriment at a humorous incident. Once he chuckled, and once he laughed outright in class. Sometimes he would run through the whole class from A to Z asking the same question and drawing out what various answers he could. On one such occasion he reached Mr. V., who woke up, rose to his feet blinking, and said, "I didn't understand the question." The class broke into a spontaneous laugh and Baldwin chuckled. When he *laughed*, the event was recorded in the *Yale Shingle*, 1898 (p. 57). Addison S. Pratt tells the story that in Private Corporations, a student was called upon to tell what had been decided in a Tennessee case. Being unprepared, he started to tell the facts in another case. Professor Baldwin interrupted him and told the story of "an Oxford student, who in preparing for an examination in Biblical History had selected the Chronology of the Jewish Kings as a likely question. But the examiner asked instead the distinction between the Major and the Minor Prophets. The student dilated at length upon the unfairness of the

82

question and continued with 'Now a much fairer question would be to give the chronology of the Jewish Kings,' which he proceeded to give in full. In the hearty laugh which followed, Judge Baldwin was seen to join—the only time he was ever known to upset the gravity of the Bench in the recitation room."

He cared not at all for the ceremonies and social perquisites of his offices. He carried the simplicity of his living almost to an extreme. When as Chief Executive of the state he went from New Haven to Hartford, he took his lunch with him and ate it in the Governor's office. On one railroad trip accompanied by his staff, when told that places had been reserved for them in the dining car for luncheon, he replied that he had his lunch with him, and taking a bag from his pocket, he ate his sandwich.

We have seen that as a college student, he was interested in boating, baseball, and chess. As a young man he was fond of swimming. Later he rode a bicycle, but gave it up for walking. Rain or shine, according to George E. Woodbine (*Dictionary of American Biography*, I:546), he walked four miles a day. An apparently frail figure, "he walked unhurriedly alone, stooping somewhat, buried in thought, compelled by poor eyesight to keep his gaze fixed upon his path a few feet ahead of him." During the youth of his children he read to them often. He was a member of a book club which supplied fiction as well as more serious works. He enjoyed playing whist, and gave it up only because he could not sleep after it, and he was a courteous and gracious host to guests in his home. He never forgot a favor, and sooner or later repaid it; but his gratitude was seldom put into words. He regretted his inability to be more expansive in his personal relationships, and on one occasion let Judge Beach know that he was conscious of it as a weakness. He was visibly touched

83

when, in 1893, his former pupils rallied to his support and overcame opposition to his appointment to the Supreme Court of Errors, and there is reason to believe that he took his election as Governor "as proof of a popular esteem which he never courted, and, perhaps until then, did not know that he possessed."

Although, as Harrison Hewitt, one of his devoted admirers, put it, he belonged to a "generation of New England Yankees, part of whose creed it was that one's heart should not be worn on his sleeve, and that it was not appropriate to disclose either deep affection or deep grief, or similar emotions, in public and to the public," this fact did not account fully for the intense preoccupation and drive of his work to the exclusion of personal companionship. His contemporaries knew that there was a tragedy in his life, but how deeply it was affecting him they could only guess or infer from isolated instances. One of his students tells that in a class where causes for divorce in various states were being discussed, Professor Baldwin came to a jurisdiction in the courts of which the only ground for divorce was incurable insanity. He stopped an appreciable moment, caught his breath, and went on. Only those students who knew of the history of his own marriage realized that the pause was caused by his very deep feeling. There is a key to the philosophy of his own life, in the circumstances in which he found himself, in words spoken by him at the memorial exercises to William K. Townsend, June 18, 1907. "There are those," he said, "to whom hard work brings its daily blessing as a banisher of sorrow. Melancholy is a foe to be expelled at any cost, and pre-occupation is often the only thing that avails to shut it out." But more significant and revealing than this is the letter which he wrote to his children and executors on July 17, 1910, when he put into

84

their hands the diaries that he had been keeping since 1851. He asked that they be deposited in the New Haven County Historical Society and be kept in a locked box for fifty years. "In this drawer," he wrote, "are the journals which I have kept for nearly sixty years. I should prefer that you should not read them. They have been my confidant, and I have written in them very freely of things I might have talked over with a wife, had I had one (except in name), and for want of her sympathy and counsel have entered here." Work, the satisfaction of getting things done, had been only partly his salvation. He was lonesome and heartsick. In the daily entries of his journals, he provided himself with an escape for his pent-up emotions, still presenting to the world the appearance of imperturbable calm.

INDEX

A

Abbott, Benjamin Vaughan 85
Adams, James T. 251
Adams, John Quincy 8
Abbott, John S.C. 91
Adler, Max 215
Aiken, William P. (Yale Law
School 1892) 182
Alexander, Clarence A. 197
Allen, Mr. 6
Alling, John W. 157
Alvord, Alwin A. 96
American Baptist Union 221
American Social Science Associa-
tion 226
Amistad case 8
Andrew, George W. 177
Andrews, Nathan 129
Andrews, S.J. 14
Anketell, Edward A. 206
Anketell house 207, 211
Athletics 193-200
Atkin, Edgar 199
Atkinson, Edward 226
Atwater, Rev. William Woodruff
(Yale 1846) (law school
librarian 1873-1874) 172, 174-
175,178
Atwood, Charles 13
Averill, Frederick L. 215

B

Babcock, Thorpe 195
Backus, Reverend Azel 15
Bacon, Custis S. 212
Bacon, Francis 125

Bacon, Leonard, Reverend 30, 87,
105, 119, 124-125
Bailey, Mark 125
Baldwin, Rev. David Dwight
(Yale 1821) 174
Baldwin, David Dwight (law school
librarian 1874) 174-175, 179
Baldwin, Henry 4
Baldwin, Roger Sherman (Yale
Honorary Master of Arts 1768,
Treasurer of the College 1765-
1776) 8, 68, 105, 107, 266
Baldwin, Roger Sherman [1793-
1863](Yale 1811, Yale L.L.D.
1845) Governor of Connecticut
1844-1846, United States Senator
1847-1851) 52, 197, 215, 266
Baldwin, Simeon [1761-1851] (Yale
1781) 7, 266
Baldwin, Simeon Eben [1840-1927]
7, 52, 69, 72,92, 96, 117-120, 122,
124, 126-127, 132, 136, 143, 150,
153-154, 157-158, 162, 166, 171,
182, 186, 188, 189, 205, 207-208,
215, 217-218, 220, 226, biograph-
ical sketch 265-287
Bangs, Merwin and Company 9
Barnard, Daniel D. 63
Barnard, Henry 224
Barnes, Clarence A. 200
Barnes, E. Henry 215
Barnes, T. Attwater 215
Barnes, William 13
Barstow, Francis S. 224
Baseball team 197-200

www.ingramcontent.com/pod-product-compliance
Lightning Source LLC
Chambersburg PA
CBHW030717250326
R18027900001B/R180279PG41599CBX00021B/33